John Sawyer is Senior Research Fellow in the Department of Religious Studies and Social Ethics at the University College of St Martin, Lancaster.

JOURNAL FOR THE STUDY OF THE OLD TESTAMENT
SUPPLEMENT SERIES
227

Sheffield Academic Press

Reading Leviticus

A Conversation with Mary Douglas

edited by
John F.A. Sawyer

Journal for the Study of the Old Testament
Supplement Series 227

Published by Sheffield Academic Press Ltd
Mansion House
19 Kingfield Road
Sheffield S11 9AS
England

Printed on acid-free paper in Great Britain
by Bookcraft Ltd
Midsomer Norton, Bath

British Library Cataloguing in Publication Data

A catalogue record for this book is available
from the British Library

ISBN 1-85075-628-7

CONTENTS

PREFACE

This volume contains an edited version of the proceedings of a colloquium held on 30 May-1 June 1995 at Lancaster University. Originally entitled *Unity, Purity and the Covenant: Reading Leviticus*, it was dreamed up by Mary Douglas, Paul Morris and myself. Unfortunately Paul Morris had already moved to New Zealand before it took place and was unable to attend, and at the last minute Jacob Milgrom also could not join us. In any case it was Mary who was really the prime mover and our inspiration from the start: hence the revised title. No scholarly work on Leviticus can fail to take account of her writings: from *Purity and Danger* and *Natural Symbols* in the late sixties and early seventies to the stream of fascinating and original articles that have been appearing in the nineties. 'Atonement in Leviticus', 'The Forbidden Animals in Leviticus', 'Poetic Structure in Leviticus' and 'The Stranger in the Bible' are some of them. The colloquium was built round Mary, and, although I know she will never admit it, in many important respects it was held in her honour.

A conference entirely devoted to Leviticus is a fairly rare occurrence. We had a few surprised and somewhat sceptical reactions to the very idea. One reason for this is of course that among the books of the Hebrew Bible, Leviticus has had a particularly bad press. Ritual texts, legal texts and, for that matter, priests, are red rags to a good many Christian bulls, especially Protestant ones. But things are changing. A daily newspaper here recently had an article with the title 'The Revolutionary Moral Insights of Leviticus'. In it Haim Maccoby exposed the ignorance and amateurishness that fuel that kind of prejudice, and his rehabilitation of the book continues in this volume. Graeme Auld's unashamedly tendentious title 'Leviticus at the Heart of the Pentateuch?' shows he has something similar on his agenda.

Of course there may be other reasons why conferences on Leviticus are rare events, literary reasons for example. One of these is discussed by Rolf Rendtorff and Kathryn Gutzwiller, who tackle the question of whether it is possible to read it as a separate book at all. Maybe it can only be read in the context of some larger literary stucture. Jacob Milgrom's paper on the redactional role of the Holiness School, and John Rogerson's response to it, focus on another literary problem that has prevented people over the years from looking at Leviticus as a literary work in its own right. Maybe it is not a unity but composed of several sources, each part of a larger literary unit.

Probably the most unusual feature of this colloquium, however, was its interdisciplinary approach. The participants are by no means all full-time biblical scholars: there are strong contingents of anthropologists and lawyers here too—and surely that is how it should be. As well as Mary's paper 'Sacred Contagion', there are Adriana Destro's 'Anthropological Reading of *Niddah*' and occasional interventions from the local anthropologists Paul Heelas and Geoffrey Samuel. Jonathan Magonet, also sadly unable to attend, contributes a short paper to this section of the volume. Calum Carmichael, an expert in Comparative Literature, examines the sequence of rules in Leviticus 19 and Alan Watson who is a specialist in Roman Law, looks at Leviticus in the Gospels. Bernard Jackson, another lawyer, gives a response to Mary's paper.

Whatever the origins of Leviticus, its role in the evolution of Second Temple Period Judaism, including Chronicles and what has been called 'New Testament Judaism', is obviously important. So Alan Watson's paper on the Gospels is joined by Hannah Harrington's on 'Struggling with Ambiguity' and William Johnstone's on Chronicles. Philip Davies and Philip Budd contribute responses to two of the papers in this section.

I gladly acknowledge financial assistance from the British Academy. I would also like to thank Deputy Vice Chancellor Joe Shennon, Professor John Clayton, Head of the Religious Studies Department, and the staff of Furness College for their hospitality and Diane Collier and Alison Pryce for invaluable administrative and other assistance. Special mention must also be made of Sylvia Cooper who bravely typed up transcripts of the taperecorded discussion.

John F.A. Sawyer

LIST OF CONTRIBUTORS AND PARTICIPANTS

Professor Graeme Auld, New College, Edinburgh
Dr Philip Budd, Westminster College, Oxford
Professor Calum Carmichael, Comparative Literature, Cornell University
Dr Philip Davies, Biblical Studies, University of Sheffield
Professor Adriana Destro, Cattedra di Antropologia Culturale, University of Bologna
Professor Mary Douglas, University College London
Dr Kathryn Gutzwiller, Department of Classics, University of Cincinnati
Dr Hannah Harrington, Patten College, Oakland, California
Dr Paul Heelas, Religious Studies Department, Lancaster University
Professor Bernard Jackson, Faculty of Law, University of Liverpool
Professor William Johnstone, King's College, University of Aberdeen
Dr Hyam Maccoby, Leo Baeck College, London
Dr Jonathan Magonet, Leo Baeck College, London
Professor Jacob Milgrom, Hebrew University, Jerusalem
Professor Paul Morris, Religious Studies Department, Victoria University of Wellington
Professor Rolf Rendtorff, Unversity of Heidelberg
Professor John Rogerson, Biblical Studies, University of Sheffield
Professor Geoffrey Samuel, Religious Studies Department, Lancaster University
Professor John Sawyer, University College of St Martin, Lancaster
Dr Robert Segal, Religious Studies Department, University College of St Martin, Lancaster
Professor Alan Watson, School of Law, University of Georgia, Athens

ABBREVIATIONS

AB	Anchor Bible
ANET	J.B. Pritchard (ed.), *Ancient Near Eastern Texts*
BDB	F. Brown, S.R. Driver and C.A. Briggs, *Hebrew and English Lexicon of the Old Testament*
BKAT	Biblischer Kommentar: Altes Testament
BZAW	Beihefte zur *ZAW*
CB	*Cultura bíblica*
CBQ	*Catholic Biblical Quarterly*
EncJud	*Encyclopaedia Judaica*
ExpTim	*Expository Times*
HAT	Handbuch zum Alten Testament
IB	*Interpreter's Bible*
ICC	International Critical Commentary
IDBSup	*IDB*, Supplementary Volume
JB	*Jerusalem Bible*
JBL	*Journal of Biblical Literature*
JJS	*Journal of Jewish Studies*
JSJ	*Journal for the Study of Judaism in the Persian, Hellenistic and Roman Period*
JSOT	*Journal for the Study of the Old Testament*
JSOTSup	*Journal for the Study of the Old Testament*, Supplement Series
JSPSup	*Journal for the Study of the Pseudepigrapha*, Supplement Series
LCL	Loeb Classical Library
NCB	New Century Bible
NICOT	New International Commentary on the Old Testament
NJB	H. Wansbrough (ed.), *New Jerusalem Bible*
NRSV	New Revised Standard Version
OBO	Orbis biblicus et orientalis
OTL	Old Testament Library
RB	*Revue biblique*
RSV	Revised Standard Version
SANT	Studien zum Alten und Neuen Testament
SBLDS	SBL Dissertation Series
SBS	Stuttgarter Bibelstudien
SJLA	Studies in Judaism in Late Antiquity
STDJ	Studies on the Texts of the Desert of Judah
ThWAT	G.J. Botterweck and H. Ringgren (eds.), *Theologisches Wörterbuch zum Alten Testament*

VT	*Vetus Testamentum*
WBC	Word Biblical Commentary
ZAW	*Zeitschrift für die alttestamentliche Wissenschaft*

THE LANGUAGE OF LEVITICUS

John F.A. Sawyer

I hope this short paper will provide something of an introduction to the colloquium, partly by picking out some of the issues involved for preliminary discussion, and partly by raising at the outset the general question of what exactly is this text that we have come here from all over the world to discuss? In particular, can its grammar and vocabulary give us a clue as to who in this text is trying to do what to whom? For present purposes, I mean the grammar and vocabulary of Leviticus as whole, not the first 16 chapters on their own, or P or H or any other corpus, but the book of Leviticus on its own as a complete literary unit, coming after the Book of Exodus, in which 'Moses finished the work' of erecting the tabernacle and the tent of meeting, and which ends with the formula, 'these are the commandments which the Lord commanded Moses for the people of Israel on Mount Sinai' (27.34). Subsequent discussion may well challenge this procedure as rather arbitrary, but I think I can show that there are some useful conclusions to be drawn from it. If that is the case, then I am only too happy to add my evidence—as a linguist—in support of Mary's literary/anthropological conclusions on Leviticus.

With the advent of the computer it is a lot easier to handle minute grammatical data than it used to be, and I begin with the grammar of Leviticus. Of course statistical data can be misleading, especially in the case of a text like the Hebrew Bible in which all sorts of complex, arbitrary and often unknown factors have operated, from speakers' or writers' choices in their original universe of discourse in ancient Israel and Judah, right down to the fixing of the canon at Yavneh and the activities of the Masoretes in the first centuries of the Common Era. But in a survey like that published by Frank Andersen and Dean

Forbes a few years ago,[1] a few features stand out as statistically so extraordinary as to be significant. Here they are.

In most respects—the frequency of verbs, nouns, the definite article, passive forms, pronouns, prepositions, numerals and the like—Leviticus is normal in comparison with Biblical Hebrew as a whole. But there are two very striking characteristics of the grammar of Leviticus which distinguish it from most other books of the Bible. First, Leviticus is characterized by the extreme infrequency of imperatives (42/35: that is, a total of 42 occurrences, corresponding to 35 per 10,000 words). Most books of the Bible have three or four times as many imperatives per 10,000 words as Leviticus. Imperatives are most frequent in the language of the Prophets and the Psalms—in Psalms for example, imperatives are 10× more frequent than they are in Leviticus (693/354). The nearest parallels to the situation in Leviticus are Esther (11/36) and Ezra (15/40) where imperatives are equally rare. Significantly, the relative frequency of imperatives in the Holiness Code on its own, that is Leviticus 17–26 (15/34), is almost exactly the same as for the book of Leviticus as a whole—a nice example, incidentally, of continuity or consistency from ch. 1 to ch. 27. Direct commands using the imperative are rare in Leviticus: the incidence of direct negative commands or prohibitions (using *yiqtol* forms rather than imperatives) is not significant. The relative frequency of negatives (298/249) is not much higher than average (6233/204), and exceeded by Deuteronomy (445/311), Isaiah (525/310), Jeremiah (633/290), Job (366/439), Proverbs (233/337) and several of the smaller books. When it is remembered that a large proportion of the imperatives that do occur are those addressed by God to Moses (דבר אל־בני ישראל 'speak to the people... ', קח את־אהרן ואת־בניו 'take Aaron and his sons... ' and so on), then the lack of direct commands addressed to the listener or reader is very remarkable indeed.

The other feature of the language of Leviticus, which distinguishes it from narrative texts like Esther and Ezra, is the relative infrequency of plain statements of fact, describing what happened or how things actually are. No book in the Bible has fewer *qatal* forms per 10,000 words than Leviticus; most have over twice as many. Similarly, no prose work (with the exception of Qohelet) has fewer *vayyiqtol* forms per 10,000 words than Leviticus. Conversely, *v*^{e}*qatal* forms are

1. F.I. Andersen and A.D. Forbes, *The Vocabulary of the Old Testament* (Rome: Pontifical Biblical Institute, 1989).

almost three times as frequent in Leviticus (721/603) as they are anywhere else. Deuteronomy, Ezekiel and some of the minor prophets come a long way behind in second place. The relative frequency of *yiqtol* forms, although not so high, is nonetheless above average for the Hebrew Bible as a whole.

So what can we conclude from this? The book is described in the closing formula as a collection of 'commandments'—אלה המצות אשר צוה יהוה את־משה, and throughout it there are such expressions as זאת תהיה תורת המצרע (14.1), ...והיתה לכם לחקת עולם... (16.29), ...את משפטי תעשו ואת חקתי תשמרו... (18.4). But the language in which God addresses the people and the priests through his prophetic spokesman Moses, seems almost to avoid the normal direct means of phrasing obligations. The author seems instead to want us to imagine a state or a society in which some elaborate procedures are to be carried out, some things are to be done and some are not to be done. Sanctions are there, including the death penalty; and what looks very much like one of the celebrated 'do what I say or else...' passages appears in Leviticus, as well as Exodus and Deuteronomy (Lev. 26; cf. Exod. 23.20-33; Deut. 28). But the emphasis is different. Direct commands concentrated in chs. 18 and 19 seem to be exceptions rather than the norm. At the end of ch. 26, the sanctions are greatly mitigated, as they are at the end of Deuteronomy: the memorable hapax legomenon ואף־גם־זאת 'Yet in spite of everything...' makes that clear (26.44). Of course this is not reflected in our English translations. The *yiqtol* and *w^{e}qatal* forms are notoriously hard to translate: should it be 'he shall bring his offering...' or 'he will bring his offering' 'or 'let him bring his offering...'? Should it be 'you shall not steal...' or 'do not steal' or 'you will not steal'...? And what about the terms for 'law', 'commandment' and the like. Should תורת המצרע not be translated 'this is what you (Moses) are to teach concerning people suffering from צרעת', rather than 'this shall be the law of the leper' (RSV)?

This brings me to the second part of my paper, which is about the vocabulary of Leviticus. Word frequency is a notoriously unreliable guide to how things were or are in the universe of discourse from which a text derives. The fact that the word for a 'sneeze' (עטישה, Job 41.10) only occurs once in the Bible, for example, doesn't mean that sneezing was rare in ancient Israel, any more than you can argue that ancient Israelite houses were very clean places from the fact that there is no everyday domestic word for 'dirty' in biblical Hebrew, corresponding to post-biblical מלכלך. Conversely, the fact that Leviticus contains a disproportionately high concentration of words for 'ritually clean', 'impure' and the like, has to be investigated very carefully before you can conclude the author was obsessed with matters of purity or sacred contagion. They may, for example, mainly be confined to one short passage on the subject, and only alluded to in passing elsewhere. Maybe Leviticus is not all about ritual purity and holiness as has often been thought.

But what I think might be significant and often overlooked, is that Leviticus contains some key-terms and phrases not found elsewhere, or very rare elsewhere, in the Bible. One obvious example is עזאזל which occurs only in Leviticus 16 and, with it, יום הכפרים which occurs only in Leviticus 23 and 25. Another word which appears alongside יום הכפרים in the last of these passages, Leviticus 25, is the highly emotive term דרור 'liberty', 'freedom' which occurs in the Torah only here, and another is יובל 'jubilee'. Another obvious one is the phrase ואהבת לרעך כמוך ('and you shall love your neighbour as yourself')which occurs twice in ch. 19 and nowhere else in the Hebrew Bible (it recurs often enough in post-biblical texts, including half a dozen times in the Gospels and Paul). The significance of this cannot be overestimated. While in many contexts the perception of the Book of Leviticus is that of a ritualistic, legalistic priestly work, it is not called Leviticus 'the priestly book' in Jewish tradition, and could instead be understood as the book which uniquely focuses on 'loving one's neighbour', the ideal of a 'jubilee' of justice and freedom and *yom kippur*. A further reason why Leviticus has been so undervalued and its true meaning misunderstood, is that many Christian commentators, ancient and modern, have no idea of the religious significance of *yom kippur* as a day of spiritual renewal, a high point in the Jewish liturgical year, both before 70 CE (cf. Sir. 50) and after, and right down to the present.

I would like to raise one other point about the vocabulary of Leviticus, which may be rather more controversial. It is often said that priestly terminology—and that refers to most of Leviticus—is characterized by an almost technical precision. Terms are used very carefully and with great attention to detailed distinctions between related terms, with 'unmatched precision of terminology and formulation'.[2] I would like to question this on two accounts. First of all there is the obvious problem of the somewhat crude anthropomorphisms in Leviticus such as ריח ניחוח ליהוה 'a pleasing odour to the Lord', לחם אלהיכם 'food for your God' and similar expressions. Are contemporary readers permitted to turn a blind eye to these expressions, so to speak, and call them 'fossils', as commentaries frequently do, and feel free not to take them literally? If they can do that with some expressions, what is to prevent readers and listeners from doing it with others? If לחם אשה in 3.16 is not to be understood literally, for example, why should they take חקת עולם 'an everlasting law' in the next verse literally. Or if ריח ניחוח ליהוה in 2.2 is purely metaphorical, how should the term קדש הקדשים in the next verse be interpreted? Is this not the stuff of rhetoric, working on the general associations and nuances of these terms and the cumulative effect of repetition, rather than concern for the choice and exploitation of precise terminology? Another example of an entirely non-technical use is the 'elegant variation' in one of the most celebrated passages in Lev. 19.15-18, where no less than four different terms are used for the other person, 'neighbour, brother, companion, fellow-countryman' or the like.[3]

The second point I would like to make on the vocabulary of Leviticus concerns supposed differences in terminology and lexical usage between different sources. What would happen when two sources, in which the same terms occur both with a technical meaning and a less technical or figurative meaning, are combined in one text—in this case P (Leviticus 1–16 and 27) and H (the Holiness Code in 17–26)? To a reader who knows nothing at all about source criticism what do they mean? The term מעל, for example, 'desecration', טמא 'ritually impure' and נדה 'bodily discharge' may originally have had some precise, narrow, restricted, technical sense in some ancient contexts, painstakingly and convincingly reconstructed by modern critical scholarship, but they no longer occur in that original context. Now they are in a context in which the original source is combined with another source or sources in which these same terms are used figuratively or in a less precise or less technical sense. Is it not then

2. J. Milgrom, *Studies in Cultic Theology and Terminology* (Studies in Judaism in Late Antiquity, 36; Leiden: Brill, 1983), p. 122.

3. M. Noth, *Leviticus: A Commentary* (trans. J.E. Anderson; London: SCM Press, 1965 [1962]).

the case that the less precise, less technical or figurative sense is bound to be uppermost in the reader's mind? Surely terms like מעל, טמא and נדה can no longer be understood as narrow technical terms with a restricted meaning, and all the passages in which they occur should perhaps be interpreted accordingly. Are not the minute details of ancient priestly terminology now submerged in the rhetoric of a larger literary work whose aims and interests are perhaps more theological than practical, more prophetic than priestly. Perhaps the Hebrew title of the book ויקרא, focusing as it does upon God's first words to his prophet Moses from the newly established אהל מועד, gets closer to its overall purpose than the tendentious and misleading Greek or Latin title we use in English.

Part I

QUESTIONS OF TEXT AND COMPOSITION

Is it Possible to Read Leviticus as a Separate Book?

Rolf Rendtorff

Recently, Mary Douglas has surprised her readership with articles and even books on matters of the Hebrew Bible. In particular she offers new ideas about the structure of biblical books. First she proposed a possible way of understanding the structure of *The Glorious Book of Numbers*,[1] and now she is turning to the Book of Leviticus as well.[2] Being a bit of a specialist on Leviticus, I now feel called into the arena. What is she doing with our Leviticus? Is it possible to approach it that way? What are the criteria to decide what is right or wrong?

For me, her proposal is surprising and attractive. I always like new approaches, in particular if they are well-founded and not too fantastic. In the case of a non-specialist, one will accept that there is no detailed discussion of earlier positions about the structure of Leviticus and in particular no argument about its supposed sources and the like. Nevertheless, even if I appreciate such an approach for myself, I have to check its validity in the framework of the rules of scholarship. For Mary is a scholar and she has to be taken as a scholar, even if she is provoking the established scholarly guild. Therefore let me try to evaluate step by step her new proposal to understand the structure of the Book of Leviticus.

I

The first question has to be: Is it at all possible and permissible to read Leviticus as a separate book? The answer is: Yes, of course. Jewish

1. *Jewish Studies Quarterly* 1 (1993/94), pp. 194-216; see also *In the Wilderness: The Doctrine of Defilement in the Book of Numbers* (JSOTSup, 158; Sheffield: JSOT Press, 1993).

2. 'The Forbidden Animals in Leviticus', *JSOT* 59 (1993), pp. 3-23; 'Atonement in Leviticus', *Jewish Studies Quarterly* 1.2, pp. 109-130.

exegesis since earliest times has taken Leviticus as a separate book. *Leviticus Rabbah* is one of the oldest Midrashim, and *Sifra* or *Torat Kohanim* is one of the halakhic Midrashim ascribed to the so-called 'school of Rabbi Aqiba'. For them, it was quite evident that Leviticus was a book on its own. There is other evidence as well. The name *Pentateuch* is derived from the Greek ἡ πεντάτευχος βίβλος 'the five volume book' which shows that already in early times the Pentateuch had been written on five separate scrolls. The same notion is expressed in Hebrew by חמשת ספרי התורה 'The five books of the Torah' or חמישה חומשי התורה 'the five fifths of the Torah' which terms appear early in rabbinic literature.

From this perspective, it is evident that Leviticus *is* a book on its own. Some scholars might not be satisfied by this answer because their scholarship tells them differently. This brings us to a touchy point. Who decides in a case like this? Who is 'right'? Were the rabbis 'wrong'? Are the modern scholars right against the biblical and rabbinic tradition? I am sure, no one would say so. Right and wrong are not the appropriate categories. But what better expressions are there for what is at stake? Perhaps to say 'original' and 'later' or 'secondary'? But if this were used in answer to the question whether Leviticus is a book, one would have to say: There is no Leviticus at all. There are only sources like 'P' (the so-called 'Priestly code' or 'source') with a number of sub-sources like 'Pg', 'Ps' or simply 'P_1', 'P_2', 'P_3' as in Jacob Milgrom's commentary[3] and in addition 'H' (the so-called 'Holiness Code' or 'source'), perhaps also to be subdivided. But why then write a commentary on Leviticus and not on 'P' or 'H'? And the other way around: If they finally came together why not take Leviticus as a book?

I shall come back to this question later. Let us first continue to speak of Leviticus in its given form. There is another question with regard to the separateness of Leviticus. It is evident that the Book of Leviticus is not independent of what precedes and what follows. It is part of the story of Israel at Sinai, which itself is part of Israel's journey from Egypt to the borders of the promised land, which in turn is closely connected with the story of the creation of the world, the Flood, the calling of Abraham and the history of his family up to their moving to Egypt. This is, so to speak the case against speaking of Leviticus as a book on its own. In this case there is no controversy between a

3. J. Milgrom, *Leviticus 1–16* (AB, 3; Garden City, NY: Doubleday, 1991).

traditional and a modern scholarly argument but rather an intra-biblical question how to read Leviticus: whether as a continuation of the story of the Pentateuch or as a book on its own.

II

Let us go one step deeper into this question. What about the rest of the books of the Pentateuch? In the final shaping as 'Torah' its five books do belong closely to each other. On the other hand, it is obvious that Deuteronomy is a separate book. It is clearly framed by a new beginning and a definite end; it has its own style, its own topics, and its own theology. Yet it is not independent of the preceding books. At the beginning Moses says to the Israelites: 'The LORD our God spoke to us at Horeb, saying "You have stayed long enough at this mountain. Resume your journey... See, I have set the land before you; go in and take possession of the land that I swore to your ancestors, to Abraham, to Isaac, and to Jacob, to give to them and to their descendants after them".' (Deut. 1.6-8) The reader has to know about Israel's stay at the mountain, that is of things told in the Book of Exodus; but has also to know about the patriarchs and God's promise to them, that is of the Genesis tradition. Otherwise what Deuteronomy says would be unintelligible to the reader. At the same time, nobody would deny that Deuteronomy can and should be read as a book on its own, and nobody would object to attempts to find out the structure of this book.

I turn to the opposite end of the Pentateuch, to the Book of Genesis. It has a marvellous beginning, the beginning of the whole world and of the whole Bible: בראשית ברא אלהים את השמים ואת הארץ 'In the beginning God created heaven and earth'. Here there is no problem in seeing the beginning of a book. But what about its end? Jacob and his sons are finally settled in Egypt, but there are links forward and back. Jacob had asked his son Joseph, who had made a career in Egypt, to bury him after his death in the land of his ancestors (Gen. 49.29-30), and Joseph did (50.7-11). Later Joseph himself said to his brothers: 'I am about to die; but God will surely come to you, and bring you up out of this land to the land that he swore to Abraham, to Isaac and to Jacob... When God comes to you, you shall carry up my bones from here' (50.24-25). Now the reader is aware that the story must continue. Nevertheless, when entering the Book of Exodus there is a new beginning, a new style, new problems. Israel is now a nation, oppressed by another nation. So again both occur: a continuation and a new beginning. In this case, too, nobody would deny the right to read Genesis as a book on its own.

Now we come closer to the specific problem: the relationship between the end of Exodus and the beginning of Leviticus? Are they two separate books or not? Exodus tells the story of Israel's being rescued from slavery in Egypt, wandering through the wilderness, arriving at Mount Sinai and then receiving several kinds of commandments. Among those there is the order to build a sanctuary for God's dwelling among Israel and for Israel's cultic worship of him. The building is completed, but the cult has not yet begun. So on the one hand, Exodus is incomplete, and on the other hand Leviticus would be without basis if Exodus did not precede it.

Let us have a look into the more recent commentaries. Baruch Levine in his commentary on Leviticus in explaining the structure of Leviticus does not mention its relation to Exodus explicitly. Only later in his commentary to Leviticus 8–9 does he write that chs. 8–9 'serve to describe the fulfillment of what was ordained in Exod. 29.1-37 and also overlap in content with the final chapters of Exodus'.[4] But this does not effect his taking Leviticus as a book on its own. John E. Hartley in his commentary on Leviticus is also very brief on this point: 'The material contained in Leviticus has its setting in a larger block of material on priestly matters that runs from Exod. 25.1 to Num. 10.10. Nevertheless, a heading and two summary statements (26.46; 27.34) demarcate Leviticus as a book in itself.'[5]

Jacob Milgrom is more specific:[6]

> One would expect the account of the building of the Tabernacle (Exod. 35–40) to be followed by the account of its dedication (Lev. 8). This expectation is reinforced by the observation that Exodus 39, Exod. 40.17-33, and Leviticus 8 reveals the same septenary structure (see ch. 8, Comment A). Thus, Leviticus 1–7 is an insertion, but one that makes sense because the dedicatory and inaugural sacrifices that follow (8.14-29; 9.1-21) cannot be understood without it.

I want to ask what the term 'insertion' could mean if the surrounding text cannot be understood without it. Could it ever have existed

4. B.A. Levine, *Leviticus* (JPS Torah Commentary; Philadelphia: Jewish Publication Society of America, 1989), p. 48.

5. J.E. Hartley, *Leviticus* (WBC, 4; Dallas: Word Books, 1992), p. xxx.

6. Milgrom, *Leviticus 1–16*, p. 61.

without that 'insertion', and would it then have been unintelligible? If not, what does 'insertion' mean? The main question in this context is, what consequences this observation might have for reading Leviticus as a book.

Milgrom continues:[7]

> The closing verses of Exodus (Exod. 40.36-38), however, are clearly intrusive; the information that the divine cloud will lead Israel in its wilderness trek belongs in the Book of Numbers. In fact, the same information is repeated, but in greater detail, just before Israel begins its march (Num. 9.15-23). This repetition, however, instead of creating a problem, provides an answer, and a significant one at that: the Exodus passage is a proleptic summary of its Numbers counterpart and serves with it to bracket the intervening material, Lev. 1.1–Num. 9.14, which comprises all the laws revealed to Moses at Sinai.

Here is another structure combining Leviticus with the first chapters of Numbers through a kind of inclusio. In this case the end of Leviticus is involved. Does it mean that Leviticus does not have its own ending but continues up to Numbers 9? So far we do not have Milgrom's second volume so we do not know how he will answer this question.

Two things seem to me to be obvious. First, with regard to its contents Leviticus is closely related to the preceding Book of Exodus and cannot be understood independently from it. Secondly, Leviticus contains a very specific collection of texts, describing the rules and the meaning of the cultic proceedings at the sanctuary on Sinai, in particular the sacrifices. There can be no doubt that these texts actually do speak about the cult at the temple in Jerusalem, notwithstanding the question of dating. From that point of view, the texts beginning in Leviticus 1 for the religious community in Jerusalem are of much higher importance than the preceding ones, because they offer the actual guidance for the central events of its cultic life. Leviticus 1.2 begins to tell the Israelites what to do אדם כי יקריב מכם קרבן ליהוה 'When any of you presents an offering to the Lord'. Therefore there are good reasons to speak of these texts as at the centre or 'the heart' of the Pentateuch.

That means that Leviticus is not simply the continuation of Exodus. One could even put it the other way around. What precedes in Exodus 25–30 and 35–40 is the preparation for the central religious and cultic

7. Milgrom, *Leviticus 1–16*, p. 61.

texts beginning in Leviticus 1. From the point of view of the reader of the Hebrew Bible this is what is really effective. There is another indication of the important position of this beginning. God 'calls' Moses (ויקרא, which is the Hebrew name of the Book of Leviticus) as he did earlier on Mount Sinai when he summoned him on the seventh day to enter the cloud which was covering the mountain and in which the glory of the LORD was present (Exod. 24.16). Now in Leviticus 1 begins the second part of this revelational event which will be of the highest relevance for Israel. And with it begins a new book within the five books of the Torah.

There is one more argument. Numbers begins with a date: 'On the first day of the second month in the second year following the exodus from the land of Egypt.' Here obviously is a new beginning which is not explicitly related to the preceding Book of Leviticus but rather to the Book of Exodus. Within the scope of the question whether it is possible to read Leviticus as a separate book, it is a clear argument for an ending to the Book of Leviticus.

III

Now I turn to the question of the structure of the book. Again, look first at some traditional positions in Old Testament scholarship. Usually, Leviticus is divided into two main parts that are taken to belong to two different sources. The first half of the book, chs. 1–16, are seen as belonging to 'P', the so-called 'Priestly Code' or 'Priestly Source'; and chs. 17–26 (with the appendix in 27) are seen as belonging to 'H', the so-called 'Holiness Code'. This makes it very easy for scholars to have a clear view of the book. There are a number of problems with this widely accepted theory. Let me begin a general remark. With regard to the notion of the 'Holiness Code'. It is well-known that it was August Klostermann who coined this term in 1877. I tried to find out where and how he did it, and when I finally found the place,[8] I was surprised and amused to see that he did it 'by the way' in the true sense of the word: in a parenthesis within a longer sentence. His topic was the refutation of the thesis that Ezekiel wrote these chapters of Leviticus (p. 385): Ezekiel 'ganz besonders mit den

8. A. Klostermann, 'Ezechiel und das Heiligkeitsgesetz', first published in a journal in 1877, reprinted in *idem*, *Der Pentateuch: Beiträge zu seinem Verständnis und seiner Entstehungsgeschichte* (Leipzig: A. Deichert, 1893), pp. 368-418.

Worten unserer Gesetzessammlung, die ich von nun an kurz "das Heiligkeitsgesetz" nennen will, redet... ' (Ezekiel particularly speaks with the words of our collection of laws, which from now on I will call 'the Holiness law' for short...). It was originally just an abbreviation, but eventually it became a title of a book. It came to be taken as one of the three most important law codes in the Hebrew Bible, alongside the so-called 'Bundesbuch' (Book of the Covenant) in Exodus 20–23 and Deuteronomy.

Another interesting point about 'H' is that for decades almost no one questioned this theory. It was presented in the handbooks as a fact. This is all the more surprising because at the same time everybody declared that it was difficult if not impossible to find a clear structure in this so-called 'book'. Many scholars also overlooked the fact that Klostermann had called it a 'fragment' and that he found elements of it in Exodus and Numbers. Moreover, his collection of laws included only chs. 18–26, but not ch. 17. That means that here a theory had been transmitted whose basis was rather weak. Only recently have there been any more thoroughgoing studies of the structure and even existence of this part of Leviticus. (I want to mention the thorough review of the history of research in Hartley's commentary [pp. 251-60] where he also uses the unpublished Claremont doctoral thesis by Henry Sun [1990].) The most influential recent theory seems to be that by Israel Knohl who speaks about a 'Holiness School' whose work is also to be found in several texts outside of Leviticus 17–26.[9] Knohl argues, in contrast to the earlier theories, that 'H' is younger than 'P'. This corresponds in general to Jacob Milgrom's view:[10] 'Knohl has demonstrated masterfully that on the basis of style, idiom, and ideology, H can be separated from P and that a comparison of the two resultant blocks proves conclusively that H is later than P and indeed has redacted P.' I have to confess a certain uneasiness with this kind of theory because, in my eyes, it is a new kind of old-fashioned source criticism. But this does not belong to my present topic.

What is relevant to this discussion is the fact that, according to such recent theories, the so-called Holiness Code cannot be taken any longer as a basic structural element for Leviticus in general. In any case, the

9. I. Knohl, 'The Sin Offering Law in the "Holiness School" (Numbers 15.22-31)', in G.A. Anderson and S.M. Olyan (eds.), *Priesthood and Cult in Ancient Israel* (JSOTSup, 125; Sheffield: JSOT Press, 1991).

10. Milgrom, *Leviticus 1–16*, p. 13.

text as we have it before us has to be the subject of a new attempt to understand the structure—or, more modestly, an attempt to find out if there is any structure, and if there is, what it is. In my view, the great advantage of questioning the so-called Holiness Code is the fact that we need not divide Leviticus into chs. 1–16 on the one hand and chs. 17–26 (27) on the other. This division is in any case not a convincing one. Leviticus 17 has no introduction but begins like many other chapters or units in Leviticus: 'The LORD spoke to Moses'. With regard to its contents, ch. 17 with its commandments regarding certain specific aspects of sacrifices belongs much more closely to ch. 16, the יום הכפרים passage, and through it to chs. 1–7, than it does to ch. 18 on sexual relations. Furthermore in ch. 18 the typical holiness formula, 'You shall be holy, for I the LORD your God am holy' does not appear. It appears in ch. 19 and previously in ch. 11 (vv. 44-45). If the latter belongs to 'H' it is even more obvious that 'H' cannot help us to understand the structure of the book.

In my view, one more point is of particular importance; it concerns Leviticus 26. This expansive chapter on blessings and curses is usually taken as the final chapter or the epilogue to the 'Holiness Code'. I never understood how such a fundamental and dramatic text could be the end of so diverse and almost unstructured a collection of laws as the 'Holiness Code' was, even in the eyes of its supporters. Now I can pose the question of the relation of this chapter to the rest of Leviticus without having to read it in such a limited context.

IV

Having prepared the ground, I am ready to ask new questions about the structure of Leviticus. My starting point is to declare that I shall read Leviticus synchronically. Of course, this is not in a naive sense as if it were entirely the work of one single author. But, to quote Mary Douglas, 'source structure does not prevent us from reading synoptically across the book'.[11]

I think it is in accordance with my general theme, that I take Mary Douglas's attempt to understand and to explain the structure of Leviticus as a starting point for my reflections. I refer to her proposal to read 'Leviticus in a Ring'.[12] In my eyes there are a number of

11. Douglas, 'Forbidden Animals in Leviticus', p. 12.
12. Douglas, 'Forbidden Animals in Leviticus', p. 11.

highly interesting observations arising out of such an understanding of the structure of the book. I want to single out some of them.

First, at the beginning of Leviticus there is a broad explanation of the ritualistic details of sacrifices, but except for חטאת and אשם, 'the sin-offering' and the 'guilt-offering' (or, according to Milgrom's terminology, the 'purification offering' and the 'reparation offering'), nothing is said about the occasions on which they are to be brought. In ch. 23 there is a calendar of festivals which includes some details about sacrifices. At the first mentioning of the basic sacrifice, the עלה (the 'holocaust'), we learn that in addition to it a מנחה, a grain offering (or cereal offering) is to be presented (vv. 12-13). This passage is concluded, as Mary Douglas observed, by the formula אשה ליהוה ריח ניחח 'a gift for the Lord, a pleasing odour'. This formula is characteristic of the sacrifice rituals in Leviticus 1–7 (and the consecration of the priests in ch. 8); but it does not appear in the rest of Leviticus until Leviticus 23 (and later in 26.31 in the framework of a curse). It is used a second time in v. 18.

There is a further addition with regard to the נסך, the drink offering, that is not mentioned in Lev. 1–7 at all. Here Lev. 23 contains an addition and expansion of the earlier sacrificial laws.

This shows clearly that there are certain interrelations between the sacrificial laws at the beginning of Leviticus and those included in the calendar of festivals in the second half of the book. The latter offers an answer to the question on what occasions to bring sacrifices which was not given in the first group of texts.

There is another connection in this area of texts, namely the declaration of certain cultic elements as perpetual portions for the priests, by the formula חק עולם in certain variations. In Lev. 6.11 it is declared that those parts of the מנחה that are not offered on the altar shall be eaten by Aaron and his sons as the respective parts of חטאת and אשם. The same is said in 7.34 of the elevation offering. Then the same formula occurs again in 24.9 with regard to the shewbread (or whatever one wants to call it) that is given to Aaron and his sons as a perpetual portion.

Here Mary Douglas' explanation of parallelism[13] has to be somewhat differentiated because of the Hebrew terminology. There has to be a distinction between Hebrew חק עולם and חקת עולם, which is not

13. Douglas, 'Forbidden Animals in Leviticus', p. 15.

discernable in the translations and is confused by some scholars.[14] The 'covenant for ever' (ברית עולם 24.8) is different from both. But it is very interesting to find two of these expressions in close connection in 24.8, 9. To put the bread on the altar every sabbath is an 'everlasting covenant' (ברית עולם) to be brought by the Israelites through the priests. But to eat it is a 'perpetual portion' for the priests.

In this field it is also important that the Day of Atonement is mentioned twice, first in ch. 16 and then in ch. 23.26-32. It would be interesting to study the congruences and the differences between the two texts in detail, but that would go beyond the scope of this paper. In this case, as well as in the other ones, it is obvious that both these texts have their individual history and their own diachronic problems. But nevertheless, I find it convincing that in the framework of Leviticus they can and must be read in interrelation to each other.

The next point I want to mention is the observation that the group of texts in Leviticus 11–15 about blemish and leprosy, including the clean and unclean animals, has its counterpart in chs. 21 and 22. Here Mary Douglas offers a quite new and stimulating interpretation of certain aspects of clean and unclean which surely will occupy us in the context of other papers on holiness, purity and the like. So I merely want to say that I find this interpretation very stimulating and look forward to the responses of other participants. For the moment my point is to agree with a reading of these two groups of chapters in the two main parts of the book in interrelation to each other.

Finally, when I saw the drawing of 'Leviticus in a Ring' I was particularly fascinated by the position of ch. 19 as Mid-Turn. It is obvious that this chapter has a very specific character. It is much less concerned with cultic questions than the majority of the chapters in Leviticus, and is often felt to be a kind of stranger in its context. In addition, it seems to contain a number of unrelated commandments so that many commentators declare themselves unable to find any order in it. But the main point is the close relation of this chapter to the Ten Commandments and related texts in the Torah. It adds a very specific new element to this tradition by saying: 'You shall be holy, for I the LORD your God am holy.' Holiness according to Leviticus 19 means to do righteousness to your fellow human beings. It is fascinating that the key word of the so-called Holiness Code appears first in a chapter

14. See R. Rendtorff, *Leviticus* (BKAT III; Neukirchen-Vluyn: Neukirchener Verlag), p. 135.

that has little to say about cultic and ritual holiness but much about human relations and righteousness. By the way, it is interesting that in the Gospels it is not only Jesus who combines the quotation from Lev. 19.18, 'You shall love your neighbour as yourself', with the *Shema Yisrael* and the following words, 'You shall love the LORD your God with all your heart, and with all your soul, and with all our might' (Deut. 6.5), but according to Luke, the scribe too (Lk. 10.25-28). This shows that in the Jewish tradition that stands behind this story in the Gospels, Leviticus 19 had a very central position.

V

These remarks should indicate that I see many points worth considering and even convincing in Mary Douglas' proposal to understand the structure of Leviticus as a book. In particular, I fully agree with the attempt to discover structures that cover the book as a whole. In this respect it is important not to take the so-called Holiness Code as a separate literary unit. In the first half of the book there are also clearly definable smaller units such as Leviticus 1–7; 8–10 and 11–15. On the other hand, it is just as easy to distinguish smaller units in the second half of the book, instead of taking chs. 17–26 as a piece on its own. At this point I take the liberty to mention that I have already questioned the separate existence of the Holiness Code in my *Introduction to the Old Testament*, whose first German edition appeared in 1983 and the English edition two years later.[15] So I had already overcome the hurdle that confronts every Old Testament scholar trained in historical-critical method, who wishes to abandon the Holiness Code as a pre-existing part of Leviticus. Therefore I feel free to consider other proposals concerning the structure of the book.

There remains for me one important point that makes me hesitate before approaching the Book of Leviticus as completely independent from the larger context of the Pentateuch. I mentioned earlier that I could not understand how ch. 26, this fundamental chapter, could be taken as just the ending of a collection of laws and commandments like Leviticus 17–26. Usually this chapter is reckoned among the genre of blessings and curses such as those found in the ancient Near East at the

15. R. Rendtorff, *Das Alte Testament: Eine Einführung* (Neukirchen–Vluyn: Neukirchener Verlag, 1983), p. 154; ET *The Old Testament: An Introduction* (London: SCM Press, 1985; Philadelphia: Fortress Press, 1986), p. 145.

end of several covenants and law codes. But if the Holiness Code is compared with, for instance, the Codex Hammurabi, it becomes quite clear that the two are incomparable with regard to their importance and their *Sitz im Leben.*

It is much more important to study the position and function of Leviticus 26 in its own context and in the framework of the Hebrew Bible. I shall, therefore, have a brief look at the structure and the main topics of the chapter. It begins with a reminder of the first two commandments of the Decalogue: not to worship foreign gods, and to keep the sabbath. Then follows the first part beginning with 'If' (אם): 'If you follow my statutes and keep my commandments... ' (v. 3). This opens a series of blessings and promises which ends with a passage of high theological importance.

> I will look with favour upon you and make you fertile and multiply you;
> and I will maintain my covenant with you...
> I will place my dwelling in your midst, and I will not abhor you.
> And I will walk among you,
> and I will be your God, and you shall be my people.
> I am the LORD, your God, who brought you out of the land of Egypt
> to be their slaves no more;
> I have broken the bars of your yoke and made you walk erect (vv. 9, 11-13).

The intertextual relations of these verses with several earlier passages in the Pentateuch are quite obvious. They go back to Genesis 1 repeating God's promise to make humankind fertile and numerous. They pick up what is said to Abraham (Gen. 17.6) and to Jacob (35.11) and has been repeated at the beginning of Exodus (1.7). They are combined with a reference to the covenant (ברית), again going back to God's covenant with Abraham (Gen. 15; 17). It is very significant that this central theological key word is used here to emphasize the high importance of keeping God's commandments. Then a new element comes in: God declares that he will place his dwelling in the midst of Israel and will walk among them. This refers to Exod. 25.8 and 29.45 where God declares that after the building of the Tabernacle he will dwell among Israel.

Then an even more important phrase is quoted: 'I will be your God, and you shall be my people.' This so-called 'covenant formula' has been used several times before. But in this context the main instances are its occurrence in relation to Abraham (Gen. 17.7) and to Moses

(Exod. 6.7). As in Exodus 6, here in Leviticus 26 the formula is a kind of explanation as to what God's covenant with Israel means. He will be Israel's God and Israel shall be his people. So Leviticus 26 is to be read in relation to Exodus 6. After having given his commandments to Israel, God repeats the basic elements of his relationship to Israel, and in addition to what he could have said in Exodus 6, now reminds Israel that he brought them out of Egypt. Let me briefly mention that the same formula—more precisely, the first part of it—appears again at the end of Leviticus 26 (vv. 42-45) where God declares that he will remember his covenant 'to be their God'.[16]

I am convinced that looking at these central theological statements, one has to read Leviticus 26 in relation to earlier texts like Genesis 17 and Exodus 6. My more recent studies have brought me to the conviction that there are certain clear intertextual signs showing that there are theological and literary concepts embracing the Pentateuch as a whole. This kind of holistic reading, which one might also call 'canonical reading', has two consequences for my specific topic. The first concerns reading the texts in their given shape and not dividing them into supposed earlier levels. In order not to be misunderstood, I want to declare explicitly that I am convinced that there are different diachronic levels within the text of the Pentateuch and also of Leviticus. But the exegetical task is not to reconstruct earlier levels that always will remain hypothetical and dependent on the respective methodological approach of the interpreter. Rather exegetes have to try to understand the biblical text in its given form and shape. From that point of view, I am close to Mary Douglas's approach as I tried to explain.

The second consequence is that it is not enough to read the books of the Pentateuch separately. Readers have also to try to understand the comprehensive literary and theological concept of the Pentateuch as a whole. I am convinced that there are clear signs and hints within the texts which make the reader conscious of those concepts. One of them, for example, is the covenant formula found twice in Leviticus 26 in close connection with the term ברית 'covenant', one of the most important theological terms of the Hebrew Bible. Therefore it is important

16. Recently, I published a little book on that topic: *Die 'Bundesformel': Eine exegetisch-theologische Untersuchung* (SBS, 160; Stuttgart: Verlag Katholisches Bibelwerk, 1995).

to take into account the relations of the Book of Leviticus to the rest of the Pentateuch.

My closing remarks are in a sense ambivalent. On the one hand I appreciate Mary Douglas's approach to reading Leviticus as a separate book, but not so much because she reads it separately from the rest of the Pentateuch as because she reads it holistically, leaving aside the traditional rules of dividing it according to 'P' and 'H' or the like. On the other hand I want to keep the relationship of Leviticus to the other books of the Pentateuch, because I am convinced that they are structured as a whole according to certain literary and theological principles. I think we have to do both and not to play off the one against the other.

Therefore, I cannot present a complete concept of how to read Leviticus. What I have tried to do is only to offer some aspects and arguments for an approach that is less dependent on traditional source critical and related arguments and more aimed at a reading of the texts in their given form and in their larger context. I should be glad if the discussion would focus not so much on the questions of right or wrong, as on striving together for certain common insights that could lead us to an appropriate approach to our biblical texts.

Comments on Rolf Rendtorff

Kathryn Gutzwiller

A discussant is in the enviable position of raising questions rather than providing answers. In my own case, this is especially fortuitous, since as a classicist and a literary critic I am hardly qualified to assess Rolf Rendtorff's detailed discussion of the structure of Leviticus. But as an outsider who specializes in the contemporary literature of ancient Greece, I have found much that is stimulating in Mary Douglas's reading of Leviticus as a text structured in a ring and in Rendtorff's attempt to situate her interpretation within current debate among Biblical scholars. The distinction he makes between diachronic and synchronic readings is important for the theoretical justification of Douglas's holistic interpretation of Leviticus. From a comparative angle, I find another distinction to be necessary as well, one that separates the process of ring composition from the concept of the book.

In modern terms, the word 'book' has two different meanings that seem relevant to the topic at hand. The word refers to a physical entity, to pages bound in a volume, but a book is also an intellectual concept, that which is composed to be read as an integrated unit. While the physical entity and the intellectual construct normally correspond, this is not always the case, so that we may have a long book published in two or more volumes, each a 'book' in the physical sense. A similar situation prevailed in the ancient world. The word βίβλος, which, as Rendtorff points out, is to be understood with the adjective πεντάτευχος, was a loan word in Greek and originally meant 'papyrus', then 'a papyrus scroll'. Books in this sense existed in Greece at least as early as the beginning of the sixth century, a period of time when the Greeks had extensive contacts with Egyptian culture.[1] A

1. See B.M.W. Knox, 'Books and Readers in the Greek World: From the Beginnings to Alexandria', *The Cambridge History of Classical Literature* I (ed.

number of fifth-century Greek vases depict the reading of literature, such as the lyric poetry of Sappho, from scrolls. But this does not mean that the material read from papyrus rolls constituted a book in the sense of an integrated unit. Such scrolls were probably private texts, a collection of favorite poems written down for mnemonic purposes, either to be recited orally or to be committed to memory for oral performance as song.

The point at which the Greeks began to compose texts to fit upon a papyrus roll, and so to be books in both senses of the word, is difficult to determine. In all likelihood, the rise of prose literature in the late fifth century is connected with this phenomenon. Herodotus appears a transitional figure, since there are records of oral presentations of portions of his work, but the length of the completed *Histories* suggests a written format. Thucydides, on the other hand, presumes a reading audience when he announces that his work is not a contest piece to be heard for the moment but a possession forever (1.22). Yet the process of gathering and organizing Greek literature, of editing it into divisions or 'books' that were coextensive with papyrus scrolls, did not begin in earnest until the first half of the third century. At that time the Ptolemaic monarchs in Alexandria set out to acquire all literary texts in their manifold variations and commissioned leading textual scholars to establish authoritative editions. Earlier Greek poetry was ordered in accordance with whatever principles seemed appropriate (e.g., by occasion of performance, meter, or alphabetically) and then divided into books on scrolls that were numbered sequentially.[2] As a result, the Greeks became accustomed, in the course of the third century, to think of a book in an intellectual sense, not just as a physical entity. From the second century, for instance, there are papyri containing two 'books' of Homer on a single roll; they are conceived separately as books in the thematic sense but are bound together physically for ease of transmission.

P.E. Easterling and B.M.W. Knox; Cambridge: Cambridge University Press, 1985), pp. 4-5.

2. Sources report, of course, that the interest of the Ptolemies extended even to the Hebrew Bible and that the Septuagint was produced in Alexandria as part of this flourish of textual activity. See Pseudo-Aristeas, 'Letter to Philocrates' (ed. H. Thackeray), in H.B. Swete, *An Introduction to the Old Testament in Greek* (Cambridge: Cambridge University Press, 1914). For a discussion of this letter in its Alexandrian context, see P.M. Fraser, *Ptolemaic Alexandria* (Oxford: Clarendon Press, 1972), I, pp. 689-90, 696-704.

Ring composition, on the other hand, is a much earlier phenomenon. Composing in a ring, or with the introverted structure ABCB´A´, is simply a way of organizing a unit of discourse. This unit of discourse may or may not correspond to a book in either the intellectual or the physical sense; it may be smaller or larger than a written work occupying a single roll. Ring composition in classical texts was studied throughout the nineteenth century and has been shown to be characteristic of much early Greek poetry. In the epic compositions of Homer and Hesiod, relatively small narrative units are commonly organized in a ring, while larger structures, like the *Iliad* as a whole, have also been analyzed on the same pattern.[3] As a basic method of organizing thought throughout the archaic period (and before as well, one assumes), ring composition apparently helped the oral composer remember and structure narrative units and helped the audience to comprehend them in a performance setting. This form of compositional structure continues to be a dominant mode of organizing discourse down through the time of Herodotus, who often forms his larger narrative units in rings with the moral lesson at the center, or pivotal point. In narrating the fall of Lydia in Book 1, for instance, he places Croesus' misinterpretation of Apollo's oracles—the king's all too human mistake—at the turning point of his ring (1.46-56).[4]

In the latter years of the fifth century, ring composition came to be replaced with other forms of organization we tend to associate with rational or logical thinking, such as linear, chronological narrative or arrangement by type and subtype. The demise of ring composition was connected with the intellectual paradigm shift that took place under the influence of sophistic and Socratic thinkers, who replaced traditional modes of thought with an emphasis on definition and rational argument. As examples of the changed form of organization brought about by this intellectual revolution, we may point to the chronological organization of Thucydides' history by year or Aristotle's method of

3. For ring composition in narrative units, see W.G. Thalmann, *Conventions of Form and Thought in Early Greek Epic Poetry* (Baltimore: The John Hopkins University Press, 1984) and Keith Stanley, *The Shield of Homer* (Princeton, NJ: Princeton University Press, 1993). For an analysis of the *Iliad* as a whole, see C.H. Whitman, *Homer and the Heroic Tradition* (Cambridge, MA: Harvard University Press, 1958), ch. 11.

4. For additional details about Herodotus' narrative structure, see my review of Douglas' *In the Wilderness* in *Religion* 26 (1996), pp. 78-81.

breaking down in outline form the subject he is discussing. Organization by rings does later reappear in artistically contrived poetry books, such as Vergil's *Eclogues*. However, the matching of poems in concentric rings hardly represents the same unselfconscious method of organization that is found in early Greek poetry and seems rather to be modeled on the example of archaic and classical texts. It is apparently this same disappearance of ring composition as a dominant manner of thought that accounts for the absence of any discussion of it in the rhetorical and literary critical treatises of the Hellenistic and Roman periods.

I have provided these Greek parallels in the hope that they will help in formulating some questions about Mary Douglas's analysis of Leviticus and Rendtorff's helpful remarks about Leviticus as a book. I have pointed out, simply, that structuring discourse in a ring is not necessarily synonymous with composing text in a book format. Yet in Leviticus the ring structure corresponds to the parameters of the book. How does this correspondence help us with dating the text as we now have it and with understanding the circumstances of its creation? Although cultural parallels are inexact and somewhat perilous, I would argue it very unlikely that in matters of literary composition the ancient Hebrews were more advanced than their Greek neighbors. If Herodotus' *Histories* is taken as an appropriate parallel, it may be assumed that Leviticus became a fixed text at a time when traditional methods of composition were being incorporated into texts that were designed to be preserved in written form. In Greece this process dates to the fifth century, so that Douglas's dating of Leviticus to the post-exilic period seems the earliest possible date. Since techniques of oral composition, including ring structures, have been identified even in books of the New Testament,[5] there remains a very real possibility that Leviticus was given final form, especially in its relationship with other books of the Pentateuch, at a somewhat later date.

Mary Douglas has provided us with revisionary ways of thinking about Leviticus by demonstrating that it was composed in a ring. Greek parallels support her interpretation by showing that sophisticated literary structures in written texts may coexist with very old and traditional modes of thought, that at a certain intellectually productive point in history each of the two may support and enhance the other.

5. See C. Bryan, *A Preface to Mark: Notes on the Gospel in its Literary and Cultural Settings* (Oxford: Oxford University Press, 1993).

LEVITICUS AT THE HEART OF THE PENTATEUCH?

Graeme Auld

The Third of Five Fifths—or a Book?

1.0. In a recent article, I asked whether Joshua should be read as a complete 'book' in its own right, or merely—like Leviticus within the Pentateuch—as a section of the Former Prophets. I am rather regretting now that that analogy appeared within a volume presented to John Sawyer in the same week as the Lancaster colloquium.[1] My question about Joshua still stands—it's just that I must now ask the same question about Leviticus.

1.1. It would be widely accepted that, in language and outlook, Leviticus is not as distinctive within the Pentateuch as Genesis or Deuteronomy. Genesis is the first and quite the longest of the five—but is not part of the Moses story. Deuteronomy is the last, and is so recognizably 'itself' that when we encounter similar material elsewhere in the Bible we say it is 'Deuteronomic'. But Exodus, Leviticus, Numbers are more like each other, dominated all of them by Moses and Aaron and Sinai.

1.2. Leviticus is quite the shortest of the five—and that already reminds us how flimsy the idea is that the Torah was transmitted in five units simply because they were the right length for a manuscript scroll.

1.3. The Greek name Λευιτικόν is often objected to because Levites are never mentioned; while priestly rules and ordination are. Yet Levi

1. A.G. Auld, 'Reading Joshua after Kings', in J. Davies, G. Harvey and W. Watson (eds.), *Words Remembered, Texts Renewed: Essays in Honour of John F.A. Sawyer* (JSOTSup, 195; Sheffield: Sheffield Academic Press), pp. 167-81, see pp. 167-68.

was the traditional ancestor of the Aaronites; and there may also be some traditional connection between the third book of the Pentateuch and the third book of the Psalms, dominated by songs of the Levites Asaph, Korah and Ethan.

1.4. תורת כהנים ['Priestly Torah'] is rightly urged as a more transparent title. There are two panels each of five תורות in chs. 6–7 and 11–15, and much of the rest of the content may well have been the business of priests to teach. Yet that last point is true of material in the surrounding books as well, and there are four other rules actually called תורה within Numbers. Is it sensible to talk about Leviticus as the heart (as the lively centre, and not just the middle) of the Pentateuch? Milgrom has in fact read much of the 'Hexateuch' as a vast chiastic structure—with the discussion in Exodus 33 of Yahweh's פנים (traditionally 'face' or 'presence') at its core.[2]

Leviticus and Unity

2.0. One way of plotting the relationship between Leviticus and the rest of the Pentateuch is to return to the question (1.1 above) whether Leviticus is any more or less united or consistent or coherent than the rest of the Pentateuch?

2.1. In terms of classical Pentateuchal criticism, we can approach the issue by a *via negativa* and note that at least the 'sources' JED provide no complication in Leviticus: it is a P-book. Yet that observation is no sooner stated than it has to be balanced by noting that the so-called 'Holiness Code' is a larger and more distinctive component of P (or resident alien within P) than we find elsewhere. If Leviticus does not raise questions of unity by exhibiting Yahwistic or Deuteronomic material alongside Priestly, it compensates by insisting that we pose more radically than in much of the Pentateuch questions about the unity of the Priestly material.

2.2. Another familiar way of focusing on issues of unity or consistency in P is to distinguish between story and instruction, between narrative and תורה [or תורות]. On this scale, Leviticus can be contrasted with its immediate neighbours: its only narrative is in Leviticus 8–10, while

2. J. Milgrom, *Numbers* (JPS Torah Commentary; Philadelphia: Jewish Publication Society of America, 1989), p. xviii.

they have many more stories to relate. If it is a book, this may be more remarkable. If it is part of a larger book, then less so—Leviticus may simply be the centre where narrative has paused, and all but stopped, to permit full attention to the teaching.

2.3. Leviticus and Pentateuch are read by Jews and Christians, by men and women, by religious scholars and literary critics, by vegetarians and carnivores, by mixtures of all these categories who bring their own expectations and prejudices to their reading. They are in the hands of readers who consider that Leviticus or any of its four neighbours is the basic 'reading unit', and of others who know that that basic unit is the whole Pentateuch—not to speak of those who hold to a Primary History stretching from Genesis to Kings. It is easy to document how differently it may be read. But can we answer the question what it is—how it was written to be read?

What Sort of Beginning is ויקרא?

3.0. Mary Douglas has urged a strong reading of במדבר ('in the wilderness') as a better title for the following book than 'Numbers', and not just a suitable word chosen from the opening of the first verse.[3] We might similarly ask whether the words ויקרא אל־משה ['and he/one called to Moses'] were original to Lev. 1.1, or whether they were framed as a later title prefaced to 'and Yahweh spoke to [Moses] from the tent of meeting, saying'. LXX has reproduced exactly the striking word-order of MT, with the divine subject not identified until after the second verb of the verse. Peshitta, however, placed 'the Lord' alongside 'called'; and most English versions so translate. The matter has long interested the commentators.

3.1. The position of the divine name in MT and LXX has been explained with backwards reference to Exodus, and in two overlapping ways:

3.1.1. The phrase repeats, or perhaps more precisely recapitulates, from Exod. 24.16b 'and he called to Moses on the seventh day from the midst of the cloud'. There the subject of 'called' did not require specification, as Yahweh had already been mentioned earlier in the verse.

3. M. Douglas, *In the Wilderness: The Doctrine of Defilement in the Book of Numbers* (JSOTSup, 159; Sheffield: JSOT Press, 1993).

3.1.2. It closely follows Exod. 40.34-35 which informs us that, as soon as Moses had completed the 'tabernacle', 'the cloud covered the tent of meeting. . . and Moses was unable to come to the tent of meeting. . . ' Levine, citing Rashbam, suggests this underscores the continuity of the divine address to Moses despite the removal of the divine glory from the top of Sinai to the tent of meeting.[4]

3.2. מדבר is certainly a keynote term for the whole book of Numbers. If ויקרא were also a deliberately created or deliberately placed title, we might expect a similarly clear forward reference. However, a first check proves disappointing: קרא ['call'] is never again used with Yahweh as subject, stated or implied, in Leviticus. On the other hand, the opening ויקרא does resonate with the oft-repeated מקרא קדש towards the end of the book (11× in Lev. 23)—a 'holy convocation' which, like Yahweh's 'call' in Exod. 24.16, belongs to the seventh day.

Leviticus and what Immediately Precedes/Follows

4.0. Leviticus is often read, not as something complete in itself, but as part of a larger sub-section of Exodus–Numbers. We have already noted that תורת כהנים ['Priestly Torah'] is not restricted to this 'book'. One common option is to bracket Leviticus 1–Numbers 9/10, the continuing legislation at Sinai, though no longer from the top of the mountain—the 'glory of God' now resides in the portable shrine. It is often urged against this reading, that there is no formal ending or subscript at Num. 9.23 or 10.10. Another common option is to read Exodus 25–Leviticus 26/27 as a meaningful unit. Leviticus 26.46 and 27.34 have both been identified as manifest subscripts—but of what?

4.1. Lev. 27.34 is stated more briefly: 'These are the commands [מצות] which Yahweh commanded Moses for the people of Israel on Mount Sinai.' Compared with Deuteronomy, 'command' is a rare term in Leviticus. We find 'Yahweh's commands' five times near the beginning of the book (4.2, 13, 22, 27; 5.17) and 'my commands' three times near the end (22.31; 26.3, 15). However, in Numbers it is even rarer (15.22, 39, 40; 36.13.

4.2. Lev. 26.46 talks more comprehensively in three categories, חקים,

4. B.A. Levine, *Leviticus* (JPS Torah Commentary; Philadelphia: Jewish Publication Society of America, 1989), p. 4.

משפטים and תורת, which Yahweh has 'granted/placed' between himself and the people of Israel on Mount Sinai by Moses' agency. חקים and משפטים in the plural are much commoner terms, and even more so in Deuteronomy and related portions of the Former Prophets than in the rest of the Pentateuch; תורות is much rarer.

4.2.1. משפטים ['judgments'] brackets the so-called Covenant Code in Exod. 21.1; 24.3; appears twice at the end of Numbers (35.24; 36.13); and is used some twenty times in Deuteronomy. In Leviticus, apart from the closing verse of ch. 26, the plural is used eight times in Leviticus 18–20, 25–26, and only ever with the first-person suffix, משפטי—in 18.4, 5, 26; 19.37; 20.22; 25.18; 26.15, 43.

4.2.2. חקים ['laws'] is found only in Lev. 10.11 and Num. 30.17, alongside over twenty occurrences in Deuteronomy. But the related חק[ו]ת is a feature of Lev. 18–26, used fourteen times in 18–20, 25–26: 18.3, 4, 5, 26, 30; 19.19, 37; 20.8, 22, 23; 25.18; 26.3, 15, 43. Milgrom has drawn attention to the distinction which is almost completely strictly observed in Leviticus between חק ['due'] and חקה ['law']—indeed he says in P.[5] And he nicely notes that in Exod. 30.21 and Lev. 7.36, the two exceptional passages where the usage is reversed, the Samaritan Pentateuch preserves the distinction and perhaps the correct reading. I note that in the Deuteronomic literature, the two plurals appear to be used promiscuously. I do not know whether to explain this in terms of a different linguistic milieu, or whether to suggest that there too חקים are 'dues', but in the sense of 'what is due to God', divine prerogatives or demands. However it is explained, this more promiscuous usage in Deuteronomy may have led to inattention in the later scribal tradition of other books too.

4.2.3. The Pentateuch uses the plural תור(ו)ת ['instructions'] elsewhere only in Gen. 26.5 and Exod. 16.28 and 18.16, 20. In all but one of its twelve biblical instances throughout MT (Neh. 9.13), this plural is written defectively; and in fact, of the five Pentateuchal instances, the Samaritan reads the form twice as singular in Exodus 18, while LXX offers νόμος at each opportunity in Exodus and Leviticus. In Deuteronomy, of course, the Torah is always singular.

5. J. Milgrom, *Leviticus 1-16* (AB, 3; Garden City, NY: Doubleday, 1991), pp. 618-19.

4.2.4. Can a pattern be discerned amid all this information? I see two; and remain unclear whether to choose between them or try to embrace them both.

4.2.4.1. One deals in larger generalities, but confines itself to the Book of Leviticus. This understands Lev. 26.46 as a subscript to a larger block of text. Yahweh's משפטים and חקת have appeared frequently, both separately and together, in Leviticus 18–26; and חקים, as we have seen, is an acceptable alternative to חקת. Then ten instances of תורה have been taught within the earlier chapters of Leviticus—five in Leviticus 6–7 and five in Leviticus 11–15. On this understanding, Yahweh's 'laws and judgments and instructions [תורות]' will usefully summarise much of Leviticus.

4.2.4.2. The other pattern interprets this concluding verse within two contexts, one of which is much more restricted than Leviticus or even Leviticus 18–26 and the other much wider. Within Leviticus 18–26, it is in chs. 25–26, after a break in chs. 21–24, that many instances of חקת and משפטים are clustered. The first of these chapters underscores the importance of sabbath and jubilee for both land and people; the second threatens an enforced sabbath for the land if the people are disobedient. 'These are the laws and the judgments. . . ' very appropriately resumes the dense clustering of these terms in Leviticus 25–26. So far, the restricted context. But תורות ['instructions'] in the plural has not been used since Genesis 26 and Exodus 16 and 18. Significantly, in Exodus 16, the immediate context concerned manna on the sabbath; and in Genesis 26 we are told that the promise of blessing to Isaac and through him to all nations was 'because Abraham [before him] listened to my voice, and kept my charge, my commands, my laws, and my instructions'. Leviticus 26 ends with a passage (vv. 40-45) which promises, consequent on Israel confessing and making amends, that Yahweh will remember his covenant with Jacob, with Isaac and with Abraham. The scholar who added the current v. 46 to this passage deftly pushed behind Jacob–Isaac–Abraham towards Noah and even creation by using the words 'between him and the people of Israel': the divine 'between me and you' is used in the Pentateuch only of the covenant promises to Noah (Gen. 9.12-17) and Abraham (Gen. 17.10-11), both of which have a 'sign' attached; and of the sabbath, that other sign (Exod. 31.13). So read, Lev. 26.46 is neither subscript to the so-called Holiness Code nor, one chapter early, to the whole book of Leviticus. It is a final comment on Leviticus 25–26 alone—or, better, a peroration that does not leave these two chapters isolated, but places them within a context that embraces key moments of Genesis and Exodus. Indeed, as Rendtorff makes clear elsewhere in this volume, elements of Leviticus 26 already resonate with this wider context. Levine offers a personal 'epilogue' to what he calls the epilogue to the Holiness Code (26.3-45)[6]—however, Lev. 26.46 is the text's own epilogue.

4.2.5. This reading may be in tension with Douglas's ring-cum-chiasm approach to Leviticus.[7] It certainly binds together two chapters which occupy separate positions within her schema. If a choice does have to be made, I have more confidence in the smaller than in the larger structures she detects.

Instruction and Narrative—Which Comes First?

5.0. I suspect that this is not at all a simple question—indeed that it has a chicken-and-egg quality. It overlaps with another question: how to differentiate between 'priestly' and 'P'.

5.1. It is quite possible that there once existed individual collections of instructions regulating a number of areas of life. It is perfectly plausible that the actual cult was the basis of P; and Levine proposes as its 'primary codes' Leviticus 1–7; 11–16; 27 and Num. 5.11-31; 6; 15.37-41; 19.[8] As these were combined to produce the familiar Pentateuchal materials, narrative may have been used in or for the redactional process. Again, in Levine's terms, the narratives may have sought 'to rationalize cultic practice'. The teaching in the codes would have been prior; the story, secondary. Do 'the dietary laws [Lev. 11.2-25] systematically pick up the order of creation in Genesis',[9] or

6. B.A. Levine, 'The Epilogue to the Holiness Code: A Priestly Statement on the Destiny of Israel', in J. Neusner, B.A. Levine and E.S. Frerichs (eds.), *Judaic Perspectives on Ancient Israel* (Philadelphia: Fortress Press, 1987), pp. 9-34, see pp. 31-32.

7. M. Douglas, 'The Forbidden Animals in Leviticus', *JSOT* 59 (1993), pp. 3-23, see pp. 8-12.

8. B.A. Levine, 'Priestly Writers' (IDBSup; Nashville: Abingdon Press), pp. 683-87.

9. Douglas, 'Forbidden Animals in Leviticus', p. 16.

does the prologue to Genesis follow the structure of this Torah?

5.2. Sometimes instruction and narrative are quite integrally related as demand and illustration. There are many good examples in Deuteronomy and Joshua/Judges: matters of חרם and warfare (Deut. 20.10-18 and Josh. 6–7); the appropriate ways to destroy illicit cultic materials (Deut. 7.5 and Judg. 6.25-32). And it should be asked, case by case, whether the story was first conceived as illustration of the rule, or whether the legislation was abstracted from an already existing story. This has of course been a particular interest of Calum Carmichael.[10]

5.3. Comparable pairings of story and Torah within a broadly P context have not been so much discussed, though they begin at the very beginning, with sabbath fundamental to creation. One case that has long interested me is the relationship between Moses' commands relating to the taking and settling of the land of Canaan in Numbers 27–36, and the report in the second half of Joshua about how the land was settled and divided. There I am still persuaded that the divine demands transmitted via Moses were drafted in knowledge of the reports in the book of Joshua. Indeed one of my difficulties, not in reading Mary Douglas's *In the Wilderness* but in allowing myself to be persuaded by it, is thinking together her structure with my own conviction that the closing chapters are a substantial supplement to the material in Numbers. It seems to require positing that the book was given its present shape, and related to Deuteronomy and Joshua, only after the supplements towards the end were added.

5.4. How do shorter narratives relate to the 'big story'? In an obvious sense, the big story is made up of the little constituent stories. Yet there are also opportunities within the big story for new little stories to be generated. Did several of the narratives and תורות in Numbers take the opportunity of space, במדבר, that was available to be 'colonized', of room between the holy mountain and the promised home, of a chance to expand forty days of Moses' mediation into forty years? And, if so, did Leviticus pioneer the way for this sort of extension of an earlier received tradition?

10. C.M. Carmichael, *Law and Narrative in the Bible* (Ithaca: Cornell University Press, 1985).

5.5. One way of gathering some of these questions together is to note a detail of the discussion about the relationship of Exodus 29 to Leviticus 8. Levine had earlier argued,[11] and also Elliger,[12] that Leviticus 8 was drafted before Exodus 29, that the report of Aaron's ordination existed prior to the command to ordain him.

5.5.1. Levine's more recent commentary[13] does not return to the matter. Milgrom, however, makes a powerful case for the priority of Exodus 29, with arguments noted throughout his commentary on Leviticus 8[14] and summarized in an appended comment.[15] My own more recent work on Samuel/Kings and Chronicles[16] would predispose me to be more sympathetic than Milgrom to the hypothesis of a shorter draft than to either Exodus 29 or Leviticus 8 as source of them both.

5.5.2. The one detail I select for mention is the notable use in Lev. 8.15—and again in 9.9—of יצק for 'pouring' blood, rather than the regular שפך, as in Exod. 29.12. Even those who would reconstruct a shorter source-document, must choose which of these terms that document used. Elliger argued that the chapter using the more striking term יצק was the more original; for him, the reviser of the secondary Exodus 29 had perhaps been reminded by the regulations quoted in Leviticus 4 (5×) that שפך was the proper term. Of course, that argument assumes that the narrative is prior, and the sets of regulations inserted into it. Milgrom, on the other side, has advanced the suggestion that the unusual יצק was chosen in Leviticus 8 to underscore the central importance of the blood-rite among all the verbs, or actions-words.

Conclusions

6.0 It is time to draw together some threads, though these may be too easily snapped to permit strong conclusions.

11. B.A. Levine, 'The Descriptive Tabernacle Texts of the Pentateuch', *JAOR* 85 (1965), pp. 307-18, see pp. 311-12.
12. K. Elliger, *Leviticus* (HAT, 4; Tübingen: Mohr, 1966).
13. Levine, *Leviticus*; see n. 4 above.
14. Milgrom, *Leviticus 1–16*, pp. 494-542.
15. Milgrom, *Leviticus 1–16*, pp. 545-49.
16. A.G. Auld, *Kings without Privilege* (Edinburgh: T. & T. Clark, 1994).

6.1. In preparing this paper, I have become increasingly attracted to the idea that Exodus, Leviticus and Numbers were conceived serially and not together.

6.1.1. Exodus reports the people's paradigmatic deliverance, the key commands from the holy mountain, the discussion of the divine presence (to which Milgrom so rightly attaches prominence), and the provision of an alternative, humanly constructed residence for the divine glory. It may not tell the whole story with which we are now familiar, but Exodus, so understood, is no more vulnerable to the familiar 'torso jibe' than the Pentateuch as a whole: a people is led from slavery to free worship of their deity at a mountain of his choice.

6.1.2. Leviticus, opening with a striking resumption of the divine call at the end of Exodus 24, makes plain that the Lord's commanding and providing were not just mediated through Moses in forty days at the top of a holy mountain—he could continue to convoke and proclaim from within the new shrine. The divine provision for the (priestly mediated) cleanness and holiness of Israel before Yahweh, already instructed—and therefore implicitly realised—in Exodus, is reported in Leviticus. It is the book which can properly and simply conclude: 'These are the commandments which the Lord commanded Moses for the people of Israel at Mount Sinai.' Conceived admittedly as a supplement, it is still a supplement complete in itself.

6.1.3. Numbers goes further. (For Numbers as later than Leviticus, see Milgrom.[17]) Its theme במדבר is also resumed from both Exodus (10×) and Leviticus (2×): God continued to teach his wandering people from the portable shrine even after it had left Mount Sinai. The categories of Exodus remain normative, even when extended. As in Exodus, so in Leviticus and Numbers, the people of Israel never reached the promised land, though they continued to hear their God's call in the wilderness.

6.1.4. I would suggest that the addition first of Leviticus then of Numbers was in part a device for extending the revelation, for allowing still later ages to claim Mosaic authority for their ideas and practices. Several teachings of Leviticus/Numbers may have been

17. Milgrom, *Numbers*, p. xxi.

widely current before being written down and attributed to Moses' mediation. The spatial setting of Leviticus and Numbers—each at a further remove from the top of the mountain in Exodus—reminds me of the implied argument of Solomon's prayer (1 Kgs 8 and 2 Chron. 6). The later situations envisaged there offer a hope that Yahweh may be addressed on another holy mountain from distant exile as well as by the congregation gathered at his house. Here in the Pentateuch the claim may be being made that later additions, later books, are quite as 'Mosaic' as the earlier. So read, these books embody a discourse on revelation. Indeed Leviticus and Numbers may have deliberately included the admission that their contents were subsequent to, dependent on, the teaching from the mountain-top—yet, like the exiles of Solomon's prayer, not less than it.

6.2. A serial approach to the conception of these books helps to explain their differences, including the many instances of updating—Leviticus 8 later than Exodus 29; the four תורות in Numbers later than the two sets of five each in Leviticus; Leviticus 4 used in Numbers 15;[18] Numbers 28–29 later than Leviticus 23; as well as their many similarities. I would prefer a more nuanced statement than Rendtorff's (pp. 22-35 above) that the Pentateuch contains the instructional material in force within the community at the time of its canonization. Such an approach may also help to explain the varied nature of the non-Priestly instructional material in each of the central three Pentateuchal books. The so-called 'Book of the Covenant' and surrounding material in Exodus is distinct from the so-called 'Holiness Code' in Leviticus, though many of the topics handled are the same. The closing ten chapters of Numbers (27–36) could be deemed to be analogous (largely) non-Priestly instructional material in close proximity to (the largely) Priestly Numbers 1–27. Yet the end of Numbers is more closely linked in content to the book of Joshua than to the 'Book of the Covenant' or the 'Holiness Code'. However, Deuteronomy as a whole could be viewed as a massive insert towards the end of

18. M. Fishbane, *The Garments of Torah: Essays in Biblical Hermeneutics* (Bloomington: Indiana University Press, 1989), p. 9. See also, I. Knohl, 'The Sin Offering in the "Holiness School" (Numbers 15.22-312)', in G.A. Anderson and S.M. Olyan (eds.), *Priesthood and Cult in Ancient Israel* (JSOTSup, 125; Sheffield: JSOT Press, 1991), pp. 192-203.

Numbers; and, so viewed, would provide a better comparator (cf. Fishbane on Lev. 21.5-6 used in Deut. 14.1-2).[19]

6.3. Of course, such a serial approach to issues of Pentateuchal composition, is far from answering all questions. Any neat pattern is immediately disrupted. If the completed Pentateuch is part of a wider biblical chronological system which dates the construction of the Tabernacle to 1333 years before 164 BCE, then its completion can be no earlier than the middle of the second century BCE. We have to distinguish between composition and many later adjustments. Yet we must question whether Leviticus is the heart of the Pentateuch (Damrosch[20])—whether indeed the Pentateuch has a heart!

19. Fishbane, *Garments of Torah*, p. 14.

20. D. Damrosch, 'Leviticus', in R. Alter and F. Kermode (eds.), *A Literary Guide to the Bible* (Cambridge, MA: Harvard University Press, 1987), pp. 66-77.

Discussion

Watson: Speaking not as a biblical scholar, but as a comparative legal historian who can choose which areas to work on, what astonishes me is the enormous extent to which laws are borrowed from one place to another with very minor changes, and set forth in a new context, where, if you know something of the social, political, economic, religious background, you would not believe that these were actually the laws of that place. For example, in sixth-century Byzantium, which I am told was a hot-bed of Christian debate, the basic students' textbook for law, Justinian's *Institutes*, has not one mention of Christianity apart from in the preface. The only reference to God is right at the end where it says, 'God willing, you will learn more next year'. This is because it is lifted in very large measure from a pagan textbook written about 160 CE from a very different society, that of Rome, in the Roman West. This is not an isolated example. I could give literally hundreds of examples. The whole of the French law of torts basically comes from a discussion of rules of Roman models that the French have rejected. The rejected rules frame the whole parameter of the debate. It is in that sense that I have to take exception to some of the references to the meaning of the final redaction. At least in my field the final redaction has very little real meaning.

For me, the best example is the Turkish civil court in 1926. Turkey made the mistake of fighting on the wrong side in World War I. The Allies would not give Turkey a peace treaty until it had a better modern system of law. A committee was set up which made very little progress and Atatürk told his minister of justice that he wanted law made quickly. So Turkey adopted Swiss law, almost entirely, not just the code but also decisions, customs, juristic opinions and so on. There is an enormous difference between Switzerland at the turn of the century and Turkey in 1926. How did it work? To begin with badly, because Turkish lawyers could not read German, French and Italian; but eventually it became the law of the land. What, to me, is interesting about that is that there is little regard for particular political circumstances in a new code being adopted, and no attempt was made to put particular Turkish solutions into Swiss law. Looking at that sacred biblical text in which there are none of the surrounding political economic social contexts, I just do not see how one can be very definite at all about a particular message intended by the final redactors.

Gutzwiller: I think your Turkish example is very interesting but it may refer to a very different set of circumstances where nations are imposing upon one another the need for a law code. Sometimes these law codes do not just go back five centuries and pick something up that's wrong. Maybe there was already a tradition there leading up to Justinian's code.

Watson: It goes on in areas which are beyond Justinian's code. For example in seventeenth-century Scotland, if an advocate was arguing a case and there was no precedent, which was usually the situation, the standard thing was to look at Roman law and argue from that. Because it is a tradition it does not mean that the laws, without the background, would tell you a great deal about seventeenth-century Scotland in general. My problem with Rolf's and Mary's approaches is that if we don't know anything about the background, we cannot tell to what extent the past history has shaped the final redaction.

Carmichael: Rolf said that the heart of Leviticus was the cult instructions which were the rules that the people had to live by, or did I misunderstand it? On this assumption these rules were designed for the direction of the people reading the book. That therefore constitutes what you called the heart of Leviticus. But what if the entire book is historical recollection? After all it is a fictional composition. It is given a fictional historical setting which should presumably be taken with some seriousness. So I would question your assumption if only to ask, how do you know these rules are to be taken as directives from an actual situation in the Second Temple period?

Rendtorff: There are two different approaches to the question. To the latter one, I am unable to imagine that the canonized texts about sacrifices in the Temple (or the Tabernacle) are not in agreement with what happened in the Temple. Of course nobody knows: even Jack

Milgrom does not know. Maybe the same things happened over a very long period, for many centuries maybe. Maybe it's many, many centuries old. But that is my problem. I find it impossible that they canonized a text that was not in agreement with what actually happened in the Temple.

Carmichael: Why should that not be a reconstructed, idealized description of what people thought was the way in which they did things, or even how they remembered some of it. One would have at least to consider that possibility, given that so often literature is committed to writing precisely because what it is about no longer exists. A crisis of identity leads to the need to recollect it.

Rendtorff: In this particular case I learned a lot from post-biblical Jewish rabbinic literature because it always takes the text as referring to something that really happened. It gives a lot of additional explanations as to how it worked. I think the beginning of this rabbinic tradition was written down by people who were still there before the destruction of the Temple or at least had oral traditions from which they could know what really happened. I think there are so many hints in the post-biblical literature about an actual working cult. Even Jack Milgrom would agree.

That is one approach. The other concerns the traditional suspicion among modern scholars about all the later stages in the process, and later redactors who put things together and did not know what they were doing. Do we know any more about the earlier stages? We do not know the date of the Yahwist, or the date of the Book of the Covenant. Nobody knows when it was written, for what society. We have almost no chance of determining a clear date for anything that happened before the canonization of the text. My approach is thus mainly to understand what ideas those who preserved the text had and whether they had real intentions. For example, one of the most interesting problems is to understand how things are to be read which seem to be self-contradictory. How can we read—just ask the Pentateuch experts—about the 'tent of meeting' in Exodus 33 which is totally in disagreement with everything around. Didn't they know that? If they did, why did they put it there? So I want to direct all my efforts towards trying to understand that.

Watson: My problem, Rolf, is that when you said that there were many intentions, we do not know that. I believe that in the case of law at any rate, a lot is without intention and I would believe, without knowing, that something similar could easily happen in the case of Leviticus.

Maccoby: Could I just make a distinction in what you were saying about Byzantine law being really a null quantity?

Watson: Not null, limited.

Maccoby: When law is brought in to fill a gap, that is one situation. I think that was the case in Byzantium because law was required in that situation for practical reasons. It was not required for any theological reasons because Christianity, unlike Judaism, is not a religion of law in which salvation is gained through law. That is a quite different situation from the redaction of Leviticus where the laws that are discussed are really part of the writer's heart's blood, so to speak. This is the way in which he gains salvation: through these laws. That writer is not taking over a body of Babylonian laws. There is no gap there which needs to be filled with directives like traffic directions. I think it is a very different situation. Even if he was taking over laws from Babylon, he was moulding them in a way which tended towards salvation and therefore there was a very strong intention in the redaction. The Byzantium example was a gap-filling exercise, but Leviticus was not.

Jackson: I think we are driving ourselves into a series of corners, simply by the use of the one English term 'law' to refer to an immense diversity of different kinds of sources. To make an argument, for example, by comparing the use of Roman materials in the period of Justinian which conventionally we would call law, with the normative material in Leviticus, on the assumption that we use the same term 'law' for both, because it is essentially the same kind of material, begs the interesting and important questions. I would like to bring us back to the main issues, I think, that were raised by Rolf's paper and the two responses that we heard. I found the dating material that Kathryn gave us extremely provocative. One question which I wanted in any event to ask Rolf was this: he based his argument for at least the possibility of autonomous books at an early period, in part on the early rabbinic material, *Sifra*, *Torat Kohanim* and so on. I think there are questions that can be posed as to when that itself came to be conceived as a set of books. Even if one uses that example, one is still several centuries later than the one we are talking about. What Kathryn seemed to suggest to us was that the organisation of discourse structures through rings is much earlier in the classical tradition than the division of material into literary units which correspond to a *biblos*. She suggested that that was not known before the third century. It seems to me that this is a very fruitful hypothesis to try to date what we are talking about here. What it would suggest, as a hypothesis I would put to you, is that the ring structure in Leviticus could have existed long before Leviticus was separated as a book. It may have been the recognition of that which led to the decision, once the genre of book division came about in the third century, that that is where one would divide it. Does that make sense?

Rendtorff: Yes, the distinction between book and ring composition could bring us a step further, towards an understanding of how the material is to be construed. I would like to add one more remark, about dating and historical setting. The majority of us think that the creative period in the formation of the Pentateuch is post-exilic and yet we know so little about the actual political and social situation at that time. If we are honest, we do not know too much about the earlier periods either. But we suddenly feel that we enter an era that in our handbooks is still described as the Dark Age, between, say the time of Haggai and the beginning of the Hellenistic age. Ezra and Nehemiah suddenly appear and nobody knows from where and why and we do not know what the situation in Jerusalem was. Today we do not know what Ezra and Nehemiah really found in Judaea. We just know what they tell us and they hardly mention the priests. Ezra acted as if there were no priests at all. Yet only the priests and Ezra and Nehemiah could have acted as if they were responsible for anything that happened. It is very strange and hard to understand what happened in this period.

Carmichael: Why is that strange? Unless you pre-suppose that this is historical reporting one would have to enquire into the ideological basis of the composition of Ezra and Nehemiah. It is too easy to leap between the description of the historical situation in Nehemiah and the laws in the Pentateuch.

Rendtorff: If we do not have these two books we have nothing at all about post-exilic times.

Carmichael: Then it might be wiser to admit that we know so little that we must adopt an alternative approach.

Douglas: I believe we can get quite a lot out of Ezra and Nehemiah, from the text, about attitudes and ideology.

Sawyer: Indeed we can, and from other texts as well, including Leviticus, because if the hypothesis that Leviticus owes its existence to social and political factors in the Second Temple Period, fits all the evidence we have, and some has come from Kathryn today in terms of the development of the ring structure and the origin of books, then surely that hypothesis becomes all the more convincing. It is a circular argument of course, but the more evidence it fits in with, the more convincing it becomes.

Carmichael: There is no evidence for ring composition. I know no discussion of it in the Hellenistic sources. It comes from nineteenth-century scholars. I personally find many problems with this ring composition theory. For example, Mary, when you say we should read chs. 21 and 22 in relation to 11 to 15, I disagree. I think it is crucial to read 20 before 21 and 22. Do I have to throw out the necessity to understand 20 before 21 because we have to bow to a particular ring structure? Remember, these chapter divisions are mediaeval.

Douglas: I have a different ring structure now.

Gutzwiller: You are right that the ancient traditions of rhetorical criticism have nothing to say about rings. This is a question that Mary put to me. One answer of course is that they are wholly modern constructs as Calum suggests. But I say an alternative explanation is simply that scholarly thinking about literary texts can be traced back exactly to the sophistic period in the second half of the fifth century which is that period of reaction against traditional ways of thinking such as we see embedded in ring composition. It is a break away from that, and the whole ancient tradition of literary criticism then proceeds from there. What I find interesting is that when the rings do reappear, they are in highly sophisticated literary texts, particularly poetry books, where enough people would agree about their presence that there does seem to be something in the text to suggest this kind of structure.

Jackson: I think this also addresses Calum's earlier question. He asks whether he has to throw away the need to read ch. 20 before 21 and 22, if he is going to endorse the ring structure. I think the answer to that is clearly 'No'. Reference has been made already by Graeme to the existence of overlapping structures. The existence of one literary structure does not exclude the existence of others. But—and this gains support from what Kathryn has told us—the more sophisticated a literary structure, the more difficult I find it to believe that that was the very beginning of that material. If you accept that premiss, then the very fact of a sophisticated literary structure requires us to seek to reconstruct a literary history.

Carmichael: Why do you think that follows? Why cannot it be sophisticated on the spot?

Jackson: I could well envisage a course of literary history in which the simpler literary connection, which for the sake of the argument we will take to be that between 20 and 22, existed in a body of material before that material was incorporated into a larger corpus, the structure of which was created as the ring structure. When I say I think this was supported by what Kathryn told us, she may reject this. If her example comes from collections of poetry, then what I think she is saying is that the individual poems existed already and they have their own internal and simpler literary structure. Then the ring is imposed from the collection.

Douglas: I cannot see why Calum thinks the ring composition precludes reading 20 before 22. I think that is nonsense.

Sawyer: Could I ask what other biblical works have a ring structure apart from the ones we are considering? How widespread is it in the Bible?

Douglas: The 'Garden of Eden' story in Genesis is a beautiful ring, and so is Noah's flood.

Sawyer: Although it was not given a name by the ancient literary critics, did you imply that the differences between Herodotus and Thucydides were recognised by the ancient literary critics?

Gutzwiller: Since they do not discuss it, we cannot say that. Literary criticism begins just at a period of time when the whole way of thinking that is embedded in ring structure is being rejected as not being logical and not getting us to where we want to go. So literary criticism is an attempt to find other structures and may be deliberately ignoring this pervasive way of thinking.

Sawyer: In a way it is a very obvious way to arrange material—though in the case of Leviticus no-one noticed it till Mary. It is very natural to find a pivotal chapter in the centre of a work once you start looking for that kind of structure. The book of Jonah is a good example. Scholars for centuries argued that the psalm in ch. 2 was extraneous, not by the original author and therefore to be removed. Then more recent, one might say more sophisticated, literary critics, like Jonathan Magonet, noticed that it is the pivotal point, the centre, although written in a different style. Job is another example: starting from ch. 28 as the pivotal point of the book, a really remarkable symmetry appears, right from the beginning to the end of the book.

Douglas: Apart from the pivotal structure, there are complex series of interlocking rings. In order to discount that structure, you would have to say that everything was coincidence, and there are just too many coincidences.

Jackson: In the context of these examples, can I ask you how you regard both conceptually and also historically, the relationship between your ring structure and the chiasmus, particularly the elaborated chiasmus which has been around for ages in biblical scholarship in these areas?

Douglas: To me there are two differences. One is the way you draw it, which is minor, but I would like to talk about it. The other is the one I am interested in, the macro-compositional one. As Graeme says, we tend to have more confidence in the little structures, which themselves are in little rings very often. But it was the fact that the whole book of Numbers panned out like this, though I did not know anything about rings when I started, that convinced me. Now the chiasmus is just drawn wrong, if you draw it so that the ends get farther and farther apart, when they are really coming closer and closer together.

Jackson: This is not a chiasmus but a graphic representation of it: so there is no conceptual difference. You return to the same point and you have an emphasized middle.

Douglas: That is right. If you put all the beginnings together and turn it into a ring, then you see the properties of the structure, which you cannot see if they are spread out as a series of numbers, or as a series of inclusive panels.

Jackson: If I ask a child to draw me a set of circles, starting with a very small one and then ever-widening ones, then I am sure the larger the circumference of the circle, the more inaccurate the drawing would be and the worse the circle would appear. I use this as a metaphor. Is it the case that we start off from very small units (after all, the basic chiasmus is no more than ABA)? Then you add on and add on until one can show that virtually the whole gamut of biblical laws is built on this kind of literary pattern. Once you move from something like a chiasmus, for example the law on blasphemy in Leviticus 24, into something which seeks to describe the structure of a whole book, are we not imposing on the editor a cognitive task which is comparable to that of a child who is trying to draw the widest possible circumference? It is just not going to come off fully. This is the reason why we are going to have the greatest difficulty with it, because it is going to have these jagged edges.

Douglas: Just read the book of Numbers, it is fantastic when you recognize the structures.

Maccoby: I would like to suggest that perhaps the complication of the structure is not necessarily an argument for being later. You do not necessarily go from being simple to complicated. You can sometimes go from being complicated to simple. For example, metrical compositions come before prose compositions, at least lengthy ones; and in grammar you go from more complicated structures to simpler structures where you are using endings, etc. I think it might be a function of primitive society to think that things need to be more complicated than they actually need be, simply to get them down in a form of composition at all. They have to perform complicated dances, so to speak, in order to do something which at a later stage of sophistication, you can do more economically.

Gutzwiller: Rings seems to be a basic way of organizing a unit of discourse. You find very brief narratives organized this way, within much larger narratives, so that no matter how large the narrative, it is still essentially going to come out as a ring because that is the only way an individual in this culture knows how to tell a story. We think of stories in a different sort of way, in a chronological progression and when the chronology is disturbed we see this as sophisticated and literary, etc. But this is not the way in which we find many of the early narratives told. We are already beginning in the middle of narratives with Homer and the natural structure seems to be a ring, whether it be small or large. I would agree that there would be certain jagged edges.

Auld: Then it has to be tested at each stage. What I was suggesting in the reading I offered of the end of ch. 26, was that one should read chs. 25 and 26 closely together but Mary's pattern has them in different places in the ring.

Gutzwiller: Certainly the text is linear in the sense that the person experiencing it goes through it sequentially, so 25 is going to be set next to 26. It is just that the chiasm creates another connection on top of that, in addition to the juxtapositions.

Auld: Perhaps you are saying that the answer to my problem is the same as was suggested to Calum. Yes, 20 should be read alongside 21 and 22 but that does not mean that 21 and 22 do not resonate very loudly with another bit of the book as well.

Sawyer: You have not mentioned again the point you made in your paper, Kathryn, that in Luke's Gospel there seemed to be evidence that rabbis in those days were already aware of Leviticus 19 being a focal point. This is not quite evidence that readers recognized a whole ring structure in Leviticus at that time, but it does suggest awareness of the existence of a significant central or pivotal point. Is there evidence of such an awareness in the examples that you have been studying in Classics? Although the complications and circles around it may make it more or less complicated, the importance of the centre point seems to be absolutely basic.

Gutzwiller: Yes, I saw that as an interesting parallel with what I see in Virgil who is chronologically comparable. I do not for a moment believe that he still thought in that archaic pattern. It was just a structure that he knew from earlier literature and wanted to repeat, as a purely literary structure now, and something which is just a good way to put together a poetry book. But a kind of recognition of earlier ring structures is certainly observable in his *Eclogues*, that is to say, in the way the poems are arranged within the *Book of Eclogues* as a whole.

Carmichael: I thought that Rolf's paper was arguing that Leviticus 19 is central to the book because there are no ritual laws in it, and that is the connection with the Decalogue. That is not in fact so. There are at least two ritual rules in ch. 19.

Rendtorff: Maybe I should have referred to the traditional feeling that it does not fit in very well to the so-called 'Holiness Code'. It is obviously such an important text, and I mentioned its relation back to the Decalogue. It might be placed in the middle of things in order to organize them, but in a ring, or whatever. My remarks were that it did not fit into the separate collection known as the Holiness Code where nobody knew what to do with it. If it has a position in a larger context, its function might be very important as a central point.

Carmichael: Why do you mention the Decalogue, implying that there may be a link? Why should a rule that says 'Fear your father and your mother'—which is quite differently formulated from 'Honour your father and our mother'—why should that lead us to think there is a link? After all, rules about being nice to parents have been around at all times and places. Rules about what should be done about idolatry and the sabbath, are of such general concern in so much literature, why should one single out the Decalogue as somehow leading to these particular rules in 19? Neither in language, nor in structure, nor in order does one find much trace of that.

Sawyer: Hosea 4.1-2 is another example where it is very hard to work out the exact relation to the Decalogue for the same reasons.

Carmichael: The link need not be with the Decalogue: the lawgiver may have had other reasons for setting down these particular rules. I thought your implication was that some way, somehow, he was modelling himself upon something you called the Decalogue.

Rendtorff: Yes, but my point was that the Decalogue was put where it is because it was felt to be a kind of summary. From the perspective of the history of ideas the Decalogue is not so unique. But the fact that it is given in Exodus 20 and Deuteronomy 5 suggests that it holds a central position in the Pentateuch. Only these ten commandments were what God himself spoke to Israel. The rest were spoken through the mediation of Moses. I think scholars overlooked the relevance of the Decalogue for a long time because they did not look at its literary context. The Decalogue is placed at a crucial point in the literary structure, from many different points of view. It is very interesting to discuss with non-specialists. For once I do not have to fight against Wellhausen and against dividing the Pentateuch into all kinds of pieces. Here we are much more interested in the history of the traditions, and in reading the text as a whole.

Carmichael: I understand your point. But the position of the Decalogue, which is not in one place but two, means we have to assume that these are such pivotal positions, in Deuteronomy 5 and Exodus 20, that they colour everything else we see about, for example, Leviticus 19. Is that the link you are trying to see?

Rendtorff: I am personally convinced that the one who put Leviticus 19 where it is now, had in mind the place of the Decalogue at Sinai.

Maccoby: Surely the remarkable point about ch. 19 is not its pivotal position and not even the content of its rules which are found in every society, but that they are fundamental moral rules which have to be distinguished from ritual rules, and what is so surprising is to find such rules in Leviticus at all—apparently it's not that kind of book.

Carmichael: What kind of a book is it?

Douglas: Maybe it is not a lawbook at all, in which case we can deflect the lawyers' criticisms and return to our ring structures.

Watson: My point basically has nothing to do with lawbooks as lawbooks. Traditional subjects, including law and religion, tend to have ancient books which are not changed even when belief patterns change. The formulation is already there.

THE CHANGING CONCEPT OF HOLINESS IN THE PENTATEUCHAL CODES WITH EMPHASIS ON LEVITICUS 19

Jacob Milgrom

In the Semitic languages, the concept of 'holy' is expressed by the root *qdš*. In Akkadian, the D-stem *quddušu* means both 'to purify' and 'to consecrate' (persons, buildings, divine images, ritual appurtenances; *CAD*). Through euphonic metathesis *dš* = *šd* (cf. *GAG* §36b), the verb *qašādu* denotes G-stem (mostly as a stative) 'become, be pure'; D-stem (*quššudu*) 'purify, consecrate'; adjective *qašdu* 'pure, holy' (*AHw* 906); *quššudu* 'most holy' (*AHw* 930). These listed derivatives of *qdš* are, almost without exception, found in a religious-cultic context containing a qualified subject of places and persons, which have been 'purified' and thereby 'consecrated', that is, brought in close relationship to the deity. In West Semitic inscriptions (e.g., Ugaritic), *qdš* as a verb means 'consecrate' but not 'purify', as is possible in Akkadian texts. In either case, the consecration of people or objects to the deity implies no moral dimension (on the etymology, see further Kornfeld and Ringgren).[1]

An examination of Semitic polytheism (and indeed of any primitive religion) shows that the realm of the gods is never wholly separate from or transcendent to the human world. Natural objects such as specific trees, rivers, stones and the like are invested with supernal force. But this earthbound power is independent of the gods and can be an unpredictable danger to the latter as well as to people. 'Holy' is thus aptly defined, in any context, as 'that which is unapproachable except through divinely imposed restrictions' or 'that which is withdrawn from common use'.

In opposition to this widespread animism, we notice its absence from the Bible. Holiness there is not innate. The source of holiness is assigned to God alone. Holiness is the extension of his nature; it is the agency of his will. If certain things are termed holy—such as land

1. W. Kornfeld and H. Ringgren, '*qdš*.', *ThWAT* 6 (1989), pp. 1179-1204.

(Canaan), person (priest), place (sanctuary), or time (festival day)—they are so by virtue of divine dispensation. Moreover, this designation is always subject to recall. Thus, the Bible exorcizes the demonic from nature; it makes all supernatural force co-extensive with God. True, as in the polytheistic religions, the *sancta* of the Bible can cause death to the unwary and the impure who approach them without regard for the regulations that govern their usage. Indeed, though biblical קדש attains new dimensions, it never loses the sense of withdrawal and separation, as will be demonstrated below.

The following analysis is limited to the pentateuchal codes (JE, D, P and H). Diachronically, these four codes can be considered as two: JE leading to D, and P leading to H. H is the successor to and the redactor of P.[2] In P, only the sanctuary, its *sancta*, and those authorized to serve them (the priests) are holy by virtue of being sanctified with the sacred anointing oil (Lev. 8.10-11, 15, 30). A temporary status of holiness is also bestowed upon the Nazirite as a consequence of his vow of abstinence (Num. 6.2-8), especially the prohibition against shaving or trimming his sanctified hair (cf. Num. 6.5, 7, 9, 18). Prior to the selection of Aaron and his descendants, the firstborn served as priests, to judge by the tradition, acknowledged by P, that they were 'sanctified' by God (Num. 3.13; 8.17). To be sure, P maintains that they were replaced by Levites, not by priests. However, the Levites did not inherit the firstborn's holiness. In fact, P goes out of its way to deny the term קדש 'holy' to the Levites and employs, instead, the neutral verb נתן 'assign' (Num. 8.16; 18.6)[3]—an indication of the enduring obsession of the Aaronid priests to deny priestly status to the Levites.

The term 'holy' (rather מקרא קדש 'a proclamation of holiness') is also bestowed on the fixed festivals (Num. 28–29), because they are characterized by the prohibition against work. This term is, therefore, absent from the injunctions concerning the New Moon (Num. 28.11-15), which is not a day of rest. It is also missing in P's prescriptions for the sabbath (Num. 28.9-10), despite the fact that it is the day of rest *par excellence*. In this case a different consideration prevails: The sabbath is not proclaimed—it automatically falls every seventh day—

2. I. Knohl, *The Sanctuary of Silence: The Priestly Torah and the Holiness School* (Minneapolis: Fortress Press, 1995). See also, J. Milgrom, *Leviticus 1–16* (AB, 3; Garden City, NY: Doubleday, 1991), pp. 3-16.

3. J. Milgrom, *Numbers* (Philadelphia: Jewish Publication Society of America, 1990), pp. 63-64.

and, hence, the term מקרא (from קרא 'proclaim') does not apply.[4]

In sum, the root קדש in all its forms (*piel* 'sanctify [by ritual]'; *hiphil* 'consecrate [by transfer from common to sacred status]'; adjective 'holy'; noun 'sacred place or object') bears the basic meaning 'set apart for God', and applies in P only to *certain* space, persons and time.

In H, the root קדש occurs 66 times in chs. 19–23 (*niphal* 1×; *piel* 9×; *hiphil* 2×; *hithpael* 1×; adjective 10×; substantive 36×; מקדש 7×). However, as demonstrated by Zimmerli,[5] God's holiness is implied by his self-declaration אני יהוה אלוהכם 'I [am] the Lord [your God]', especially when it is followed by his salvific action אשר־הוצאתי אתכם מארץ מצרים 'who has freed you from the land of Egypt'. The addition of these two formulae enlarges the compass of H to Leviticus 18–26. Furthermore, the root קדש referring to God and the two formulae are attested within P contexts, inside and outside of Leviticus, in passages also attributable to H (Lev. 11.43-44;[6] Exod. 6.2-8, 29; 7.5; 12.12, 29.43-46; 31.12-17; Num. 3.13, 44-50; 14.26-35; 15.37-41; 35.34).

H introduces three radical changes regarding P's notion of holiness. First, it breaks down the barrier between the priesthood and the laity. The attribute of holy is accessible to all Israel. Secondly, holiness is not just a matter of adhering to a regimen of prohibitive commandments, taboos; it embraces positive, performative commandments that are ethical in nature. Thirdly, Israel as a whole, priests included, enhances or diminishes its holiness in proportion to its observance of all of God's commandments. The key to all these changes is a new understanding of the holiness of God as expounded in Leviticus 19.

Chapter 19 opens with the imperative: 'You shall be holy, for I, the Lord your God, am holy' (v. 2aβ, b). This chapter is thereby radically different from the preceding one, which is headed by the divine self-declaration 'I am the Lord your God' (18.2b). This latter formula opens the Decalogue (Exod. 20.2a; Deut. 5.6a). In ch. 19, however, H has altered the formula to emphasize the Lord's holy nature and that Israel should emulate it. The chapter then enumerates some thirty commandments grouped into eighteen units by which the goal of holiness can be attained. These commandments are a mixture of both rituals

4. Milgrom, *Leviticus 1–16*, pp. 120-21.

5. W. Zimmerli, '"Heiligkeit" nach dem sogenannten Heiligkeitsgesetz', *VT* 80 (1980), pp. 493-512.

6. Milgrom, *Leviticus 1–16*.

and ethics, the latter taking predominance. Holiness is no longer just a matter of 'divinely imposed restrictions' but also embraces positive ethical standards that are illustrative of God's nature: As God relates to his creation so should Israel relate to each other. Thus, all the commandments enumerated in ch. 19 fall under the rubric of holiness. An example is the שלמים prescription (vv. 5-8). It is a repetition of P (7.16-18), but in its rationale (v. 8) it adds the terms קדש and its antonym הלל. However, before I enter into a detailed analysis of ch. 19, the concept of holiness in the JE and D codes needs to be discussed.

H also differs sharply from earlier JE and its subsequent evolution into D. The epic tradition had also proposed that Israel could become a holy people, but only if it would accept the covenantal obligations of the Decalogue (Exod. 19.6), the two distinctive elements of which are the rejection of idolatry and the observance of the sabbath (Exod. 20.3-11). This tradition also added abstention from טרפה 'torn flesh [by prey]' as a holiness requirement (Exod. 22.30). These three injunctions, abstention from idolatry, sabbath labor and torn flesh, are therefore JE's prescription for holiness.

D incorporates them in its holiness prescriptions by its repetition of the Decalogue (Deut. 5.7-15), its emphasis on the rejection of idolatry (Deut. 7.6; 14.2) and its dietary code (Deut. 14.3-21, esp. v. 21). D, however, institutes a change of its own: Israel *is* a holy people by virtue of its covenant. To be sure, D acknowledges that Israel's retention of its holy status is dependent on its adherence to the Lord's commandments (Deut. 26.17-19; 28.9). This condition recalls H's view of the priesthood: although priests are genetically holy, they diminish, and can even forfeit, their holiness by their violation of the commandments. Conversely, by observing the commandments, they augment their holy status ('I the Lord sanctify them [him]', Lev. 21.8 [LXX], 15; 22.9, 16). Thus for H, holiness is a dynamic concept, towards which all of Israel, priests and laity alike, must continuously strive: priests to retain it, lay persons to attain it.

Here H serves as a polemic against P, which rigidly reserves the notion of קדוש solely for the priests, Nazirites and the *sancta*. To be sure, H—also a priestly school—does not deny the genetically transmitted holiness of the priesthood. But even this holiness, limited to the exclusive prerogative of the inherited priesthood to officiate at the altar, can only be sustained by the priests' adherence to a rigorous ritual code (see Lev. 21). Israel, on the other hand, achieves holiness by its obedience to all the revealed commandments, ritual and moral alike.

This divine imperative, however, bears the seed of H's greater innovation, one directed to members of H's own priestly class. No differently than Israel, God also is מקדש of the priests (Lev. 21.23; 22.9, 16) and even of the high priest (21.15). Indeed, it is not enough for the priests to abstain from ritual impurity themselves (e.g., 22.9). They, like their fellow Israelites, must obey all of God's commandments, and they must beware lest they become 'impure' by causing Israelites to sin (e.g., 22.16)—and *thereby diminish their own holiness.*

It should not go unnoticed that the participal expression 'YHWH the sanctifier' is the first of seven occurrences in H (20.8; 21.8, 15, 23; 22.9, 16, 32). It is also noteworthy that the outer two are directed to Israel (rather, to all of Israel including the priests), the second, third, fifth and sixth occurrences refer to the priesthood (reading 21.8 with the LXX), and the fourth, the middle occurrence, probably to the *sancta.* It is also no accident that the two outer passages are extensive, giving initially the method by which God sanctifies all of Israel, namely, by Israel's following his commandments (20.7-8), and closing with the rationale for YHWH's indisputable right to impose his holiness demands on Israel, namely, by freeing them from Egyptian bondage and, thereby, acquiring his lordship over Israel (22.32-33). This motif, YHWH the sanctifier, also shows that 21.1–22.33, the unit on the priests, was not inserted at random into the H corpus but is integrally and inextricably bound to its surrounding pericopes (chs. 20 and 22.17-33). This motif reappears outside of Leviticus in Exod. 31.13 (H) and in Ezek. 20.12 (citing Exod. 31.13) and Ezek. 37.28 (based on and expanding Lev. 26.11).

Nonetheless, this overlap in goal should in noway mask D's innovation. Whereas H, in agreement with JE (cf. Exod. 19.6; 21.30), regards holiness only as an ideal towards which Israel should aspire, D establishes Israel's holiness as inherent in its biological nature. Thus, from the diachronic viewpoint, D has extended H's axioms regarding priestly holiness to all of Israel. Knohl adds a further nuance:[7] In D holiness is the *reason* for the prohibitions; in H, the prohibitions are the *means* for holiness. Both D and H, however, condition priestly holiness (H) and Israel's holiness (D) on obedience to God's commandments.

As has been demonstrated,[8] D's diet laws are modeled on Leviticus

7. Knohl, *The Sanctuary of Silence*, p. 183 n. 43.
8. Milgrom, *Leviticus 1–16*, pp. 698-704.

11, and the attachment of the holiness ideal to Israel's diet (11.43-45) is the contribution of H. H also bans idolatry and emphasizes the sabbath as part of its holiness prescriptions (19.3, 30; 20.1-8 and 26.2a). H, however, goes much further: It adds many other regulations, ritual but mainly ethical, as itemized in ch. 19 (see below, pp. 72-73), and enjoins the wearing of distinctive tassels as a daily mnemonic so that Israel can attain holiness by observing the Lord's commandments(Num. 15.37-41 [H]).[9] Moreover, it polemicizes against P's dogmatic insistence that priestly holiness is unchanging and permanent by implying that the violation of the Lord's commandments not only bars Israel from attaining holiness but also priests from retaining it. H's dynamic concept of holiness is best explained by resorting to the following diagrams:[10]

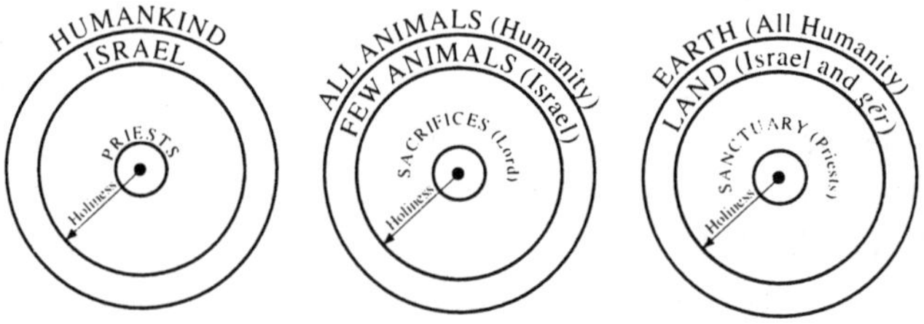

PERSONS ANIMALS SPACE

In P's world view, the tripartite division of the human race corresponds to its three covenants with God: persons (Gen. 9.1-11, including the animals), Israel (via the patriarchs, Gen. 17.2; cf. Lev. 25.42), and the priesthood (Num. 25.12-15; cf. Jer. 33.17-22). The cross-comparison of these three congruent sets of concentric circles reveals, first, that priest, sacrifices and sanctuary (the innermost circles) must be unblemished and unpolluted. They are deliberately set apart from the middle circles, implying that the realms of priests, sacrifices and sanctuary must never be fused or confused with the realms of Israel, edible animals and holy land, respectively. H breaks apart this static, immutable picture. It declares that the innermost circles are neither fixed nor frozen. All three innermost realms are capable of a centrifugal movement enabling them to incorporate their respective middle circles. According to H, although priests are innately holy, all Israel is enjoined to achieve holiness. Not that Israel is to observe the

9. Milgrom, *Numbers*, pp. 410-14.
10. Also in Milgrom, *Leviticus 1–16*, pp. 722-25.

priestly regimen or attain priestly status in the sanctuary. Rather, by scrupulously observing the Lord's commandments, moral and ritual alike, lay Israel, can achieve holiness, and priestly Israel can retain it.

Signs of this mobility are reflected in the animal sphere: H insists that the blood of permitted non-sacrificial animals (game) must be buried so that the animal's life force can be returned to its creator. H also harbors an old tradition that the entire camp in the wilderness cannot tolerate severe impurity (Num. 5.1-4; cf. 31.19). This tradition is echoed in D, which explicitly stipulates that the camp must be holy (Deut. 23.10-15). It is H, however, that extends this view, logically and consistently, to the future residence of Israel—the Promised Land. Hence, impurities produced by Israel, by violating the Lord's prohibitions, pollute not only the sanctuary but the entire land. Because God dwells in the land as well as in the sanctuary (e.g., Lev. 25.23; 26.11; cf. Josh. 22.19; Hos. 9.3-4), the land cannot abide pollution (e.g., Lev. 18.25-30; cf. Num. 35.33-34). It is therefore no accident that H enjoins upon both the Israelite and the resident alien (גר)—that is to say, all who live on the land—to keep the land holy by guarding against impurity and following the prescribed purificatory procedures (e.g., Num. 15.27-29; 19.10b-13; the גר is an H addition), so that the Lord will continue to reside in it and bless the land and its inhabitants with fertility and security (Lev. 26.3-11).

The dynamic catalyst that turns H's view of the Lord's covenant from a static picture into one of flux is its concept of holiness. For H, the ideal of holiness is not only embodied in a limited group (priests), animals (sacrifices), and space (sanctuary) but affects all who live on God's land: persons and animals, Israel and the גר.

As noted above, the commandments, the observance of which generates holiness, are performative as well as prohibitive, ethical as well as ritual. In contrast with P, which touches on the dangerous, even fatal aspect of the *sancta* (e.g., Lev. 10.1-4; Num. 4.15, 17-20), H focuses on the beneficial aspects of divine holiness. It generates blessing and life; it is the antonym and ultimate conqueror of impurity, the symbol of death.[11] This dynamic power of holiness can also be represented diagrammatically:

11. Milgrom, *Leviticus 1–16*, pp. 733, 766-68, 1000-1004.

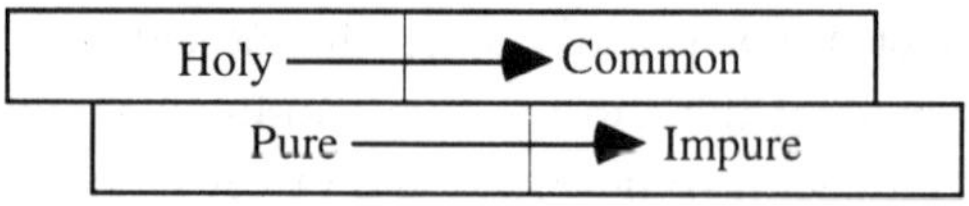

Persons and objects are subject to four possible states: holy, common, pure and impure. Two of them can exist simultaneously: pure things may be either holy or common; common things may be pure or impure. (These relationships are represented in adjoining boxes in the diagram). However, the holy may not come into contact with the impure. (Their respective boxes do not touch). These latter two categories are mutually antagonistic and they are dynamic: they seek to extend this influence and control over the other two categories, the common and the pure. In contrast to the former, the latter two categories (the pure and impure) are static. They cannot transfer their state; neither the common nor the pure are contagious. Indeed, in effect they are secondary categories. They take their identity from their antonyms. Purity is the absence of impurity; commonness is the absence of holiness.[12] Hence, the boundaries between the holy and the common and between the pure and impure are permeable, represented by a broken line. There is no fixed boundary. Israel by its behavior can move the boundaries either way. But it is enjoined by H to move in one direction only: to *advance the holy* into the realm of the common and to *diminish the impure*, thereby enlarging the realm of the pure.

Leviticus 19 provides the prescription to effect this transformation. Under the call to holiness (v. 2), it enumerates sixteen units containing commandments by which holiness can be achieved. The first two units echo the Decalogue. The sabbath (v. 3b) must be sanctified (Exod. 20.8-11; Deut. 5.8-15), and parents must be honored, revered (v. 3a; Exod. 20.12; Deut. 5.16); the worship of other gods and images of Israel's God (v. 4) are strictly forbidden (Exod. 20.3-6; Deut. 5.7-10), and as proposed by the epic tradition—which H has adopted—obedience to the covenantal Decalogue renders Israel a גוי קדש 'a holy nation' (Exod. 19.6).

Unit three: the well-being offering (vv. 5-8) expressly mentions the terms קדש 'sacred' and its violation, חלל 'desecrate' (v. 8). Unit four: horticultural holiness (vv. 9-10) lacks these terms, but its inclusion

12. See, W. Paschen, *Rein and Unrein* (SANT, 24; Munich: Kösel, 1970), p. 64.

under the call to holiness is significant. The emulation of God's holiness, *imitatio dei*, must include materializing God's concern for the indigent. Also, these gifts from the harvest are equivalent to firstfruits and tithes; thereby, symbolically, YHWH has assigned some of his due to the poor. Unit five: ethical deeds (vv. 11-13) includes oath desecration (הלל, v. 12), implying the concomitant diminution in holiness. The remainder of this ethical series (vv. 14-18) includes unit six: exploitation of the helpless (v. 14); unit seven: injustice and indifference (vv. 15-16); and unit eight: reproof and love (vv. 17-18), all of which emphasize the divine attribute of compassion, essential to God's holy nature. As neatly encapsulated by the rabbis: 'As he (the Lord) is gracious and compassionate (cf. Exod. 34.6) so you should be gracious and compassionate' (*Mek. Shira*, par. 3; *b. Šabb.* 133b).

> As he clothes the naked (Gen. 3.21), you should clothe the naked; as he nurses the sick (Gen. 18.1), you should nurse the sick; as he comforts the mourners (Gen. 25.11), you should comfort the mourners; as he buries the dead (Deut. 34.5), so you should bury the dead' (*b. Soṭ.* 14a).

Unit nine: mixtures (v. 19), proscribes the breeding of different animals, sowing mixed seed, or weaving fabrics made from mixed seed because these mixtures are reserved for the sacred sphere, the sanctuary and the priests. Unit ten: the betrothed slave-woman (vv. 20-22) involves a reparation offering prescribed in cases of *desecration* (5.14-16). Unit eleven: horticultural holiness (vv. 23-25) focuses on the fruit of the fourth year which is declared קדש 'sacred' and belongs to the Lord (v. 24). Unit twelve: eschewing the chief form of impurity, death and the dead (vv. 26-28), is essential in adhering to the God of holiness—life. Unit thirteen: prostitution (v. 29) is a form of desecration (cf. Lev. 22.7, 9). Units 14–16: sabbath and sanctuary (also 26.2), consulting the dead (also 20.1-7), and respecting elders (vv. 30-32) parallel the opening verses (vv. 3-4) and, hence, echo the Decalogue, the basic prescription for holiness. Units 17–18; the גר and business ethics (vv. 33-37) are appendices.[13]

To recapitulate, in Leviticus 19 H, in effect, writes a new 'Decalogue'. The Lord's self-declaration becomes a call to holiness, followed by a series of commandments (addressing the most pressing

13. B.J. Schwartz, 'Selected Chapters of the Holiness Code—A Literary Study of Leviticus 17-19' (Hebrew University of Jerusalem dissretation [Hebrew], 1987), pp. 120-22.

problems in H's time; see below) by which holiness may be achieved.

The basic text of Leviticus 19 (vv. 1-32) and, indeed, the bulk of H reflect the Priestly response to the indictment by the prophets of the eighth century (especially by Isaiah of Jerusalem) of Israel's cultic and socio-economic sins. Isaiah's revelation of the thrice-repeated declaration of the Lord's holy nature (Isa. 6.3), to judge by the prophet's reaction (v. 5), indicates to him that the divine imperative for Israel is to be ethical: 'The Lord of hosts shall be exalted by his judgment and the holy God shall be shown holy by his righteousness' (Isa. 5.16), a statement which is both a prediction of doom upon unrighteous Israel (vv. 24-30)[14] and an indictment of the moral failings of Israel's corrupt judicial leaders, who blur the distinction between right and wrong (5.20) and pervert justice for the sake of bribes (5.22). Isaiah's indictment of the leadership includes the prophet *and the priest* (28.2), but it is especially directed against the civil leaders (3.14) and the rich (5.8), who rob the poor and seize their land. That is to say, for Isaiah the Trisagion implies that the Lord who governs his world by justice expects Israel to do the same. In Isaiah's gloomy forecast, only those who do not participate in these social evils will survive the forthcoming purge, and these few—provided they truly repent—will be called קדש 'holy' and be admitted into the New Zion (4.3).[15]

The text of H testifies that its priestly authors have been stung by their fellow Jerusalemite's rebuke. Their response is twofold. First, they adopt Isaiah's revelation that the Lord's holiness implies that Israel must be ethical; and then they go beyond Isaiah by prescribing specific commandments (Lev. 19) by which holiness can be attained; and by prescribing a revolutionary program that will reverse the extant socio-economic wrongs (Lev. 25). Moreover, H takes issue with Isaiah's pessimism concerning Israel's inability to repent. (Note that after pronouncing Israel's irrevocable doom in ch. 6, Isaiah never again calls upon his people to repent).[16] In ch. 19, H brims with hope that all Israel will heed the divine call to holiness, and hence there is no reason to anticipate a purge of the nation (the dour forecast of ch. 26 has not yet dawned).

14. J. Milgrom, *Did Isaiah Prophesy during the Reign of Uzziah?*, *VT* 14 (1964), pp. 164-82, see pp. 167-72.

15. Milgrom, *Did Isaiah Prophesy?*, pp. 167-72.

16. Milgrom, *Did Isaiah Prophesy?*, pp. 167-72.

The rabbis follow up on H's insight and extend it into new dimensions. To be sure, they accept the Torah's basic notion that holiness implies separation and withdrawal, and hence, they interpret the injunction to be holy to mean that Israel must separate itself from the nations of the world and its abominations (Lev. 20.26; cf. *Mek.* 63a; *Sifra Qedoshim* 93b; *Lev. Rab.* 23-end), but they add, in agreement with H: 'Be holy, for as long as you fulfill my commandments you are sanctified, but if you neglect them you become profaned' (*Num. Rab.* 17.6); 'when the Omnipresent enjoins a new precept upon Israel, he endows them with a new holiness' (*Mek. de-Kaspa* 20); and the rabbis exemplify these statements by specifying that holiness is added to Israel by observing the sabbath (Lev. 19.3b, 30a; *Mek. de-Shabbata* 1) and by wearing tassels (Num. 15.37-41; *Sifre* Num. 115).

RESPONSE TO JACOB MILGROM'S CONCEPT OF HOLINESS

John Rogerson

Rogerson: Because I expected his paper and the defence of it to be the main part of this session, my response is directed to one or two specific points with regard to the text, but they may be useful here in the light of the discussion we have been having, although the points are rather different. First, the statistic that Milgrom cites about the occurrence of the stem קדש 66 times in chs. 19–23 of Leviticus was one which I did not find very impressive when I looked at the actual occurrences. In a number of instances (Milgrom numbers them), you have on a number of occasions the word מקדש or מדשי ('sanctuary' or 'my sanctuary'), and my question is whether this usage had reference rather than sense. In other words, it was referring to a sanctuary. No-one wants to suggest that a sanctuary is not sacred or holy in some sense but one wonders if you are simply using מקדש to refer to the sanctuary, whether that occurrence has the rhetorical power that might be thought if one were thinking of a statistic of 66 occurrences. I think the same thing could be argued about the word קדש, in מקא קדש or the use of קדש to denote a sacrifice or sacred thing. Does such a usage have the same rhetorical power as the word קדשים has, for example, in 19.1? Is it rather a matter of reference than sense?

I think these are points that could be argued, therefore I do not want to insist on them, but simply to raise them. But this moves me to the more substantive point I wanted to make, and that is that is you ask about the use of the stem קדש in statements that say to Israel that they must be an עם קדש, because the Lord is holy, there are far fewer of these. I think if we had 66 occurrences of such a rhetorical injunction to Israel rooted in such a motive clause, I would find the case very impressive, but when you look at them there are not more than about a dozen; and it is very interesting to see how they are distributed. I have brought with me this old but very interesting commentary on

Leviticus by Kalisch (2 vols. 1867, 1872), which incidentally anticipated much of what we associate with Wellhausen and is particularly interesting as coming from the Jewish side of things. He very helpfully prints the Hebrew text at the back and I went through, marking all the occurrences of words containing the stem קדש. It is very interesting to me, in view of the whole question of whether there is such a thing as H, and I am not sure that I am convinced that there is, that there are no instances at all in chs. 17 or 18. It is when we get to ch. 19, v. 2, that we have the first occurrence and it is one of these rhetorically important usages. I am now talking within the confines of Milgrom's paper. 'You shall be holy because I, the Lord your God, am holy.' This is at the beginning of ch. 19. There are thereafter only three other instances in ch. 19 of words with that stem, one is מקדשי 'my sanctuary', and the other two instances are in vv. 8 and 24 in connection with the fruit of the tree which you plant in the land which you have to regard as uncircumcised. I think the usages are interesting but do not carry anything of the rhetorical force that one might think. As one further looks at the distribution of the stem in chs. 19–23, one finds that they occur mostly, though not entirely, with material that seems to be dealing with priests and offerings and holy things. Now, that may or may not be significant.

At the end of ch. 22, if I may introduce another term to add to ring and chiasmus, we have a very nice inclusio. Verse 32 ends 'I am the Lord who makes you holy' and one could argue that 19.1 and 22.32 mark a beginning and an ending, beginning with the prescription, 'You shall say to them. . . ' and ending at 22.32 with the words 'I am the Lord who makes you holy'. When one looks at subsequent occurrences of the stem, in ch. 23 there are quite a few but they are all in connection with the proclamation of a holy feast or festival. There is one in ch. 26 but that is מקדשי, and the only occurrences in ch. 25 are in vv. 10 and 12 in connection with the fiftieth year, the jubilee.

So it seems to me to be important to ask Milgrom what he thought was the significance of the deployment of these specific instructions to Israel to be holy, justified by the motive clause that it is the Lord who is holy, and to ask him how this affected his view about the composition of Leviticus. I wanted to ask him whether he thought that 19–22 was the original core with clearly marked beginning and ending, because my own feeling about the talk about all these structures and things shows that I tend only to be convinced by them if they are clearly marked in the text. I am very bothered about things that have gone undiscovered for nearly 2,000 years and are suddenly discovered. Forgive my degree of scepticism but I am of the view that you can only know things if you have evidence and if you do not have evidence, you do not know. I do not mind not knowing. I think it is as important for scholars to discover what we do not know as to discover the little that we might know. I am prepared to accept that there might well be at the beginning of ch. 19 and the end of ch. 22 a clearly marked inclusio. If that were the case, I think that goes some way in supporting the point that Milgrom wants to make, that here you have some kind of deliberate extension of the what 'holiness' means. I think there is enough purely non-sacral material in between 19 and 22 to suggest the notion of holiness extends beyond what we loosely call the sacral per se to the moral and ethical more broadly. I wanted to ask Milgrom whether he thought chs. 17 and 18 on the one hand, and 23–26 on the other, were in some sense a kind of enlargement of this core. That would seem to me to bring H up to the sort of strength that it has been traditionally thought to have, assuming that one believes in H.

Discussion

Rendtorff: I found it extremely interesting and I think it fits nicely into what we have been saying already about ch. 19 being the centre of a ring structure. I was also very glad to hear your critical remarks on the occurrence of the root קדש and in particular the way in which you combined that question with the formulas at the end of ch. 22. In my paper I mentioned these important priestly formulas which are too often overlooked. They seem to have a structuring function and in particular this very rare, or even unique אני מקדשכם 'I am the one who makes you holy' at the end of ch. 22 clearly points back to 19.

Jackson: We keep talking about Leviticus 19 as if it was a single homogeneous unit. Most of what I have heard said about it in various contributions this morning, stressing the moral element, and possible relationships with the Decalogue etc., seems to refer only to the earlier half of that chapter and to have little to do with the rest of it. I know that Calum is going to talk about that, but does Milgrom help us any further with the internal structure of Leviticus 19?

Rogerson: Not in the paper he has given here. Perhaps he will in the commentary. But to defend his position, he might argue that various bits of material have been imported into ch. 19, maybe in a somewhat disordered way, but with the clear aim of achieving a broadening of the view of holiness.

Sawyer: I think we have also been using the expression 'Leviticus 19' as a sort of shorthand to refer to a chapter that has, not only at the beginning but also at the end, some unusual moral injunctions, on for example loving the גר (19.34).

Douglas: Can I ask about the disorderliness we find in ch. 19? I come from reading it as if each part had to be related to the other in a chronological sequence, but the order you are looking for is missing. Supposing you read it as confronting and fulfilling ch. 24, I think you would find that the two chapters, which are both on talion actually, would match each other in ways that are much more satisfactory, although it seems disorderly in a chronological sense. Chapter 19 has some general preface about idols and false gods and then it goes right into the ethics of just measure, lying and false witness. Then it ends with a general injunction. Chapter 24 then explains about an eye for an eye and a tooth for a tooth, which fulfils and puts on to a covenantal level the injunction about just measures.

Rogerson: I think in one way this is a discussion about reading and there is the first-time reader and the second-time reader. There is the reader who may be convinced from the outset that there is no coherence. There may be the reader who is convinced that there is coherence. They both may deploy different strategies. I have already said that for my own part I am naturally sceptical, but I would never deny anyone the desire to read the text coherently: attempts have been made from the time of the rabbis onwards.

Douglas: That is a kind of negativism which is very helpful and constructive because, although it sounds destructive, it is telling people to watch out, while at the same time you are keeping them honest about what they are saying. The only cost you have to pay if you take that line absolutely consistently is that anything might be true, and the opposite is true too. I get this from the Hindu doctrine of negation in which the philosopher's obligation is said to be performing this very important function of warning philosophers, priests and others that what they say may not be true at all. But they were never allowed to say anything. Do you agree with that?

Rogerson: I have my own opinions and am always willing to be persuaded by others. For example, I find reasonably convincing the view that there is a clearly marked inclusio in the language at the beginning of ch. 19 and the end of ch. 22.

Sawyer: Did anyone else take up Milgrom's point about Isaiah? He says quite specifically these people have taken up Isaiah's interpretation of the קדוש and are now in a sense using his authority, perhaps, in what they are now writing in the Second Temple Period.

Rogerson: Yes, that was his view. My own feeling about that is twofold. With Rolf here, I think there is an awful lot we do not know about when these texts were written; and with everything being put into the post-exilic period, which may well be right, I am reminded of something which Evans-Pritchard used to say in his books, about explaining what we know something about, by what we know nothing about. So I wasn't really convinced by that. But on the other hand, if one wanted to read the text synchronically rather than diachronically, and one was simply coming to the text and taking it as a whole, it seemed to me to be a very interesting point. From the point of view of intertextuality, one text very interestingly illuminates another. Personally I could not go further than that.

Jackson: You do accept that Isaiah was an eighth-century prophet?

Rogerson: Yes. I take it that Milgrom is working from the assumption that there was an eighth-century prophet called Isaiah who had a vision in the Temple of the thrice holy God. He has written an article about this.

Jackson: It is reasonable to say that there is common ground that H, whatever its actual date, is not likely to be earlier than the eighth century. It is likely to be the later of the two texts. Hence, if you are claiming any kind of intertextuality, it is in that direction. If you are being sceptical, I would be interested to know the grounds for it. It seems to me to be an illuminating hypothesis that Isaiah influenced H.

Rogerson: Yes, I would be sceptical in the sense that I do not know enough about the people who put Leviticus into its final form, or what traditions were available to them. But I could readily conceive, at the level of plausibility as opposed to probability, that the book of Isaiah is reaching its final form at the same sort of period and perhaps in the same sort of circles as Leviticus, and that there could well be cross-fertilization.

Carmichael: I am a bit shocked with Milgrom's position. It seems to me, unless I have misunderstood it, that he is saying that the moral stuff which is attached to notions of holiness is an advance over the ritual—that they have moved on. Is not that the traditional, Christian, anti-theological position vis-à-vis Judaism? Also, I am very sceptical about the particular position he has laid out. For one thing, one has to look very carefully at rules where the formula is not used, where the term קדוש is not used, and so on. I think you will find any time it is used it is always vis-à-vis Canaanite or Egyptian practices, so that the notion of holiness there is always in the context of separation from what these dreadful foreigners do. Of course, that notion of separation today is not surprising and there is no sense in which that would represent an advance. One would not compare the ritual material along with notions of separation in the same way in which you would compare the rules about not doing what the abominable Canaanites do. It is a much more straightforward explanation of why they used the term קדוש.

On your point about the use of the formula at the start of ch. 19, I would really stress that the material that comes before it is very much about separation too, the separation of the people from the abominable practices of the Canaanites, in particular incest and bestiality. Then it goes on about how, if you do what they do, you will be spewed out of the land, and so on. Of course it is well known that the chapter divisions are nothing to do with the original, so that I do think one has to take very seriously what comes before. I would be sceptical about any suggestion that 19.1 begins something quite new.

Rogerson: On your first point about Milgrom seeing this as an advance, it is interesting that one of the books he refers to in the body of the text and in the bibliography is Otto's *Das Heilige* (*The Idea of the Holy*) where you will remember that precisely that argument was put forward, that the notion of holiness is the experience of the numinous which is then filled up with ethical content. So that may well reinforce the point that you are making. That is what Milgrom is doing and perhaps that is something one should think about more deeply. On the other matter, I do not want to suggest that something new begins in 19. The question I want to put to Milgrom is that, if he thinks that there is such a thing as H, does he believe that chs. 19–22 constitute some kind of a core in H, clearly marked by rhetorical formulae within the material, which is then expanded before and after? It certainly does seem to be clearly marked.

Then there is the further question as to whether 'clearly marked' necessarily entails something new.

Maccoby: In relation to Calum's point that Milgrom seems to be putting forward a sort of Christian point of view that morality is superior to ritual, I do not think that is his point. As I understand it, the point of the prophets was not that they raised morality above ritual, but that they reminded people that this ritual was supposed to mark the Israelites out as a special people who therefore had special *noblesse oblige* obligations to at least keep the elementary laws of morality. They were supposed to be better than the ordinary people but in fact they were being worse. So what Leviticus is saying here is: 'Yes, these special laws apply only to Israelites. They put them in a special position as a priest nation. But do not forget, that does not make you Nietzschian supermen who are above the normal laws of morality. On the contrary you have an even stronger obligation to keep these ordinary laws than non-Israelites do.' That is the function of ch. 19.

Rendtorff: That would be a criticism of Milgrom's idea that Leviticus is in some way dependent on Isaiah, and that the priests learned from Isaiah that there have to be moral elements as well. That is the kind of historical dependence and development that I personally cannot accept.

Part II

PURITY AND HOLINESS

Sacred Contagion

Mary Douglas

The Biblical Law of Talion

According to Raphael Draï, a French professor of law, the biblical law of talion is a false and dangerous myth which has defamed Jewish thought over 2,000 years.[1] He considers that the general misunderstanding of 'an eye for an eye, a tooth for a tooth' in Exodus 21 is a myth that is as much a threat to the existence of the Jewish people as the myth of the Jews as assassins of the Son of God. The eye-for-an-eye myth presents a cruel and vindictive Jewish God. First Draï shows that the idea of exact repayment for injury is antipathetic to the spirit of Torah, which enjoins forgiveness and compassion. For this he relies on Exodus. Then he unravels the misconception that the law of talion is the early basis of Jewish law. This calls forth from him a deep excavation of anti-semitic bias in Western thought.

After discussing the role of the Jew in literature, (in Marlow, Shakespeare and in German romance, as well as in Sigmund Freud), Draï compares this image of the Law with what the Talmud says, and with later Jewish commentary on talion. His complaint against *The Merchant of Venice* is that it is sheer malignant fantasy to imagine a Jew claiming the flesh of his debtor as legally his by right of contract. It is inconceivable for a pious, informed Jew to make such a claim and pretend that it is in accord with biblical law. The case is that biblical origins in Exod. 21.23, 24, 25 and other laws of restitution need to be placed in the full context of laws requiring generosity and respect for life. Draï is writing in the tradition of the rabbis who 'made an intense polemic effort to demonstrate the milder intent of biblical law'.[2]

1. R. Draï, *Le Mythe de la loi du talion, une introduction au droit Hebraïque* (Aix-en-Provence: Editions Alinea, 1991).

2. B.A. Levine, *Leviticus* (JPS Torah Commentary; Philadelphia: Jewish Publication Society of America, 1989), p. 268.

However, one cannot say that the religion is not retaliatory. It depends what you mean by the term. Curiously, Professor Draï says nothing about the strong retaliatory talk in Leviticus 24, where the Lord says:

> 19 and if a man cause a blemish in his neighbour, as he hath done, so shall it be done to him:
> 20 Breach for breach, eye for eye, tooth for tooth: as he caused a blemish in a person, so shall it be done to him.

My support for Draï's argument is that Exod. 21.23 and Leviticus 24 where the negative retaliations occur are balanced with positive laws; both positive and negative should be read in the spirit of generosity. So at the end of *The Merchant of Venice*, when the hounded, defeated Shylock is asked to be generous to his daughter, he ought to recognize the voice of his own religion.

The Bible is retaliatory in a perfectly proper sense of requiring reciprocity. Marcel Mauss in his *Essay on the Gift*[3] showed that a principle of cosmological reciprocity upholds the social theory of ancient civilisations. Positive retaliation means the return of good for good, matching the law of returning harm for harm. Leviticus repeatedly insists that the covenant between God and his people is a reciprocal obligation, and also that God is always the more generous partner.

I make common cause with Professor Draï because I would wish to say the same for biblical ideas of purity as he says for biblical ideas of retaliation. A dangerous myth attributes to the Bible (and especially Leviticus) a trivializing prurience about body, food and sex. Add to the idea of a vindictive legal system the idea of a squeamish, purity-obsessed religion and you have an unedifying view of Judaism and the God of the Bible. There is an interesting difference between the two cases: Jewish believers tend to agree with Draï against outsiders on the subject of talion; at the same time many subscribe to the idea that impurity is the dominant concern of the priestly laws. The result is a rift between the priestly books and the rest of the Pentateuch.

In what follows I will try to show the unity of the book in a traditional way. One idea is simply that the metaphor of uncleanness summons established ideas about contagion to the support of the covenant and particularly to defend the first commandment against other gods. Sexual debauchery and spreading disease are figures here,

3. M. Mauss, 'Essai sur le Don', in *Sociologie et Anthropologie* (Paris: Presses Universitaires de France, 1950).

as elsewhere, of unfaithful Israel. This needs more elaboration than I have space for here. The other idea is to use the doctrine of divine compassion as an interpretative principle for this book. This follows the traditional idea that the Bible has unity through the Pentateuch, instead of following historic protestant prejudice against the priestly caste.

Some have sought to protect the religion from contempt by downgrading Leviticus to the status of a handbook of cultic practice. This strategy seems to assign only low level responsibility to the book, as if purity was the concern for officiants, and ceremonial details a minor matter compared with the grand philosophy and theistic doctrines. To take this line is to support Wellhausen's project[4] of separating the characteristically Priestly themes from the rest of the Bible by reading the prophets without the Law, and implicitly taking license therefrom to read the law without the prophets. In consequence, only a few Bible scholars, almost all present in Lancaster today, treat purity as a central theological doctrine. Most have separated it from their work, and sent it into the margins of biblical scholarship.

Holiness and Ritual Cleanness

My procedure will be to focus particularly on verses in Leviticus which imply a conflict between the compassionate mercy of God and the requirements of holiness. I will ask why God does not want lepers in the camp (Num. 5.2-4)? Why are leper priests (Lev. 22.4) and blind, lame, hunchbacked, dwarfed and mutilated members of the priestly line excluded from the sacrifice of his sanctuary (21.16-24)? In Deuteronomy, the Lord even rejects the mutilated from the congregation (Deut. 23.1). And why does he class some animals of his creation as abominable and unclean?

If I were asking why his law is harsh on sexual offenders, on incest, adulterers and homosexuals (Lev. 20.13), I would be reproached for applying anachronous moral standards. But I am less interested in archaic moral ideas and more interested in interpretations that attribute inconsistency to the Bible. Deuteronomy (15.7-11) recommends kindness to the poor, the psalms are full of praise for the Lord as the comfort of the afflicted, the Chronicler can cry out to the Lord in affliction (2 Chron. 20–29), in Leviticus the Lord is sensitive to the

4. R. Rendtorff, 'Two Kinds of P? Some Reflections on the Occasion of the Publication of Jacob Milgrom's Commentary on Leviticus 1–16', *JSOT* 60 (1993), pp. 75-81.

trials of the blind and the deaf (Lev. 19.14). Leprosy and mutilations are terrible afflictions; but the Lord wants to reject lepers and cripples from his service. Is not this a contradiction?

One common reply is that the symbolism is the issue, it has nothing to do with the pain of the mutilated body: kindness has nothing to do with cleanness; the levitical texts explain the meaning of holiness, being set apart, pure, by contrasting it with bodily imperfections, smeared and broken boundaries. This answer confirms that purity as a value in itself is the dominant idea, and takes the puzzle back to God's hardheartedness. Commentators on Leviticus go to pains to insist that uncleanness concerns ritual status and is a technical term. Only Wellhausen seems to have taken seriously the apparent conflict between the Lord's holiness and his compassion.

After reading two recent commentaries on uncleanness, I began to wonder about the traditional translation.[5] In some religions several words indicate different kinds of transgression: violation, corruption, spoiling, breaking, causing to be sick; and such a word may refer to a person, a deed, an object or place. Sometimes a general term refers to transgression and its effects. In the Bible defilement seems to be just such a portmanteau term. I wondered if it was over-used perhaps by the translators, and whether a less metaphor-laden term would do, such as sacred contagion. The priestly editors' apparent obsession with dirt and cleansing might be an effect of a too literal translation. However, not very far into my reading of the JPS commentaries on Leviticus and Numbers,[6] I found I was wrong. The scholarly Hebrew translators were exonerated, and I was humbled.

The dictionary tells me that Leviticus uses several ideas for sin: טמא, defilement, means becoming unclean by sin or by contact, and to be at fault; חטא means to miss the mark, miss the way, the goal, the path of right and duty, to err, to go astray, to do wrong. It is applied to breaking the law, incurring a debt, breaking faith, and to incurring guilt. For indicating what has to be done to put the transgression right there are various resources, asking the priest to purify (טהר), to make

5. W. Houston, Purity and Monotheism: Clean and Unclean Animals in Biblical Law (JSOTSup, 106; Sheffield: JSOT Press, 1992); P.P. Jenson, *Graded Holiness: A Key to the Priestly Perception of the World* (JSOTSup, 106; Sheffield: JSOT Press, 1992).

6. Levine, *Leviticus*; J. Milgrom, *Numbers* (JPS Torah Commentaries; Philadelphia: Jewish Publication Society of America, 1990).

reparation (אשם) or to atone, make good, or expiate (כפר). The latter word has very wide applications in the Bible, including and going beyond the metaphor of purifying, to include acquittal, ransom, penalty, repentance, keeping to the right path.

Moses told the priests to teach the people the difference between clean and unclean (10.10); the next chapters (11–16) give a peculiar ritual significance to bodily states declared unclean, and through the rest of the book the people are adjured not to sin *and* to avoid defiling themselves. To me at this stage it is not clear whether these are two separate commands or whether the injunction against defilement is a literary intensifier of the command not to sin. An example of the intensifier use is: 'You shall keep my charge not to engage in any of the abhorrent practices that were carried on before you, and you shall not defile yourselves through them' (18.30). Sins which involve intention, such as sexual misconduct, defile (Lev. 18.25, 27); idolatry defiles sacred places (2 Kgs 23.8, 2 Chron. 36.14), and any of the doings listed in 18 from vv. 1-24 will defile the land (Lev. 18.25, and 27). The same word used for the defilement of sin applies to certain bodily conditions which exemplify and convey it (Lev. 12–15). I am not sure that it makes sense to sort out sin from defilement, as the book's literary form tends to use ideas in paired similars (leprosy and blemish, as I shall show below) as well as in contrasts. But in any case, no one but the Priestly editor is to blame if the book has a reputation for devoting a lot of attention to defilement. We have to assume that he meant to do so.

This becomes part of the puzzle. What has Leviticus achieved by gathering together a wide variety of transgressions under the head of clean/unclean? Is the idea of contamination part of a new synthesis or was it there before the P of the cult rules wrote it down? As Raphael Draï wants to see the law of talion set in the full context of laws of restitution, so also should the laws of contagious uncleanness be set in the full context of holiness. This is a bigger task than I am competent to undertake. At least as an anthropologist I can suggest why the Bible is harsh on cripples and lepers and certain non-human creatures. I can do this by sketching in different kinds of context for sacred contagion. One is the context of comparative religion. One is social, how do purity ideas get put to use? One is the literary context of this particular text, and lastly, but perhaps impossibly, the context of history.

The Universal Model of Sacred Contagion

Our ideas of ritual uncleanness are largely derived from a nineteenth-century model of power in nature. French scholars in the Section V of the École Pratique des Hautes Études were trying to develop a comparative basis for religion that would relate Judaism, Christianity and Hinduism.[7] They focused on sacrifice as the particular point at which humans relate to the transcendental sphere in which divine power is located. Their elementary model used images of lightning conductors and the harnessing of electricity to explain sacrifice.[8] The case of electricity was fashionable as an example of a power that might be for good, but had to be channelled and contained; we could use nuclear power. Zeus carried a bunch of thunderbolts, Apollo used to send plague in his arrows, Genesis used flood water and Numbers used fire and plague as instruments of the wrath of God. At first sight it also seems as if Leviticus describes God inflicting contagious skin disease as a punishment, but there is a difference. The disease is not caused by the wrath, the disease and the associated uncleanness are circumstances which call down the wrath of God.

The fixed parts of the universal model are two worlds, a secular one for the humans, and a sacred one, a source of unlimited power for good or ill; in between the two lies a dangerous liminal area, the interface with both worlds; the fourth element in the model is sacred contagion. Religions vary according to how they believe that the sacred power in World 2 can be tapped and what humans can do to bring it out to help their lives in World 1; and according to how they can stop undesired intrusions and attacks. On this approach magic and ritual are handles for persons in World 1 to get a grip on World 2. Doctrines about the reliability of these techniques range from high confidence in their efficacy, to denial that they have any influence at all, especially no power to constrain the freedom of God to dispose as he wishes.

Jacob Milgrom, quoting Ben Zakkai, would put Judaism at the extreme end of that gamut. He insists that in biblical Judaism magic

7. I am grateful to Ivan Strenski for this understanding of the beginnings of the modern discussion of comparative religion.

8. I. Lévi, 'Le sacrifice d'Isaac et la mort de Jesus', *Revue des Études Juives* 64 (1912), pp. 161-84; S. Lévi, *La doctrine du Sacrifice dans les Brahamanas* (Paris: Leroux, 1898), p. 27; H. Henri and M. Mauss, 'Essai sur la Nature et la Fonction du Sacrifice', in *L'Année Sociologique*, II (ET *Sacrifice: Its Nature and Functions* [trans. W.D. Halls; Chicago: University of Chicago Press, 1964]).

does not work, ritual does not work, only God's will is effective.[9] In his view magic is repudiated in Judaism as an impugning of the perfect doctrine of monotheism. God may be angry, or stay his anger, but no human or spiritual being can oblige him to do one or the other. No one can promise to put things right with God, or claim to be able to bring rain, or to heal the sick. The only miracles are God's. There is no magic, and no minor spiritual being to whose intervention a desperate cause can be entrusted. Robert Markus has drawn a close parallel between this thinking and that of Augustine.[10] I hope that what follows will serve to confirm this view of the foundations of Judaism and add something about Leviticus's contribution to the pure unmagical monotheism of the Bible.

The universal model was intended to explain why a religion was more biased this way than the other: Why more monotheism here and more polytheism there? Why more magic, or less? For the school of l'Année Sociologique answers would be in terms of how the doctrines were embedded in institutions. Religion was thought to be a vital influence in society (who would deny it?), and the pressures of social life were likewise expected to influence its doctrines (why not?). For them the context of comparative religion pointed on to the philosophical and social contexts. But for others there still is no way to justify such comparisons. Beyond an intellectual account of doctrine lie the evils of reductionism. Religions can be described but not further explained; reductionism leads to shallow and false conclusions and must be avoided.

Histories of anthropology describe how in the 1930s the armchair view of the subject came to be superseded by the fieldworkers' view. In the history of religion the intellectualist interpretation is being superseded by one that expects the religion to be implanted in the lives and institutions of the believers. Explanations of beliefs show how they are used to serve the worldly concerns of the congregation. The anthropological approach is modest in respect of claiming to know the divine purposes, but bold in claiming to analyse the human purposes to which religious institutions are bent. To compare religions we have to compare the uses to which doctrines are applied.

9. Milgrom, *Numbers*, Excursus 48, p. 438.

10. R. Markus, 'Augustine on Magic: A Neglected Semiotic Theory', *Revue des etudes Augustiniennes* 40 (1994), pp. 375-88.

Ritual Impurity as a Branch of Contagion in General

Essentially, sacred contagion is a variant of ordinary contagion. Who would try to understand it without knowing something about the secular sort? Contagion is a causal notion, it is a theory of transmission, usually but not always based on proximity. It is a perfect theory for enforcing order by holding persons to account. Sickness and misfortune are co-opted into the universal model by making someone responsible, someone can be accused of unleashing the power against the victim. Sacred contagion directs blame.

In any community, but specially in one that is poorly organized as to the effectiveness of its judicial apparatus, the neatest sort of blame points the finger at transgressions which bring down their own punishment. No one needs to do anything unpopular, whisper and rumour are enough. In an unstable society accusations can be rife, flying in all directions: then contagion theory contributes an accelerator to the general destabilizing by making hate and envy effective.[11] In a stable situation contagion theory tends to be regulated and the religion tends to settle down to a universe whose dangers are coded for enhancing social control.

Once the classes of sins and the classes of contagions they launch are classified, a community can sit back and watch the course of events. Inexorably the punishments will be found to fall on offenders. Apparent exceptions are only deferrals of what is bound to happen, for eventually trouble does catch up with the sinner, everyone dies in the end. The concept of contagion is also useful socially for defining identity. A person who is assigned to the class of the less pure can legitimately be put down. This gives everyone an interest in defining themselves as more pure. Signs of purity in character or descent prove eligibility for marriage, or for office.

It is useless to treat the biblical rules for containing sacred contagion as a purely intellectual system, however beautiful, however consistent. Tracing how purity rules mesh with the exigencies of social life is the only way to demonstrate that a local theory of contagion has been understood. God is not arbitrary. Borrowing from Einstein's theology that God does not play dice, we can suppose that he devised his law for the kind of society that he chose for his people to live in.

11. G. Paicheler and A. Quemin, 'Une Intolerance diffuse: Rumeurs sur les origines du sida', *Sciences Sociales et Santé* 12.4 (1944), pp. 41-76.

Social Uses of Secular Contagion

We do not have to dig into ancient religious archives to learn about contagion when we have examples all round at all times. Some are used as rituals of separation, to clarify identity. For example, in Paris when my mother-in-law was young, after a death in the family the clothes of the defunct were given away, but the pollution of death had first to be removed. It was simply a matter of asking the dry cleaner to put them through the regular treatment used for the purpose.

Here follow some contemporary examples collected by sociological colleagues.

a) Contagious mental handicap:[12] This is a theory about how to protect those who receive mental patients in their own homes from contamination; neighbours who suspect that they may have acquired mental illness by contact and make it a reason to refuse inter-marriage, are rebutted by proof of extreme care to prevent contact by commensality.

b) Contagious HIV conveyed through the eye:[13] Nurses caring for AIDS sufferers need to prove they are trustworthy by demonstrating their care to insulate and protect against contamination; when an HIV positive patient leaves the leisure room after watching television with other patients, the nurse ostentatiously disinfects the television screen.

c) Contagion from proximity of an alcoholic:[14] Patients suffering from lassitude and depression explain it by the contamination of their living space shared with an alcoholic.

d) Contagion from passive smoking (the newspapers): In England and America active smokers are warned that they can harm their own babies by their habit. One friend told me that she had despaired of persuading her son and daughter-in-law to give up smoking, sorrowfully predicting early deaths for both, and added that she only hoped that they would have a

12. D. Jodelet, *Folies et representations sociales: Sociologie d'Aujourd'hui* (Paris: Presses Universitaires de France, 1989).

13. M. Calvez, 'Composer avec un danger: Approche des réponses sociales à l'infection du VIH er au SIDA' (Institut Régional du Travail Social de Bretagne, 1989).

14. S. Fainzang, 'L'alcoolisme, un maladie contagieuse? Reflexions anthropologiques sur l'idée de contagion', *Ethnologie Francaise*, Melanges 4.24.4 (1994), pp. 825-32.

> child, for then they would be forced by public opinion if not by their own parental anxiety to stop, because of the dangers for the foetus. This is like the form of social control embodied in the African idea that a woman endangers her baby by adultery.

Rolf Rendtorff recently asked how Leviticus is related to the rest of P.[15] I wish to narrow the question by asking how the cultic idea of holiness shows up in the narrative books. Is sacred contagion the same in Samuel and Kings as in Leviticus? At first glance the answer is that in the Bible narratives sacred contagion behaved just like anywhere else. Transgressions come to light, and prophecies are justified because of misfortunes. Divine anger uses contagion to protect God's law.

For example, the disaster which befell the old priest Eli's two sons, both killed in the one day, is traced to their exorbitant demands, their neglect of their priestly duties and generally debauchery (1 Sam. 2.22, 30–36; 4.10). Sacred contagion protects sacred things from profanation by eye or touch: the Lord smote the men of Beth-shemesh (over 50,000 dead) because they looked into the ark (1 Sam. 6.19). The weather is a common medium of sacred contagion and in the Bible it responds to evil-doing with thunder and rain in the usual way (1 Sam. 12.18; 1 Kgs 18.40–45). Disease too: the widow who has sheltered Elijah immediately believes that her sins have affected her son and brought him to death's door (1 Kgs 17.18); the Lord smote the people with blindness (2 Kgs 6.18) and allowed Elisha to transfer Naaman's leprosy to Gehazi (2 Kgs 5.27). High rank is no protection: King Uzziah was struck down by leprosy when he neglected the cult (2 Kgs 15.13); the disasters which befell King David are attributed to his sin. The journey from Egypt in Exodus and Numbers is full of large scale devastation caused by disobedience or murmuring against the Lord, and by encroachment on the tabernacle.

Ritual Defilement Disarmed

All of these biblical instances are fully in accord with the way that sacred contagion works in the rest of the world. God's anger is a highly specific and precisely targeted weapon in the hands of his prophets. These narrative accounts of sacred contagion are different from the cultic account. I cannot emphasize enough how extraordinary

15. R. Rendtorff, 'Two Kinds of P?'.

it is to come back to Leviticus after reading the narrative books. First, as far as I can tell, defilement (טמא) hardly figures in accounts of sacred contagion in Samuel and Kings. Secondly, in Leviticus the free-wheeling spontaneity of sacred contagion has gone. Under the prophets and judges it was unpredictable, only a prophet could say where it was going to strike next; people would reasonably hope they might escape punishment for their sins.

The levitical rubric is a bureaucratization. In effect, ritual contagion, usually a punishing accusation, has been defanged, its claws are drawn, it is rendered helpless for defence or attack. The systematization of sin in Leviticus makes all human creatures unavoidably liable to defilement. Regardless of good intentions defilement in one form or another is going to happen to everyone and anyone at any time. Even leprosy (in spite of popular prejudice) may be inadvertent, an accident of birth. The situation is that certain exudations from living organisms automatically incur ritual contagion. Not all—our biological condition normally causes our bodies to exude tears, saliva, urine and faeces; these leaks happen all the time and do not attract pollution; but bodies also bleed, secrete sexual fluids, discharge pus and blood from wounds and festering sores. According to context, these secretions variously reduce a person's ritual status. In his mercy God has given the rite of Atonement which restores to clean and sound condition (תמם). In itself, to be unclean is not a sin. Uncleanness is something that keeps happening, and the sin lies in not doing anything about it. That 'there is no man who sinneth not' (1 Kgs 8.46, and Eccl. 7.20) is a fine principle, which Leviticus makes effective in more ways than one. Mainly, it takes away from the prophets the initiative to denounce, and brings sin within the control of the priests.

In the narrative books, sacred contagion mostly attacks intentional transgressions. There were exceptions: Uzzah was killed because he accidentally touched the ark (2 Sam. 6.6-7). Another obvious exception in which physical conditions draw direct sacred contagion is the vow of nazirites, when the hair is cut (Samson's story in Judg. 16). Numbers 5 takes up the case of a nazirite unintentionally defiled by a dead body. It is true that in the Near East leprosy and indeed most illnesses were attributed to sins of the afflicted.[16] Leprosy could be the result of a curse. David cursed the house of Joab (2 Sam. 3.29: 'Let there never cease from the house of Joab one who has an issue or who is a leper,

16. Milgrom, *Leviticus 1–16*, p. 821.

or who leaneth on a staff, or who falleth on the sword, or who lacketh bread'.[17] But, between the Book of Kings and Leviticus there is a switch of focus. In Leviticus, however much the odour of past sin may hang around the idea of leprosy, the interest is not upon the cause of the condition. It may be wrong to argue from absence, but at least in Leviticus God does not send leprosy for punishment.[18] Someone who has incurred leprosy as the result of being born into a line that has inherited an ancient curse would reasonably count as personally innocent, just as much as victims of other accidents of birth, such as being born with a disability. In the priestly books uncleanness is a sacred contagion whose conditions are independent of intention. Misfortunes are effectively decoupled from sins.

Elsewhere breach of taboo can be punished; usually a category of persons is targeted, or a particular class of transgression.[19] Here the priests have defined uncleanness so that everyone is liable to incur it; it is so common and frequent that everyone is also likely to be guilty of neglecting the prescribed means of ritual cleansing. The *tu quoque* riposte disarms the accuser: it is difficult to make a charge stick if the accuser is only too obviously guilty. Unlike the plagues sent against the people of Israel for their murmuring in the Book of Numbers, in Leviticus leprosy and blemishes are not punishments. You cannot look at an afflicted person and speculate: 'Tut, tut, which sin brought it on him?' Under this doctrine, misfortunes do not betray a sinner. Accusing is thwarted.

Morton Smith said that the levitical law of leprosy gave what he considered a frightening amount of power to the priests: 'If a priest said a man had "leprosy" the man could no longer live in an observant community; a house or a garment declared "leprous" might have to be destroyed'.[20] But a less prejudiced view would see the priestly responsibility to declare official cleanness as a way of bringing the cured person, house or garment back into society rather than putting them out. In certain forms of leprosy the sick person can have a remission,

17. I thank Hannah Harrington for clarification on this given during the Colloquium.

18. Milgrom, *Leviticus 1–16*, pp. 856-58.

19. M. Douglas, *Purity and Danger: An Analysis of Concepts of Pollution and Taboo* (London: Routledge & Kegan Paul, 1966).

20. M. Smith, *The Cambridge History of Judaism*, I (Cambridge: Cambridge University Press, 1984), pp. 219-78, see p. 247.

get ill again, and be cured again. Going in and out of the state of leprosy, the legislation allows the patient to leave and come back into the community after showing proof of healthy status. Smith underestimated the much more frightening powers of the community in adjudicating ritual contagion spontaneously and without a rule. I would suggest, contrary to his view, that the priestly doctrine of uncleanness is like a general amnesty. It would help to make it clear if I could explain the difference between structured and unstructured witchcraft accusations and my own personal horror of leaving these decisions to the mob.

When I first went to study the Lele people in present day Zaire, accusations of sorcery were only credible if they indicted old men;[21] children, young men and most women were stereotypical victims; in consequence old men had to be careful how they behaved lest they got accused and convicted and severely punished. Thus the arrow of accusation placed a control on gerontocratic power holders. When I went back thirty-five years later, that control was gone and there was no more gerontocratic power to be controlled. Accusations went in all directions, the wildest slanders were credible, women, young men, even children, could be maliciously causing death, and with the anarchy went arbitrary and cruel punishments. In the first stage witchcraft beliefs were like a house dog trained to protect the social structure from abuse of power; in the second stage the dog had gone mad and was biting the householders. At such a disorderly time in any community, when seers' accusations run wild, authorities would do well to look for some way to muzzle the dog.

Many scholars rely on Ezra–Nehemiah for the period. To bear out my point, recall how Nehemiah saw himself as beset by envious rivals, by political conspiracy, skullduggery and open attack, including that of 'the prophetess, Noadiah, and the rest of the prophets, who would have put [him] in fear' (Neh. 6.14). Those were difficult times for rulers, a theme which Hyam Maccoby's paper in this volume develops. In such a context, the expanded doctrine of uncleanness was an inspired stroke. By generalizing guilt it would work to defuse disruptive accusations; it would have calmed prophetic attack and deflected sectarian denunciation. Failure to get purification was treated as an explicit

21. M. Douglas, 'Techniques of Sorcery Control in Central Africa', in J. Middleton and E.H. Winter (eds.), *Witchcraft and Sorcery in East Africa* (London: Routledge & Kegan Paul, 1963), pp. 123-42.

rejection of God's commands, a serious sin classed with breach of the covenant and apostasy. By a brilliant stroke the revulsion against uncleanness was graphically redirected to the protection of the covenant.

This is the switch, I would suggest, that transformed Judaism into a modern religion. The prophets denounced sorcerers and soothsayers, consultations with the dead, unlawful divinations and conjurations. Anyone can denounce spiritual misdemeanour, and uncontrolled denouncing can tear a community apart. The doctrine of uncleanness effectively makes an end of accusation, it stops misfortunes being attributed to the neighbour's sins, it stops suspicion of secret magic. Illness is now attributable solely to God's inscrutable ways; repentance and atonement are the only resource. The doctrine makes the world safe for decent folks. They will not be able to be evicted or dispossessed by the arbitrary word of jealous neighbours. I would add that the dissociation between uncleanness and sin, because it generalizes liability, makes monotheism practicable. It supports at a practical level the doctrine of the perfect unity and singleness of God by tendering into God's hands, through the work of his priests, all claims of magic spells to harm and to cure. Any claims not coming from an authenticated source are invalidated.

Leprosy in General and Leper Priests

This does not explain why lepers have to be put outside the camp. The impression we gain from reading Num. 5.2-4 is that previously lepers were tended at home and went about their daily work in the ordinary way, mingling with the community as lepers do in many parts of the world. Then the people of Israel get the command, 'Put them outside' (Num. 5.1-4), and they do so. But do we know how people in the region of Palestine, at whatever period it was, treated lepers? An exaggerated idea of the risks of contagion is common, and in many regions lepers, along with other sufferers from diseases thought to be infectious or punishments from God, are treated in settlements outside the villages, without being told to go outside by God. In which case, when the Bible starts to think of examples of sacred contagion from everyday life, putting the lepers in a place apart is an example ready to hand. People will understand the meaning, because this is what they are doing already, the same as for keeping creepy crawlies out of their food. On this approach, the Lord is not being especially harsh to lepers. He is just telling people to go on doing what they are doing, and borrowing some of the horror of leprosy to bring home the lesson on sacred contagion.

When we read of leprosy in the Bible we have to realize that it is not medically defined. In any case, there are several kinds of leprosy. In parts of Africa where it is endemic a whole lot of other skin diseases are included in the same category. Because what Leviticus describes in detail in chs. 13.1–14.57 as צרעת, though it used to be translated as 'leprosy', is not, medically speaking, leprosy, Milgrom and Levine use the term 'scale disease'.[22] It seems to be more accurate, but it has a narrower range of reference and less syntactic flexibility. It is clumsier to say 'scale-diseased person' than 'leper', and צרעת is applied to a mouldy fabric or a house with rot as well as to a diseased person. The very imprecision of the concept and the traditional ideas about sin and leprosy, which probably come from Leviticus in the first place, lead me to prefer the term leprosy. I am more interested in the fact that anyone can develop a running sore, yaws, psoriasis, ulcers, other ugly skin disorders, and so anyone can be charged with the pollution of leprosy or scale disease, and be made to suffer the disabilities prescribed by the law.

The rule that puts lepers outside the camp removes afflicted office holders from the sphere of their normal privilege and responsibility. It is effectively a demotion, which makes it all the more important to institute a formal rule for bringing them back. It is curious that the general rule for lepers is not thought to be sufficient for leper priests. If they have to be outside the camp like any other lepers, how can they officiate? Why is it necessary to insist that they cannot approach the altar? Leviticus (13–14) makes the other priests competent to declare whether the uncleanness of leprosy is present, or the initial denunciation might come, as in other historical places, from the congregation.[23] The leprosy which punished King Uzziah disqualified him from kingship (2 Kgs 15.13). This is the only biblical example I know of imputed physical impurity actually being used to demote an office holder.

The rule that prevents leper priests from ministering in the

22. Milgrom, *Leviticus 1–16*, pp. 768-889; Levine, *Leviticus*, pp. 75-76.

23. See, M.G. Pegg, 'Le Corps et l'Autorité: La Lèpre de Baudouin IV', *Annales* ESC 2, March-April 1990, pp. 265-87; M. Douglas, 'Witchcraft and Leprosy: Two Strategies for Rejection', *Man* 26 December 4 1991, pp. 723-36.

sanctuary targets a defined class. In this respect it works more like taboo in other parts of the world. Hyam Maccoby (in a personal communication) has summarized the difference between being leprous and being maimed as follows: Leprosy counts as a pollution, not as a maiming, for one could be purified from leprosy, but a maimed person was maimed for life. Thus a leper priest is excluded from both serving in the Temple and from eating holy food, but may resume both when purified. A maimed priest is excluded from serving in the Temple for life, but may eat holy food—unless he becomes temporarily polluted. The priests are subject to the same laws of purity as the laity, but they face more severe penalties for breach. Milgrom pointed out to me that they may not eat carrion and nor may anyone else; but if a priest does so, it is on pain of death (Lev. 22.8-9).

By explicitly prohibiting a priest leper from officiating, Leviticus gives the congregation a shield against exploitation: just let the priest try to abuse his office and they can accuse him and demote him. Or it could be a weapon for priests in their factional strife with their brethren. The same applies to a priest with a blemish. This interpretation, which treats the priest's purity obligations as part of a system of control applied against them, supports what Hannah Harrington says about hostility between priests and laity in the post-exilic period. There were plenty of people in the Second Temple community who thought that priests ought to be kept in their place. These complex considerations suggest that we can still believe in the compassionate God of Leviticus, notwithstanding the leprosy legislation. It is harsh on the priests, but the harshness protects others from becoming their victims.

Eating Blood and Causing Blemish

I now turn to why the forbidden animals of ch. 11 should be considered as objects of divine compassion and sympathy. I will argue that the meaning of the rules is not that they be hated but rather that they are under divine protection. Blemish and leprosy are bodily afflictions. Leprosy shows as surface irruptions on the skin; blemish is morphological, parts missing or hypertrophied, and it is sometimes defined to include skin defects, 'scurvy or scabbed' (22.22). Leviticus never uses the word for blemish (מ[א]ום) for the physical characteristics of species forbidden as food. But notice the close correspondence between the forbidden animals described in Leviticus 11 (each of whom has something missing) and the description of blemish in 22.22-24. Particularly note: 'A bull or a lamb which has a part too long or too short you may present for a free will offering, but for a votive offering it cannot be accepted.' I will pursue the idea that the forbidden species are in a class with other defective bodies, having something too long or too short.

Blemish in a man is defined in Lev. 21.18-20, 'a blind man, or a lame, or he who hath a flat nose, or anything superfluous, or a man who is broken-footed or broken-handed, or crook-backed, or a dwarf, or hath a blemish in his eye, or be scurvy or scabbed, or hath his stones broken'. In one way blemish is very close to leprosy. Advanced leprosy causes decayed extremities, nose, toes and fingers, and whole limbs, to fall off leaving festering flesh exposed on the stumps. Blemish seems to be as complex and mixed a category as uncleanness, and nearly as important.

Chapter 11 gives a list of prohibited animals which have defective modes of locomotion: in the case of land animals too many or two few legs, or legs too short, or the wrong hooves, compared with the herds and flocks; for birds it is a matter of legs too; and in the case of water creatures, the forbidden species lack fins or a scaly covering, (dolphins, for instance). I suggest that the forbidden animals are in the class of blemished creatures. Remember that God, in the story of Noah, particularly requires the creeping things to be saved from the flood so that they can breed abundantly upon the earth (Gen. 8.17-20). This sets the problem of their uncleanness into the context of the covenant with Noah, where the law against eating blood is first given (Gen. 9.4; Lev. 3.17; 7.10; Deut. 12.16).

Surely the dietary rules will be consistent, and surely we should expect the list of unclean animals to relate to the law against eating blood. Blood eating cannot be inherently disgusting, as most peoples eat, and even relish, it. The reason given for the rule in Leviticus is translated as saying that the life (נפש) is in the blood. The reference to life suggests something about killing, and refraining from eating suggests something about respect. The hunter who kills an edible animal is enjoined to cover the blood with dust (Lev. 17.13). See also Deut. 12.23, 'For the blood is the life and you must not consume the life with the flesh', and Gen. 9.4, 'You must not, however, eat flesh with its life blood in it'.[24]

24. Levine, *Leviticus*, p. 115.

Would a different translation elucidate the meaning? 'For the life is in the blood', can be rendered, 'For the soul is in the blood'. If that is a legitimate translation, it makes a big difference, for 'soul' suggests personhood, creaturehood, being part of God's creation of living beings. A modern philosopher writing about changing concepts of the person in our times, says:

> Philosophers of my stripe speak of the soul not to suggest something eternal, but to invoke character, reflective choice, self-understanding, values that include honesty to others and oneself, and several types of freedom and responsibility. Love, passion, envy, tedium, regret, and quiet contentment are the stuff of the soul. This may be a very old idea of the soul, pre-socratic. I do not think of the soul as unitary, as an essence, as one single thing, or even as a thing at all. It does not denote an unchanging core of personal identity... [25]

In the same spirit, choosing the word 'soul' instead of 'life' for these passages in Leviticus need not imply any doctrine of metempsychosis, or of permanent identity or life after death. The Hebrew dictionary gives latitude for this: נפשׁ, 'soul, living being, life, self, person, desire, appetite, emotion and passion... that which breathes, anima, the soul, the inner being of man'.[26] The same source translates Deut. 12.23, 24 as 'Only be sure that thou eat not the blood, for the blood is the living being and thou shalt not eat the living being with the flesh', which is very different from saying that the life is in the blood.

One can suppose that the scholarly editors in the fifth century knew of the discussions in the school of Pythagoras about whether animals have souls, and whether they can reason, or feel pain, and whether they should be eaten at all.[27] If this is our view of the editors, the God of the Bible would be seen as adjudicating in the learned debate: he declares that living beings have got souls, and that the soul is located in the blood. By this physiographic information, he makes it all right to eat the body if the blood is drained out. The paramount sin is to eat blood.

The doctrine of Lev. 17.11 is that God has allowed blood for making atonement. If we change the translation to, 'I have given it to

25. I. Hacking, *Reviewing the Soul: Multiple Personality and the Sciences of Memory* (Princeton, NJ: Princeton University Press, 1995), p. 6.

26. BDB, p. 659.

27. R. Sorabji, *Animal Minds and Human Morals: The Origins of the Western Debate* (London: Gerald Duckworth, 1993).

you upon the altar to make atonement for your souls; for it is the blood that makes atonement for the soul', this brings talion as described in Exod. 21.23 and Lev. 24.18 within the scope of the covenant. If a life for a life can be translated as 'living being for a living being', or as 'a person for a person', or 'a soul for a soul', the phrasing implies that the sacrificed blood (which is the soul or the life of the animal) is the intended ransom or substitute for the human soul. We are back to Professor Draï's argument that biblical talion has been taken out of context.[28] It is artificial to suppose that the discussion of blood as forbidden food and blood for atonement on the altar has no evocation of blood of birth and blood of homicide. When such contrived compartmentalization is corrected, the book's teaching on blood becomes a vital part of the theology of covenant. It is a book about life and death and everything that blood stands for, violence, injustice, betrayal, killing and atonement.

I have deliberately moved the Priestly text closer to the attitudes recommended by the prophets. Now I have a platform from which I can further undermine the Wellhausen project. If it was implausible that the God of the Bible was gratuitously hard on lepers, it was implausible that God should teach his people to detest maimed creatures. Undefended widows and orphans, the vulnerable halt and the lame, all the afflicted of creation provide the paradigm for the teachings on justice with mercy, but we have had Leviticus regularly translated as saying that the people of Israel should abhor maimed animals.

Chapter 24 extends the idea of blemish from bodily defect to aggression against the divine honour and name.

> When a man causes a blemish in his neighbour, as he has done, it shall be done to him, fracture for fracture, eye for eye, tooth for tooth: as he has blemished a man, he shall be blemished (24.19-20).

The emphasis on attack and exact recompense associates blemish with victimage. Can we consider the listed unclean species as victims of aggression? That would make it a list of vulnerable creatures, showing hurt, lacking means of escape from predators, or lacking protective covering.[29] Not eating the class of vulnerable animals would be a

28. I wish to thank Bernard Jackson for some helpful discussion of talion at the Lancaster workshop.

29. Not all of the forbidden animals would come under this rubric. Many of

mark of compassion or respect. In the anthropological record dietary prohibitions on animals indicate respect due to the particular species.[30] This shift in interpretation would bring the list of forbidden animals in ch. 11 into line with the rest of the series 12–16, which is a list of 'stricken' things, to use the rabbinical phrase (Lev. 14.33-53),[31] the stricken body, animal and human, stricken garment, stricken house, and the tabernacle defiled.

The word שקץ is translated as detestable or abominable. The translation encourages the different idea that the animals themselves are abominations: 'They are an abomination for you, you must abhor/ detest them.' Jacob Milgrom lends his authority to this interpretation, pointing out that שקץ is used to tell the people of Israel to abominate idolatry, and that the noun 'stands for a detested idol or thing'; which translation he claims to support by reference to two other words in the Bible which mean abominable in the sense of 'despised' (בזה, Ps. 22.25) and תועבה, abomination (Deut. 7.26).[32] I doubt whether translating the word שקץ by an emotional revulsion is the only and always proper sense.[33] The availability of other words which carry this sense of repugnance only supports my point, since, though available, they have not been selected for this chapter. In 11.10-14 the force of the word abomination is modified each time by the addition of 'for you'. Hyam Maccoby in this volume points out that the rabbis insisted that uncleanness of certain animal species does not affect non-Jews. This suggests that its force is not ontological but a legal restriction.

A less emotional term, like 'forbidden to you, restricted for you', or 'you must avoid, keep away from', might be more accurate. The dictionary gives as one of the accepted translations of שקץ 'to shun, detest, reject'. According to that translation God's people must shun eating these things or touching their carcases: what is abhorrent is not the animal existence in itself, but eating it is abhorrent, it must be utterly rejected as food. 'Touch' is another interesting word. To touch,

those without cleft hooves would be predators themselves, and therefore to be avoided as blood-eaters. M. Douglas, 'The Forbidden Animals in Leviticus', *JSOT* 59 (1993), pp. 3-23.

30. Douglas, 'Forbidden Animals in Leviticus'.

31. Milgrom, *Leviticus 1–16*, pp. 863-85.

32. Milgrom, *Leviticus 1–16*, p. 656.

33. Milgrom has suggested (in *Leviticus 1–16*, p. 49) that I have recanted my argument (in *Purity and Danger*) that the pig was abhorred because it was anomalous. This is not so and the lines he quotes do not support what he says.

reach or strike, (נגע), also means, as it does in English, to harm. This is the sense of the same word in Genesis: 'Abimelech warned all the people, saying: "Whoever touches this man or his wife shall be put to death"' (Gen. 26.11).

New bias in translation could rehabilitate the rules about blood and blemish. They would not be teaching refined disgust at eating dirty things, but the duty of respecting God's creation. This perspective is compatible with the ancient laws which forbade blemished sacrificial offerings. It would not only be that imperfect gifts are unworthy of the Lord, but also that weaklings are protected by the 'cosmic covenant' of which spoke Genesis and the prophets.[34] On these lines a major turn around in the interpretation of uncleanness can be attempted, the Wellhausen project can be challenged and the unity of the theological teaching justified.

To conclude, the purity rules are not a technical matter that can be dealt with separately. They raise profound and difficult theological ideas. Different explanations apply to different uses of sacred contagion, one for lepers, one for leper priests and others for stricken persons and objects and for stricken species. Of these, only the case of the leper priest is out of line with the idea of a compassionate religion, and parallels suggest the exception is not an accident. The purity rules need the full resources of the Bible for their interpretation. This brief survey shows that they do not represent any withdrawal or limitation of the Lord's compassion as described in the psalms and prophets. The various statements of talion law in Exodus 21 and Leviticus 24 refer to a plan of reciprocity which is fully in accord with the doctrine of divine generosity. The people of Israel have only to repent, and the Lord will forgive. He has given them the means to reach him and to make reparation for their transgressions in the blood of atonement.

34. R. Murray, *The Cosmic Covenant* (London; Sheed & Ward, 1992).

TALION AND PURITY: SOME GLOSSES ON MARY DOUGLAS

Bernard S. Jackson

Mary Douglas sees a number of parallels between talion and contagion, both in the biblical texts and in approaches to them by modern interpreters. Her principal purpose is to elucidate the theological thought-patterns which underlie them, and which cast doubt upon the conventional ostracism of purity as a purely 'Priestly' concern. Instead, she seeks to integrate purity within a greater complex of thought and literature, that of the Pentateuch as a whole. She comes to this view, one senses, not so much as a follower of recent 'holistic' approaches to the Pentateuch, but rather as a social scientist. For 'contagion', like talion, is a 'form of social control'.

I offer here four notes to complement this important insight. The first is to suggest a diachronic parallel between talion and purity—for each assuredly had its institutional history, notwithstanding the nature of their final literary presentations. The second addresses the significance of blood, a common material factor in some of the principal applications of both principles. The third relates to the respective roles of talion and purity in the construction of identity. The fourth concerns some techniques of literary presentation which connect Leviticus with other Pentateuchal texts.

I

Douglas's conception of the functioning of contagion as a form of social control prompt further reflections on the history of biblical conceptions of talion. Sacred contagion, from the anthropological viewpoint, indicates that the sufferer is to blame for bringing into operation a divinely ordained process of cause and effect. It involves 'transgressions which bring down their own punishment'.[1] In a more stable situation,

1. M. Douglas, 'Sacred Contagion', in this volume, p. 91.

there is greater institutional regulation of the attribution of blame.

Both the concept of divine punishment and the development towards more institutionalized forms of regulation are found also in the texts on talion. Though the supposed application of 'an eye for an eye' by human agencies has dominated the literature, we should not overlook the fact that the *idea* of equivalence of punishment is one which characterizes the biblical conception of *divine* punishment.[2] Indeed, in all the narratives of the Bible, there is only one mention of the actual practice of talion as a measure of human, as opposed to divine, justice. That is the story of King Adoni-Bezek in the first chapter of the Book of Judges, and even in that context the author seeks to explain the punishment as a measure of *divine* justice. The king says, in reaction to his mutilation by the Judaites (who had cut off his thumbs and large toes): '70 kings with their thumbs and their great toes cut off used to pick up scraps under my table; as I have done, so God has requited me' (Judg. 1.7). As a measure of divine justice, talion is discretionary: God will know on all the facts of the case when it is appropriate and when it is not. Here, it may not be irrelevant that Adoni-Bezek confesses to having mutilated *many* of his own conquered rivals.

The earliest occurrence of talion in the normative sources of the Bible suggests a form of social control akin to Douglas's conception of contagion in 'a... community with weak judicial apparatus'.[3] It occurs in the 'Covenant Code' (Exod. 21):

22 When men strive together, and hurt a woman with child, and her children come out, and yet no harm follows, the one who hurt her shall be fined, according as the woman's husband shall lay upon him; and he shall pay as the judges determine.
23 If any harm follows, then you shall give life for life,
24 eye for eye, tooth for tooth, hand for hand, foot for foot,
25 burn for burn, wound for wound, stripe for stripe.

Verse 22 already presents a tension between what I have termed a 'self-executing law' (where no recourse is required to third parties in

2. H.H. Cohn, 'Talion', *EncJud* XV.741, cites Isa. 3.11, Jer. 17.10, 50.15, Ezek. 7.8, Obad. 15. See further B.S. Jackson, 'The Problem of Exod. xxi.22-25 (*Ius Talionis*)', *VT* 23 (1973), pp.273-304, reprinted in *Essays in Jewish and Comparative Legal History* (Leiden: Brill, 1975), pp.75-107, at pp. 82-84 and in the literature cited there.

3. Whether that in itself is sufficient to label it as 'poorly organized' is a question I shall not address.

order to resolve the dispute) and institutional settlement.[4] The grammatical form of talion in v. 23 presents a parallel, though less noticed problem: the Hebrew ונתתה is conventionally taken as mandatory: 'and you *shall* give'. But it could equally be taken as permission: 'and you *may* give.'[5] There is a strong argument that even in homicide, the kin originally had a discretion either to accept 'ransom' (כפר[6]) or to exact blood vengeance—and, indeed, to do so without recourse to legal institutions.[7] Even when 'cities of refuge' were instituted, adjudication took place only once the homicide reached it; the kin were still entitled to exact vengeance if they caught the killer earlier, or if later he ventured outside the city (Deut. 19.6, cf. Num. 35.19, 21, 26-27). In considering non-fatal injuries, the argument that 'talion' was non-mandatory, but could be 'compounded' by agreement with the victim, is even stronger. This, indeed, was the view of the matter taken by Josephus, in his account of this law in the *Antiquities* (4.280):

> He that maimeth a man shall undergo the like, being deprived of that limb whereof he deprived the other, unless indeed the maimed man be willing to accept money; for the law empowers the victim himself to assess the damage that has befallen him and makes this concession, unless he would show himself too severe.

This has sometimes been taken to reflect the rule of the Roman Twelve Tables: *si membrum rupsit, ni cum eo pacit, talio esto.* But there is nothing in the Jewish legal tradition to prevent monetary settlement in this case,[8] and the presence of other 'self-executing laws' in the

4. I adhere to the literary-historical solution: that ונתן בפללים is a later addition. Jackson, *Essays*, pp. 79-81.

5. This is a perennial problem for students of biblical law. There is no separate grammatical form for the permissive.

6. This is not the place to pursue the links with 'atonement', in line with the use of the verb כפר, though clearly these are germane to the parallel between talion and purity.

7. This has been a matter of dispute between Moshe Greenberg and myself. Greenberg takes the views that the references to כפר for homicide in the Covenant Code are all exceptional and do not compromise the general ban contained in Num. 35.31-32. See M. Greenberg, 'Some Postulates of Biblical Criminal Law', in M. Haran (ed.), *Yehezkiel Kaufman Jubilee Volume* (Jerusalem: Magnes, 1980), pp. 5-28, at pp. 13-17. Against this, see Jackson, *Essays*, pp. 41-50. Greenberg has replied in 'More Reflections on Biblical Criminal Law', in S. Japhet (ed.), *Studies in Bible* (Scripta Hierosolymitana, XXXI; Jerusalem: Magnes Press, 1986), pp. 1-17.

8. Indeed, the rabbis, taking this a stage further, made monetary compensation

Covenant Code supports the view that this was, indeed, the original conception.[9] In short, we have here a form of social control belonging to a 'community with weak judicial apparatus'.[10]

The self-executing nature of talionic punishment gives way in later sources to institutional regulation. The comparison, however, is not straightforward, since the context of wrongdoing also changes. In Deuteronomy 19, the very context of the offence is the judicial process:

16 If a malicious witness rises against any man to accuse him of wrongdoing,
17 then both parties to the dispute shall appear before the LORD, before the priests and the judges who are in office in those days;
18 the judges shall inquire diligently, and if the witness is a false witness and has accused his brother falsely,
19 then you shall do to him as he had meant to do to his brother; so you shall purge the evil from the midst of you.
20 And the rest shall hear, and fear, and shall never again commit any such evil among you.
21 Your eye shall not pity; it shall be life for life [נפש בנפש], eye for eye, tooth for tooth, hand for hand, foot for foot.

It is noteworthy that here, where talionic punishment is explicitly associated with a judicial process, it is applied to an offence involving a premeditated wrong: the 'malicious' witness (עד זמם).[11] The third occurrence of the talionic formula also occurs in an institutional context: the laws commanded by God in the context of resolving the case of the 'blasphemer' (Lev. 24). But this case is presented not as a

mandatory, eliminating the discretion of the victim to demand physical retaliation.

9. B.S. Jackson, 'Practical Wisdom and Literary Artifice in the Covenant Code', in B.S. Jackson and S.M. Passamaneck (ed.), *The Jerusalem 1990 Conference Volume* (Atlanta: Scholars Press, 1992), pp. 65-92, especially pp. 67-78; and further in my *Wisdom-Laws* (forthcoming).

10. Though the weakness of the apparatus (as it appears in our texts) may, I have argued, have been the result of an ideological choice. Jackson, *Practical Wisdom*, at pp. 65-67.

11. In the homicide laws, previous enmity between the parties is treated as a sign of premeditation: Deut. 19.4, Num. 35.20-21. See also Jackson, *Essays*, pp. 91-92. Enmity is also associated with bringing a dispute to court: Exod. 23.1-8, as discussed in Jackson, 'The Literary Presentation of Multiculturalism in Early Biblical Law', *International Journal for the Semiotics of Law*, 8.23 (1995), pp. 198-200.

premeditated offence, but rather as one which occurred on the spur of the moment:

> 10 Now an Israelite woman's son, whose father was an Egyptian, went out among the people of Israel; and the Israelite woman's son and a man of Israel quarrelled in the camp,
> 11 and the Israelite woman's son blasphemed the Name, and cursed. And they brought him to Moses. His mother's name was Shelo'mith, the daughter of Dibri, of the tribe of Dan.
> 12 And they put him in custody, till the will of the LORD should be declared to them.
> 13 And the LORD said to Moses,
> 14 'Bring out of the camp him who cursed; and let all who heard him lay their hands upon his head, and let all the congregation stone him...'

The case itself is resolved by oracular consultation (perhaps because of doubt whether the offence extended to the son of an Egyptian). This is not the only indication of 'priestly' interest. In the homicide laws, it is only when we reach the priestly account that we find regulation of intentional but unpremeditated killing. The earlier sources—the Covenant Code (Exod. 21.13-14) and Deuteronomy (19.4-5, 11)—had confined themselves to an opposition between premeditated killing on the one hand and pure accident on the other. The priestly writer supplies the missing case, in terms which allude to the criteria of the earlier sources (Num. 35.22-25):

> But if he stabbed him suddenly without enmity, or hurled anything on him without lying in wait (cf. Exod. 21.13), or used a stone, by which a man may die, and without seeing him cast it upon him, so that he died, though he was not his enemy (cf. Deut. 19.4), and did not seek his harm, then the congregation shall judge between the manslayer and the avenger of blood, in accordance with these ordinances; and the congregation shall rescue the manslayer from the hand of the avenger of blood, and the congregation shall restore him to his city of refuge, to which he had fled, and he shall live in it until the death of the high priest who was anointed with the holy oil.

Daube has drawn attention (in this very context) to the systematizing tendencies of the priestly lawgivers.[12] Perhaps this may be regarded

12. D. Daube, *Studies in Biblical Law* (Cambridge: Cambridge University Press, 1947), pp. 111-12, on the use of הכה נפש in vv. 17 and 18 of both the killing of a man and the killing of a beast, and noting their capacity for 'comprehensive schemata'.

as part of the 'bureaucratization' which Mary Douglas observes also in the context of purity:

> The systematization of sin in Leviticus makes all human creatures unavoidably liable to defilement. Regardless of good intentions defilement in one form or another is going to happen to everyone and any one at any time.[13]

To this extent, the priestly versions of both the homicide laws and of the contextualization of talion are comparable to the (priestly) laws of contagion. Nor was such 'bureaucratization' a matter merely of completion of a system of legal dogmatics. It is in the priestly law that we find the strongest movement away from self-executing laws, not only in the case of premeditated homicide, but also for those entitled to the 'protection' of the city of refuge (Num. 35):

> 31 Moreover you shall accept no ransom for the life of a murderer, who is guilty of death; but he shall be put to death.
> 32 And you shall accept no ransom for him who has fled to his city of refuge, that he may return to dwell in the land before the death of the high priest.

As in contagion, the law here 'brings sin within the control of the priests'; the priestly remit, moreover, is extended to cover the whole range of mental states.

II

Mary Douglas suggests a connection between talion and the dietary laws: in both the idea of shedding blood—and the implications for the נפש—are central. She takes נפש, in these sources, to mean the soul and sees the priestly editors as claiming that living beings, including animals, have souls, and that the soul is located in their blood...

> The doctrine of Lev. 17.11 is that God has allowed blood for making atonement. If we change the translation to, 'I have given it to you upon the altar to make atonement for your souls; for it is the blood that makes atonement for the soul', this brings talion as described in Exodus 21.23 and Levit. 24.18 within the scope of the covenant. If a life for a life can be translated as 'living being for a living being', or as 'a person for a person', or 'a soul for a soul', the phrasing implies that the sacrificed

13. Douglas, 'Sacred Contagion', p. 93 above.

> blood (which is the soul or the life of the animal) is the intended ransom or substitute for the human soul. We are back to Professor Draï's argument that biblical talion has been taken out of context. It is artificial to suppose that the discussion of blood as forbidden food and blood for atonement on the altar has no evocation of blood of birth and blood of homicide. When such contrived compartmentalization is corrected the book's teaching on blood becomes a vital part of the theology of covenant. It is a book about life and death and everything that blood stands for, violence, injustice, betrayal, killing and atonement.[14]

The relationship between blood (דם) and 'soul' (נפש) is not easy to disentangle in these sources: Lev. 17.11 seems to say both that the דם is in the נפש and that the נפש is in the דם (though the version in Deut. 12.23, כי הדם הוא הנפש rather than כי הדם הוא בנפש, seems to make rather better sense). I do not dissent from the semantic range offered by BDB (and quoted by Douglas), nor from the possibility of a covenant theology informed by pre-Socratic debates on the nature of the soul. But the semantics of נפש תחת נפש can lead in other, rather more mundane, directions—directions which suggest that the desirability of reading Leviticus as part of a unified Pentateuch does not entail the suppression of any pre-fifth-century history of the ideas adapted and developed by the priestly authors.

In the Covenant Code, the two ideas of נפש תחת נפש and restoration of blood are both found, but are not semantically connected: נפש תחת נפש is found in the context of the consequences of the pregnant woman caught up in a brawl (Exod. 21.22-23)—but there is no mention of דם; דם is mentioned in the context of the killing of the intruding thief, but there is no mention there of נפש. The latter text (Exod. 22.1-2, MT) reads:

> 1 If a thief is found breaking in, and is struck so that he dies, there shall be no bloodguilt for him (אין לו דם);
>
> 2 but if the sun has risen upon him, there shall be bloodguilt for him (דמים לו) He shall make restitution; if he has nothing, then he shall be sold for his theft.

The text is premised upon the assumption that the killer has indeed taken possession of the דם of the deceased; where the killing is deemed justified, such possession may remain undisturbed, but where it is unjustified, then the deceased, through his kin, has a right to restoration of the דם. As Daube puts it:[15]

14. Douglas, 'Sacred Contagion', pp. 100-101 above.
15. Daube, *Biblical Law*, pp. 122-24.

> The murderer has obtained control over the murdered man's soul. So the גאל הדם has to redeem the dead man from the power of the murderer. By killing the murderer, he takes back the victim's soul. Vengeance is compensation.

He goes on to relate this directly to the talionic formula:

> In view of the expressions discussed, two of them directly referring to homicide and its punishment, it can no longer be surprising to find that the law of retaliation, as worded in Exodus and Leviticus, speaks of retaliation as restitution. The wrongdoer has deprived another person of some faculty—life, eye, hand or the like—which means that he has added that faculty to his own. By inflicting retaliation, the person harmed or his family not only punishes the wrongdoer but regains the faculty lost. It really is, from this standpoint, a matter of exacting 'life in the place of life, eye in the place of eye, tooth in the place of tooth, hand in the place of hand, foot in the place of foot'.

But this conclusion does not necessarily follow. The version in Leviticus (below, section IV) separates נפש תחת נפש from the non-fatal examples, and gives it a different meaning. Nor does the idea of capture of another's eye, tooth, foot or hand have the same resonance as capture of the blood.

More significant, for this argument, is the existence of alternative meanings for נפש תחת נפש. The same root is used in Akkadian, and is found in a similar context in the Middle Assyrian Laws A50, in the repeated phrase *kimu ša libiša napšate umalla*: 'for the [fruit of] her womb, he shall render a person'.[16] The Hittite laws also provide for substitution of persons in the case of unpremeditated and accidental killings. I have argued that this was the original meaning of נפש תחת נפש in Exod. 21.23: for the lost foetus, a live person is to be substituted.[17] And it is this which seems to be required by the context of the formula in Lev. 24.18, 'He who kills a beast shall make it good, life for life.' Only in Deuteronomy (where the formula is נפש בנפש) does the context seem to indicate not 'life for life' but rather 'death for death'. Perhaps it was this that later led to the linking of the ideas of equivalence and restoration of the blood (= strength, personality, 'soul')—and its application to animals as well as human beings.

16. Discussed in Jackson, *Essays*, pp. 97-98.

17. Later, I suggested, the meaning changed, when this part of the law was taken to refer to death of the mother, rather than loss of the foetus. Jackson, *Essays*, pp. 104-105.

III

Mary Douglas writes:

> The concept of contagion is also useful socially for defining identity. A person who is assigned to the class of the less pure can legitimately be put down. This gives everyone an interest in defining themselves as more pure. Signs of purity in character or descent prove eligibility for marriage, or for office.[18]

Contagion is thus seen as an internal form of social control, a marker of social identity and thus of difference. Like much of the ritual law, it serves not only to differentiate internally, but also externally: the adherents of this system of purity are thus seen to be distinct from other communities.

The Bible expresses this in theological terms. Douglas connects the purity laws with the first commandment: 'One idea is simply that the metaphor of uncleanness summons established ideas about contagion to the support of the covenant and particularly to defend the first commandment against other gods'.[19] Rolf Rendtorff, similarly, connects Lev. 19.2, קדשים תהיו כי קדוש אני יהוה אלהיכם, to the Ten Commandments. Moshe Weinfeld, too, has argued that Leviticus 19, which stands out from the rest of the Priestly Code for its intermingling of ethical with ritual norms, is to be understood against the background of the Decalogue. He notes that Leviticus 19 includes 'a list of commands similar to those laid down in the Decalogue', and quotes a later rabbinic comment:[20]

> Why was this chapter (*kedoshim*) spoken at the Assembly? Because most of the principal elements of the Torah depend upon it.[21] Rabbi Levi says, because the Ten Commandments are included in it.

He concludes that Leviticus 19 'provides a sort of Decalogue in revised and expanded form'.[22]

18. Douglas, 'Sacred Contagion', p. 91 above.

19. Douglas, 'Sacred Contagion', p. 85 above.

20. M. Weinfeld, 'The Uniqueness of the Decalogue', in B.Z. Segal (ed.), *The Ten Commandments in History and Tradition* (Jerusalem: Magnes, 1990), pp. 11-15, quoting *Leviticus Rabbah* 24.5.

21. Weinfeld compares Mt. 22.40: 'On these two commandments [love of God, Deut. 6.4; love of neighbour, Lev. 19.18] depend all the law and the prophets.'

22. Weinfeld, 'Decalogue', p. 14. He too stresses the fact that, like the

Such a connection between purity and the first commandment of the Decalogue adds force to the interpretation of the purity laws as constitutive of Israelite identity. I have argued elsewhere that the Decalogue itself is structured around a distinction between particularist commands and those conceived to be universal.[23] Although the identification of individual commandments, and indeed the enumeration of them as a collection of ten, is weakly evidenced in the narrative of Sinai, there is strong expression of the view that they were written on two tablets,[24] and thus that there was (at least in graphic terms) an internal division. The traditional Jewish view of the individuation and division, represented in synagogal depictions of the tablets, goes back to an early rabbinic *midrash* (probably no later than the third century CE):[25]

> How were the Ten Commandments arranged? Five on one tablet and five on the other. On the one tablet was written: 'I am the LORD thy God.' And opposite it on the other tablet was written: 'Thou shalt not murder'... On the one tablet was written: 'Thou shalt have no other god.' And opposite it on the other tablet was written: 'Thou shalt not commit adultery'... On the one tablet was written: 'Thou shalt not take.' And opposite it on the other tablet was written: 'Thou shalt not steal'... On the one tablet was written: 'Remember the sabbath day to keep it holy.' And opposite it on the other tablet was written: 'Thou shalt not bear false witness'... On the one tablet was written: 'Honor thy father,' etc. And opposite it on the other tablet was written: 'Thou shalt not covet thy neighbour's wife.'

Such a division is based on a mere inference from the nature of the subject matter and (even more dubious) an assumption that the 'ten' (however identified) should be divided into two groups of five. However, there is good reason to doubt this as representing the original conception of the distribution of the material on the tablets: unless the text is very radically pruned (which some Biblical scholars

Decalogue, '... the commandments in Leviticus 19 begin with the declaration "I am the Lord your God" (v. 2)', and comments on the chiastic rearrangement in Lev. 19 of other aspects of the Decalogue (at pp. 12-13).

23. In outline, in 'Practical Wisdom', pp. 83-84; in more detail in 'The Literary Presentation of Multiculturalism', pp. 184-93.

24. Exod. 24.12; 31.18; 32.15, 19; 34.1, 27-29.

25. *Mekhilta ad Exodus* 20.16 (Lauterbach II. 262), quoted by G.B. Sarfatti, 'The Tablets of the Law as a Symbol of Judaism', in Segal (ed.), *The Ten Commandments in History and Tradition*, pp. 383-418, see pp. 408-409. Philo, *Dec.* 50–51, differs only in reversing the order of adultery and murder.

have sought to do),[26] the length of the material in the second pentad is very considerably smaller than that in the first, even allowing for a much greater degree of secondary elaboration in the first tablet.

I suggest that there is a better way of dividing up the material, one which rests upon an internal indication in the text itself. The Decalogue makes two explicit references to the history recounted in Genesis and the earlier part of Exodus. The first occurs at the very beginning, thus at the head of the first group (however one divides the text): 'I am the Lord your God, who brought you out of the land of Egypt, out of the house of bondage' (Exod. 20.2). There are then provisions relating to monotheism, idolatry, the divine name, and the sabbath day. Then, in v. 11, there is a reference (conventionally regarded as a 'motive clause')[27] to the beginnings of *universal* history, the creation of the world.[28] Such historical allusions also appear elsewhere in the Bible as markers of the beginnings of new sections of laws.[29]

It is easy enough to correlate the two groups of rules with the historical allusions. The reference to the liberation from Egypt—characteristic of the particular history of Israel—is followed by rules which constitute Israel's particular identity (its *ius civile*), its monotheistic faith and practice, and its particular ordering of time. The reference to universal history, on the other hand, is followed by

26. For a survey of the older literature, see J.J. Stamm and M.E. Andrew, *The Ten Commandments in Recent Research* (London: SCM Press, 1967).

27. But the opening word, כי, does not have to be translated 'for' or 'because'. It may be a deictic expression: 'Behold, in six days the LORD made heaven and earth...'

28. The Deuteronomic version substitutes here a further allusion to the Egyptian slavery. Deuteronomy does, it seems, understand the historical allusion as a motive clause, but it regards the Exodus allusion as an inappropriate motive for Israel's duty to observe the sabbath. The sabbath is taken as a symbol of freedom, denied the Israelites in Egypt, but now available to them (Deut. 5.15). And the opening injunction of the Exodus Decalogue, 'Remember the sabbath day' is transformed in Deuteronomy into an injunction to 'Observe the sabbath day', with the duty of remembrance now presented not as a motive (there is in Deuteronomy no כי, or anything comparable), but rather as a supplementary duty, 'You shall remember', וזכרת. See further B.S. Jackson, 'The Nature of Analogical Argument in Early Jewish Law', *The Jewish Law Annual* 11 (1993), pp.137-68, especially pp. 139-42.

29. Examples: Exod. 21.2 and 21.28, as argued in my 'Practical Wisdom', pp. 81-83. See also the sections commencing Exod. 22.20 and 23.9, as discussed in my 'Modelling Biblical Law: The Covenant Code', *Chicago–Kent Law Review* 70.4 (1995), pp. 1801-1804, and in *Wisdom-Laws* (forthcoming).

ius gentium: honouring parents, killing, adultery, theft, false witness, 'coveting'.

If purity is associated with that part of the Decalogue which represents Israel's particular identity, talion is associated, conversely, with that part which stresses the common humanity of Israel with the rest of creation. Though it may be correct, for analytical purposes, to distinguish 'talion' ('an eye for an eye' and so on) from the regulation of homicide, the Bible clearly associates them, by adopting the formula נפש תחת נפש and using it in immediate proximity to the talionic formula (Exod. 21.23-24, Deut. 19.21, Lev. 24.18-20). The Decalogue prohibition of murder, therefore, may not unreasonably be regarded as a paradigm of bodily injury, and was so regarded by Philo (*Spec. Leg.* 3.168).

Talion is, of course, known from other collections of ancient Near Eastern laws (*Laws of Hammurabi* §§196, 197, 200; *Middle Assyrian Laws* §A50). Indeed, the formulation of the latter (ll.63-67):

> [If a man] has struck a married [woman] and caused her to lose [the fruit of her womb, the wife of the man] who [caused] the (other) married woman [to lose] the fruit of [her womb] shall be treated as [he has] treated her...

is in a very similar context to that in the Covenant Code, while the degree of abstraction ('shall be treated as [he has] treated her') is echoed in both Deut. 19.19 ('you shall do to him as he had meant to do to his brother') and Lev. 24.19 ('as he has done it shall be done to him'). This is not the place to re-enter the question of historical influence.[30] More important, for present purposes, is the fact that the Bible itself twice associates talion with foreigners—in the narratives of Adoni-Bezek[31] and the blasphemer ('an Israelite woman's son, whose father was an Egyptian', who quarrelled with 'a man of Israel', Lev. 24.10), the latter being the dispute which gave rise to the Levitical formulation of talion. At the very least, it may be concluded from this that the

30. In an earlier study (*Essays*), I concluded that the hands of both the Deteronomist and P may be seen in the editing of the passage of the Covenant Code. M. Weinfeld, *Deuteronomy and the Deuteronomic School* (Oxford: Clarendon Press, 1972), p. 292, drew particular attention to the affinities between Deuteronomy and the Assyrian laws.

31. Judges 1, discussed above, p. 106.

Biblical writers did not regard it as inappropriate to apply the talionic principle to foreigners.[32]

IV

The larger theme of the Lancaster conference was the place of Leviticus in the Pentateuch—its unity as a book and its relationship to the other Pentateuchal sources. This is not the place to review either that issue in general or Mary Douglas's exciting contribution to the analysis of the literary structure of the priestly writings in particular. I confine myself to a comment on the literary structure of two Levitical passages already discussed above: the case of the blasphemer in Leviticus 24 and the moral commands of Leviticus 19.

The first is the passage within which talion appears as (quite literally) the centrepiece. In resolving the case of the blasphemer (Lev. 24.10-23), God issues a series of commands which appear at first sight quite disparate *inter se* and unconnected with the dispute which prompted the proclamation.[33] That this is not, however, a purely adventitious accumulation of interpolations is shown by the chiastic structure of the passage:[34]

A1	13	And the LORD said to Moses,
B1	14	'Bring out of the camp him who cursed; and let all who heard him lay their hands upon his head, and let all the congregation stone him.
C1	15	And say to the people of Israel, Whoever curses his God shall bear his sin.

32. In 'The Literary Presentation of Multiculturalism', I argue for a connection, akin to the dual meaning of the Roman *ius civile* vs. *ius gentium*, between the Biblical presentation of particularist vs. universal law, and law applied internally only to Israelites and law applied internally also to non-Israelites. The Decalogue is based on the former, the Covenant Code reflects the latter.

33. On the relationship between dispute resolution and laws proclaimed in that context in the narratives of adjudication in the desert, see further my 'Modelling Biblical Law', pp. 1824-26. In the case of the daughters of Zelophehad (Num. 27), there is a similar pattern, though the thematic connection between the decision and the proclaimed laws is closer.

34. Cf. J.W. Welch, 'Chiasmus in Biblical Law: An Approach to the Structure of Legal Texts in the Bible', in B.S. Jackson (ed.), *Jewish Law Association Studies IV: The Boston Conference Volume* (Atlanta: Scholars Press, 1990), pp. 5-22, at pp. 7-9 (and citing Thomas Boys, *Key to the Book of Psalms* [London: L.B. Seeley, 1825], p. 41, as having first identified [the major part of] this structure).

D1	16	He who blasphemes the name of the LORD shall be put to death; all the congregation shall stone him; the sojourner as well as the native, when he blasphemes the Name, shall be put to death.
E1	17	He who kills a man shall be put to death.
F1	18	He who kills a beast shall make it good, life for life.
G1	19	When a man causes a disfigurement in his neighbour, as he has done it shall be done to him,
H	20	fracture for fracture, eye for eye, tooth for tooth;
G2		as he has disfigured a man, he shall be disfigured.
F2	21	He who kills a beast shall make it good;
E2		and he who kills a man shall be put to death.
D2	22	You shall have one law for the sojourner and for the native; for I am the LORD your God.'
C2	23	So Moses spoke to the people of Israel;
B2		and they brought him who had cursed out of the camp, and stoned him with stones.
A2		Thus the people of Israel did as the LORD commanded Moses.

Chiasmus, it has been suggested, is 'a practice not uncommon when quoting, or adverting to, well-known established texts'.[35] This passage is closely connected, thematically, to the first section of the Covenant Code. Many of the individual topics are common, as indeed may be the common underlying theme: that of the possible forms and legal consequences of quarrels. It is this which provides the narrative setting of the case of the blasphemer, which commences (v. 10):

> Now an Israelite woman's son, whose father was an Egyptian, went out among the people of Israel; and the Israelite woman's son and a man of Israel quarrelled in the camp.

The term 'quarrelled' (ונגפו) is the same as that which provides the narrative setting for the case of the pregnant woman (the context of the talionic formula, which is at the centre of the chiasmus above) in the Covenant Code. Indeed, this may explain why a seemingly unconnected series of norms is promulgated in the wake of the decision on the blasphemer: in narrative (if not in semantic or conceptual) terms, quarrels are apt to lead to cursing (v. 14; also by foreigners, v. 16) and all sorts of injuries, including fatal injuries to human (v. 17) and animal (v. 18) bystanders, and non-fatal injuries (vv. 19-20). The thematic parallels with the Covenant are close. There too we find the regulation of cursing (Exod. 22.28, in addition to the Decalogue ban on misuse

35. Weinfeld, 'Decalogue', pp. 12-13 n.45, citing M. Zeidel, *Ḥiqre Miqra* (1979), pp. 1-97 (I have not had access to the latter).

of the divine name), concern for the legal position of strangers (22.21; 23.9), homicide (21.12-14), both fatal and non-fatal injuries arising from a quarrel (21.18-19, 22-25), and fatal injuries to animals (21.33-36: neither the Covenant Code nor Lev. 24 contemplates non-fatal injuries to animals). Additionally, the talionic formula—the centre of the Levitical chiasmus—is the closest *verbal* parallel to the Covenant Code. In short, the Levitical passage gains immensely in coherence if viewed as a literary reworking of themes from the Covenant Code.

Reference has been made above to the relationship between Leviticus 19 and the Decalogue. There is a further connection, if we adopt the view of the internal structuring of the Decalogue suggested in section III above. For Leviticus 19, too, is interested in the opposition between neighbours and strangers. Most of the treatment of social relations in the chapter is concerned with relations between 'neighbours'—conceived not geographically but in terms of identity as members of the community.[36] But the final paragraph turns to the treatment of the resident alien, the 'stranger' (גר),[37] and requires comparable standards of behaviour in matters of justice, and weights and measures. Significantly, the love commandment is repeated in this context:

> 19.18 You shall not take vengeance or bear any grudge against the sons of your own people [בני עמך], but you shall love your neighbour [רעך] as yourself: I am the LORD.
>
> 19.34 The stranger who sojourns with you shall be to you as the native among you, and you shall love him as yourself; for you were strangers in the land of Egypt: I am the LORD your God.

It is not, however, the Decalogue's implicit use of the neighbour vs. stranger opposition which informs Leviticus 19, but rather its role in the structure of the Covenant Code (Exod. 21.1–23.19). There, too, it is signalled by historical allusions. On the one hand, the first half of the Code begins with a law requiring the liberation of the Hebrew debt-slave after six years (Exod. 21.2), widely regarded as placed at the very beginning of the Code as an allusion to Israel's own historical experience of liberation from Egypt. This form of slavery is 'internal'—the sale of one Israelite (or a member of his family) to

36. As is seen from the stylistic variation between רעך (vv. 13, 16, 18), עמיתך (vv. 11, 15, 17) and עמיך (vv. 16, 18).

37. On the identity of this גר, see M. Douglas, 'The Stranger in the Bible', *Archives européennes de sociologie* (1993), pp. 283-98.

another, in order to work off a debt.[38] The rest of the first part of the Code (conventionally divided at Exod. 22.17, MT) continues with mostly civil (as opposed to ritual or religious) rules for the resolution of disputes amongst Israelites.[39] The paragraphs up to and including the law of the seducer (Exod. 22.15-16) presuppose the activities of insiders. Theft, for example, is conceived in the Bible as the offence of an insider (as opposed to 'robbery', or brigandage).[40] The section on agricultural delicts[41]—from the goring ox, Exod. 21.28-32, 35-36, to the shepherding laws, Exod. 22.9-12—presupposes disputes between members of the same community.

After the law of the seducer, matters change. The small group of capital offences at Exod. 22.17-19 are ones all of which were associated in the Israelite mind with the practices of foreign peoples: idolatry, witchcraft and bestiality. And the sequence which commences with Exod. 22.20 puts relations with the גר, the resident alien (the outsider who is inside the community) right up front:

> You shall not wrong a stranger or oppress him, for you were strangers in the land of Egypt.

Here, as in Lev. 19.34 and Deut. 5.15, it is no longer liberation from Egypt which is stressed (as in the opening verse of the first half, requiring liberation of the male Hebrew slave after six years, Exod. 21.2), but rather the experience of oppression within Egypt. Israel had itself been the 'other' within Egypt, and had been oppressed there: having entered as a free (if destitute) people, it had been reduced to the status of slavery. Israel is therefore warned not to treat strangers in its own midst in the same way. Israel's particular experience is to be taken as a paradigm for its own treatment of the other.

38. Argued in B.S. Jackson, 'Biblical Laws of Slavery: A Comparative Approach', in L. Archer (ed.), *Slavery and other Forms of Unfree Labour* (London: Routledge & Kegan Paul, 1988), pp. 86-101, at pp. 92-93, and further in *Wisdom-Laws* (forthcoming).

39. The opponent is frequently described as a 'neighbour' (רעהו: Exod. 21.35; 22.7, 8, 9, 10, 11, 12, 14). This term occurs only once in the second part of the Code: Exod. 22.26.

40. B.S. Jackson, *Theft in Early Jewish Law* (Oxford: Clarendon Press, 1972), ch. 1; *idem*, 'Some Comparative Legal History: Robbery and Brigandage', *Georgia Journal of International and Comparative Law* 1 (1970), pp. 45-103.

41. This includes the theft paragraph, Exod. 21.37–22.3, where the context is cattle-theft. Jackson, *Theft*, pp. 41-49, 203-212.

The provisions that follow relate to the poor, and in Exod. 23.12 the sabbath law is explicitly extended to the גר, the resident alien, here echoing the Decalogue (Exod. 20.10). The placing here of measures to protect the poor is surely not accidental. The poor could easily become enslaved—the setting of the first two paragraphs of the Covenant Code—and slavery was associated with the status of being an outsider within Egypt. This thought association was by no means fanciful, given the narrative tradition concerning the circumstances in which the Israelites came to be enslaved in Egypt—having taken refuge there, as resident aliens, in flight from famine. In this second part of the Code, there are several references to relations between Israelites and 'strangers'. The collection concludes with a famous dietary law: the ban on seething a kid in its mother's milk (Exod. 23.19), which has long been thought to be a reaction to Canaanite ritual.[42] In short, the Covenant Code, like Leviticus 19, deals first with the regulation of the behaviour of members of the community, and later with the regulation of the behaviour of outsiders resident within the community. It shares this theme with other collections of Biblical law.

How, then, should we understand the relationship between the two Levitical collections here considered and the Covenant Code? No firm answer could possibly be offered on the basis of these notes. My feeling, for what it is worth, is that radical theories of 'unity'—whether of the individual book or source (placed where it is with no change by the compilers) or of the Pentateuch as a single-authored work—are unlikely. I prefer the model of a chain novel, each author receiving and developing the 'chapters' written by predecessors—but with a feature not normally associated with the chain novel, namely the capacity of the writers of subsequent chapters to revise those of their predecessors.

42. Others have viewed the cultic laws of the Covenant Code as, in general, being of an anti-Canaanite nature: J. Blenkinsopp, *Wisdom and Law in the Old Testament* (Oxford: Oxford University Press, 1983), p. 82; cf. A. Phillips, *Ancient Israel's Criminal Law* (Oxford: Basil Blackwell, 1970), p. 121, on the interpretation of bestiality, Exod. 22.18, as a condemnation of Canaanite ritual, rather than a sexual crime related to the Decalogue prohibition of adultery.

THE WITNESS OF TIMES: AN ANTHROPOLOGICAL READING OF *NIDDAH*

Adriana Destro

The fundamental assumption on which this paper is based is that, although the rabbis' work is never documentary or historical, the literary construction of the sages Tannaim cannot be considered as an activity divorced from the socio-cultural reality in which they lived. On the contrary, in its general structure, the Mishnah is a cultural product, stemming from the intellectual and concrete experience of the rabbis. It is vital to recognize, as Boyarin does,[1] that being the result of a social process among other and similar ones, the Mishnah provides access to the sociological imagination of its authors.

The Mishnah is characterized by a dominating feature: it builds up a systemic 'world' through specific classifications and hierchical ordering of cases and rules[2] and actually elaborates solutions to many human tensions. The 'world' imagined by the rabbis is built for the benefit of the whole of Israel and not only of the group or the society in which the texts were produced. However, had the rabbis not identified themselves with this 'world', or had they not identified its background with their own, they might have written very different texts, less ethnographic[3] and more philosophical. On the basis of these

1. D. Boyarin, *Carnal Israel: Reading Sex in Talmudic Culture* (Berkeley: University of California Press, 1993), pp. 12-13.

2. J. Neusner, *Judaism: The Evidence of the Mishnah* (Atlanta: Scholars Press, 2nd edn, 1987); *idem*, 'Rabbinic Judaism: Its History and Hermeneutics', in *idem*, *Judaism in Late Antiquity: Historical Syntheses*, II (Leiden: Brill, 1995).

3. I do not mean that they discussed the body of the menstruant or of the parturient as an ethnographer would have done describing the childbearing and childbirth of an African woman, for example. The rabbis simply investigated the meaning of natural and uncontrollable facts starting from their cultural background and their doctrinal standing. See S. Cohen, 'Menstruants and the Sacred in Judaism and Christianity', in *Women's History and Ancient History* (ed. S.B. Pomeroy;

premises, for an anthropologist, reading the Mishnah means to investigate the rabbis' cultural thought and the way they implicitly correlate themselves to their culture and to those who share it.

The Scheme of Times in Leviticus

A genuine understanding of the early rabbinic writings about impurity requires a concomitant brief enquiry into levitical rules. Chapter 15 of the Book of Leviticus offers manifest and abundant evidence of the priestly concern with defilement, a religious perspective which is a 'basic condition of all reality'.[4] Within the view of the editors of Leviticus, uncleanness is a central theme that gives sense and consistency to the whole structure of the book. But the biblical idea of impurity includes transgressions and faults of different nature and origin.[5] How can the evidence of impurity be comprehensively spoken of in anthropological terms?

From a phenomenological point of view, throughout Leviticus impurity appears as something not discernible, elusive and inexorably hidden to everybody, even to the unclean person. Bodily uncleanness is either conceptually and sociologically vague. It is made accessible and decipherable exclusively through the idiom of time, and by the mechanism of temporal cycles. In its general construction, the book of Leviticus seems to convey the idea that for human beings detecting impurity means detecting or structuring times. In order to envisage concrete cases of life, the text affirms: 'when' (כי) a man has an emission of semen, or a man and a woman have sexual intercourse, or again, when a woman has a discharge of blood, each of them 'shall be' impure (that is in a state of impurity)—even after bathing—either for one day or for seven days.[6] In this descriptive context, the dimension of times is not given natural values or orders by the editors of

Chapel Hill: The University of North Carolina Press, 1991), pp. 273-99; A. Destro, 'la donna *niddah*: Ordine del corpo e ordine del mondo giudaico', in *idem*, *Le politiche del corpo* (Bologna: Patron), pp. 87-130.

4. M. Douglas, *In the Wilderness: The Doctrine of Defilement in the Book of Numbers* (JSOTSup, 159; Sheffield: JSOT Press, 1993), p. 21.

5. For Leviticus texts, translation and commentary, I depend chiefly on B.A. Levine, *Leviticus* (JPS Torah Commentary; Philadelphia: Jewish Publication Society of America, 1989) and J. Milgrom, *Leviticus 1–16* (AB, 3; Garden City, NY: Doubleday, 1991).

6. Lev. 15.13, 16-17, 18, 19, 24, 25.

Leviticus.[7] It is the overall perspective of the classification and of the division of times of Leviticus—in which the doctrine of purity was 'expanded' as Douglas maintains elsewhere in this volume—that gives intellectual access to and practical evidence of the impurity investing any human being.

In Leviticus, the use of the verb 'to be' (היה) followed by the expression בנדתה (Lev. 15.19), the simple use of the term 'impure' טמאה / טמא) or that of the verb טמא (expressions generally translated into 'to remain impure') seems to suggest a specific condition of the unclean. It would appear to convey the idea that, for a given time, individual conditions are kept stable and still. The unclean is held in a conventional immobility or status quo without alterations or reversions intervening until a prescribed (and uninterrupted) time is terminated.

Generally speaking, acts of conceptualizing and of structuring time presuppose cultural habits and enforce social conventions. Often cultures develop, on the one hand, a concept of total or whole time and on the other, an idea of partition and repetition of temporal spaces. This is crucial here: the priestly conception of time seems to derive strictly from these two interrelating principles. Time is a continuum, but time is also composed of differentiated and non-equivalent hours, days and months. In Leviticus, as I said, the natural continuity of time is 'interrupted' by uncleanness, an accident arresting the ordinary flux, the usual unfolding of human existence. The interruption, to be effective, is destined to endure over a period of time. Only the end or fulfilment of the prescribed time—a 'time of waiting'—has a resolutive outcome. It cancels uncleanness, reactivates purity along with normality.

This line of interpretation substantially implies that, in its essential features, the scheme of Leviticus is linked to God's activity at creation.[8] The editors of Leviticus conceive of time as the time of God's creation. In other words, creation has a time-defining quality which is clearly reflected in the Priestly code. On this basis, one is allowed to imagine that when Leviticus speaks of the type of uncleanness lasting 'until nightfall', it recalls the original alternation of light and darkness. Equally a seven day impurity recalls the unitary sequence of the days

7. P.P. Jenson, *Graded Holiness: A Key to the Priestly Conception of the World* (Sheffield: JSOT Press, 1992)

8. H. Eilberg-Schwartz, *The Savage in Judaism* (Bloomington: Indiana University Press, 1990), p. 225.

of creation. Within this context, human actions or institutions have little influence. The divine realm works according to its times and laws. Human will, in itself, does not intervene in them or has a limited and subordinate role. Humans have to coordinate themselves to the temporal order of God. However, while the state of stillness (the status quo) is, on the one hand, conceived on the basis of the powerful times and images of divine creation; on the other, it is envisaged as stemming from and influencing the fragility of human existence. The sense of the rule of 'he or she shall remain' derives its strength from the centrality of the precarious human world. Pushing this insight further, we may say that (from a cultural point of view) the 'time of waiting', despite the fact that it entails unchangeability, introduces an evident upheaval in the use of hours and days. When impurity intervenes, in fact, ordinary existence is strongly influenced by a two-fold force consisting of stability on one side and alteration on the other. It is this dialectic which might have interested the sages, and given impulse to their intellectual work. More explicitly, I am convinced that the sages preserve and respect the cosmology of Leviticus.[9] They certainly neither neglect the obligation of 'remaining' in the unclean state nor abandon the central tenets of the priestly understanding of time, even though they do not simply limit themselves to reiterating them. However, like any other Jewish grouping or community, historically different from that of the priests, the rabbis had to contend with then priestly construction of time categories and values. There is evidence that the Mishnah—saturated by the conceptions of time of Leviticus—demonstrates its originality precisely in this field.

The Reference to Times and Bodily Signs in Niddah

The authors of the Mishnah have two distinct ways of constructing their discourse, one of which concerns time. *Niddah* is dominated by the problem of times.The long-elaborated activity of the sages extended the temporal structure of Leviticus through wider human and cultural meanings. In this way they considerably enlarged the foundations of the scriptural system. The other way concerns the human body. The impression we gain from reading Mishnah, is that it problematizes the manifestations of corporeality. In the rabbis' vision, a clear recognition of the necessity of the body and of its material distinctiveness was intended to give practical measures to impurity. Indeed, body condition

9. Eilberg-Schwartz, *The Savage in Judaism*, p. 226.

was linked to time dimension and brought uncleanness under observation.

It is useful to treat the idea of corporeality in *Niddah* starting from the signs revealed by or observed in or on the human body. *Niddah* offers a number of categories on the intrinsic quality of materials which convey impurity and discusses how physiological fluids contaminate on the basis of their inner state. With reference to different physical materials (semen, flesh of the corpse, flow of a זב, and so on), as it is well-known, the rabbis indicate that: 'blood of a menstruant... conveys impurity when moist and conveys impurity when dry' (*M. Niddah* 7.1).[10] In an evocative way, the tractate of Niddah bases its rules also on the external appearance of the contaminating fluids. The blood that makes the menstruant unclean can be distinguished by its colours: red, black, reddish like wet earth or roasted meat (*M. Niddah* 2.6).[11] Rabbinic writings pay equal attention to *loci*—that they called 'rooms'—parts of the body that may contain or be the source of the unclean blood. Using euphemisms or metaphors, they distinguish (in the woman body) the 'room', the 'hallway', and the 'upper chamber'.[12] 'Blood from the room is impure [if] found in the "hallway", its ambiguity [causes it to be treated as] impure because it is assumed from the "source"' (*M. Niddah* 2.5). Incontestably, in these passages the rabbinic language does not describe or conceptualize physiological functions of the body. It is equally certain that the sages are not describing or commenting on the divine realm or what God has implanted in this world. They impose over the outline of creation a kind of physiography of corporal reality.

This suggests that the body is neither blemished nor exalted. It is given as a matter of fact, something through which a better awareness of reality can be reached. At the same time, in its general

10. 'But the flow and the phlegm and the saliva and the crawling animal and the carcass and semen convey impurity when moist but do not carry impurity when dry. And if they can be soaked and returned to their original states they convey impurity when moist and they convey impurity when dry. And how long are they soaked? Twenty-four hours in warm water' (*M. Niddah* 7.1).

11. 'Five bloods are impure by a woman: the red, the black, like the bright crocus, like wet earth, and like mixed (wine). The academy of Shammai say, also like the water of fenugreek and like the liquid of roasted meat' (*M. Niddah* 2.6).

12. Within the rabbinic image, these spaces are not clear. Blackman suggests considering the secret or upper room as the upper part of uterus or vagina and the room as the vagina. P. Blackman, *Mishnayot* (London: Mishna Press Ltd, 1955), VI, p. 606.

configuration, the paradigm of the body and of its *loci* is liable to indicate the domain (and the source) of human life, and how strong is the need to know and to protect it. In this sense, the transition from the priestly view to that of the rabbis implies an important evolution. The change does not chiefly depend on the fact that human circumstances are much more 'on the scene'. The inference we may make is that the rabbis' texts stress that the functioning of every single body is liable to produce different effects (blood is distinguished by different colours, origins and ways of drying). Simple physical attributes, as they were originally created, are no longer taken as the foundation for determining what contaminates. Since they are never equivalent to each other, they need attention and interpretation.

It is evident that the rabbis did not innovate abruptly or diverge totally from Leviticus. As a matter of fact, levitical impurity has clear physical effects (as far as uncleanness implies bathing and washing dresses). Priestly writings, in general, have a strong tendency to categorize objects or animals on the basis of their physical aspects or unclean characteristics.[13] Skin colour, ways of eating and of walking are recognizable manners of envisaging corporeality. However, in the levitical classification these 'physical characteristics are important because they are concrete manifestations of divine will'[14] or may be read in a wider sense to define symbols of divine justice.[15]

As I mentioned, the body-impurity relation is read by the rabbis on the basis of the inner and most secret parts of the female body, but it is always conceived within a specific time or as part of the construction of a time framework. In this sense, it is illuminating that the starting text of *Niddah* precisely concerns the onset of menses: 'every woman who has an established menstrual cycle, her time is sufficient to her' (*M. Niddah* 1.1). Menstrual time is obviously strictly connected to repetitive natural and uncontrollable cycles.[16] Yet the onset of periods of impurity is culturally channelled through appropriate

13. M. Douglas, 'The Forbidden Animals in Leviticus', *JSOT* 59 (1993); Jenson, *Graded Holiness*, p. 60.

14. Eilberg-Schwartz, *The Savage in Judaism*, p. 221.

15. Douglas, 'The Forbidden Animals in Leviticus', pp. 20-23.

16. The uncontrollability of blood flow cannot be the only criterion for determining the use of time in the impurity system. Eilberg-Schwartz affirms that it is the way to distinguish brief or long contamination. However, it may be that some uncontrollable bleeding, from the nose for instance, is not contaminating. E.L. Greenstein, 'A Mind to Savage Judaism', *Judaism* 4 (194), pp. 101-109, see p. 107.

calculations of times. Throughout *Niddah*, the rabbis construct a typology of times and define their 'forms', sequences and alternations in order to facilitate the task of the menstruant.

Terms such as 'established period' (יש לה וסת), 'her time' (*שעתה*), time that 'is sufficient to her' (די״ה) convey important but problematic temporal concepts. וסת is differently translated. The word is applied, in Talmudic writings, to a variety of things: to manners or conduct (*y. Yoma* 1, 38 c), to a diet (*b. Sanh.*101 a; *b. Ket* 110b), to dates or times which occur regularly (*M. Niddah* 1.1 and 9.8, also *b. Niddah* 63a).[17] When applied to a woman who has normal cycles, it allows her to calculate her unclean days from the moment she experiences a flow.[18] A temporal dimension is closely aligned to a specific personal dimension. Two observations in this respect can be made. First, a regular woman depends on 'her' personal time that is 'sufficient' to conceptualize the beginning and the type of her contamination. A woman's perception and physical constitution give therefore the basis for structuring her individual contamination. Second, speaking of 'sufficient' time, the rabbis are fighting against uncertainty and hazard. 'Sufficient' means neither abundant nor scarce, but simply a time which is incontestably adequate. It openly marks the lower but the correct standard within a certain scale or for a certain purpose. By its use, the rabbis (the sages Amorraim are explicit on this point) aim at shortening the impurity period that interrupts ordinary times to a minimum. In terms of rabbinic thought, as the defiling days are conveniently kept as short as possible, the woman is protected from the effects of her uncontrollable physiology. Time is positively articulated to reduce uncomfortable situations and to respond to the exigencies of ordinary life. Inexorably, if a woman is not regular, her time is not 'sufficient' for calculating cycles. Irregularity, anomaly

17. M. Jastrow, *A Dictionary of the Talmud* (London: Putnam's Sons, 1886-1903).

18. In interpreting or widening Leviticus, the rabbis ask themselves 'how is her time sufficient for her?' (*M. Niddah* 1.2). The question intends to clarify the exact moment in which she becomes unclean. The rabbis' reply is given in a descriptive idiom strictly related to the woman herself. The sages explain: take the case that she is sitting on a bed, occupied with ritually pure food, and she gets up from her bed and after that she discovers that her menses began. In this precise moment she becomes נדה (for seven days) but the food (she had touched) and the bed (on which she sat) remained pure because they were such before she perceived the flow of blood (*M. Niddah* 1.2).

and uncontrollability in a woman give greater weight to problems of purity. An irregular woman conveys impurity unexpectedly or sometimes very frequently. This is why the rabbis work differently on her time and declare that she is to be considered as retrospectively unclean (for the 24 hours before the moment she discovered her flow) (*M. Niddah* 1.2). Obviously, the retrospective principle responds to the need to face an acute risk of contamination that cannot otherwise be foreseen and controlled. In line with Leviticus, the rabbis' scheme is able to embrace and to solve problems that could produce conflicts and accusations.

A wider range of classifications is introduced by the rabbis to determine whether time is 'sufficient' or not. For a number of reasons, women may have no blood flow at all. In the rabbinic well-known taxonomic frame, they fall into four groups, namely: 'virgins', 'pregnant women', 'lactating' (nursing) and 'elderly' women (*M. Niddah* 1.3). The tendency of the rabbis is to include them in the conformable and easy category of regular women. Whenever these women experience blood, 'their time' is always said to be 'sufficient'. Under this doctrine, they do not contaminate retrospectively as other irregular women.

Within the rabbis' vision, we may conclude, regularity or irregularity, similarities and differences (precisely the attributes that have been given by God)[19] are primarily intended to emphasize the need for detailed calculations of time. It is in this perspective that the menstruant is required to be aware of her menses and must recognize 'her time'. As we will see, all this may be also restated in terms of protection of the woman and of her environment.

She who 'Saw': Coding the Menstruant's Times

Clearly, in *Niddah* the menstruant is committed by time, either 'sufficient' or not. She relies on her condition, derived strictly from the moment of her physical experience and on 'her time'. Moreover, she passes through a series of qualifying bodily perceptions and symptoms: her way of 'seeing the blood', of adapting to a 'date', of having premonitory 'sensations'.

Rabbinic long-elaborated writings demonstrate in many ways that the state of an unclean person may be concretely detected through conscious cooperation on the part of the defiling person. Such

19. Eilberg-Schwarz, *Savage in Judaism*, p. 223, has different views on the interest of rabbis in physical traits.

cooperation is brought about by the act of 'seeing'. The menstruant is an illuminating and basic case. She is invested with the responsibility of exploring regularly her body, private and secret, in order to find out the onset and the end of the menstrual flow. In rabbinic language, 'seeing the blood' therefore has the specific function of determining, as early as possible, the exact time at which blood makes the woman defiled and defiling. This delicate function of self-examination is proved by the well-known rabbinic definition of the menstruant. She is categorized as she who 'saw' (*M. Niddah* 1.2; 1.6), she who 'saw her blood' (רעתה דם) (*M. Niddah* 1.4), she who 'observes herself' (בודקת) (*M. Niddah* 1.7)[20] or she who 'watches herself day after day' (שומרת יום כנגד יום) (*M. Zavim* 1.1) (if she is irregular). A confirmation of the importance of a woman's sight, in rabbinic terminology, comes from the complementary opposite of she who 'saw'. בתולה is precisely 'a woman who in all her days never saw blood' (*M. Niddah* 1.4). Both cases are constructed on the same specific act of observation[21] and have been used to indicate an intimate relationship with one's physiological condition and dependence on one's periodical impurity.

In this framework, watching bleeding is not overtly or directly associated with metaphysical ideas, or encoded in the divine design of procreation and reproduction. By implication, we may say that it has the aim of discovering the passage from one time to another in the sequence of ordinary days. In this sense, it is an instrumental action or a cultural device that can help everyday relations and transform habits and rhythms by tracing boundaries, generating duties and expectations and preventing dangers. It is interesting to note that throughout the Mishnah the experience of the intentional overseeing of the woman becomes the paradigmatic way to control the whole range of defiling

20. In biblical language, the menstruant is she who, seeing the blood, experiences 'the separation of her impurity' (נדת טמאתה, Lev. 18.19). On general problems concerning separation see J. Baskin, 'The Separation of Women in Rabbinic Judaism', in Y.Y. Hahhad and E. Banks (eds.), *Women, Religion and Social Change* (Findley, NY: SUNY Press, 1985), pp. 3-18.

21. See R. Di Segni, '"Colei che non ha mai visto il sangue": Alla ricerca delle radici ebraiche dell'idea della concezione verginale di Maria', *Quaderni Storici* 75; XXV, 3 (1990), pp. 757-89. The definition of בתולה in rabbinic language, applies even if the woman is married. H. Zelcer, *Companion Mishnayot: Niddah* (New York: Hebrew Linear Press, 1994), p. 39 n. 1.

emissions of all humans.[22] It offers precisely the basic model for any kind of bodily inspections. I cannot elaborate on this here. What I can say is that it is symptomatic of the system of control that the model of the menstruant introduces a particular cognitive instrument within the rabbinic system of reading purity times.

Our ideas of seeing and watching are based on concepts of presumed objectivity. In reality, it is highly difficult 'to see' systematically and integrally what one needs to see. Something may be unperceived, something may be lost or may remain out of sight. Only from certain traces or parameters is one able to record the essential data that 'construct' the real fact. The reality of impurity, unperceivable in itself, is made decipherable by the time in which blood is 'visible', when it is materially and legally noticed by the sensitivity of a woman. A delicate human mediation (consisting of discretional evaluations) may be introduced between the hypothetical contaminating event and the real contamination.

The rabbinic rule of discovering the blood provides specific devices which reply to this problem of mediation. The rabbis do give great importance to personal checking but elaborate a specific syntax of seeing which assigns abilities and duties to the unclean person. Conceptualizing the entire process, they specify when, how and with which instruments controls are required. Widely elaborating their discourse they suggest that the menstruant must be correctly educated to learn how to see and how to experience physical occurrences. In cultural terms, this means that it is beyond the menstruant's choice or opportunity to give interpretation of her cycle. Her personal intentions have virtually no effect on the purity system. The rabbis simply view her as the person who is required to recognize the contaminating flow from the period in which it has been 'seen'. This implies not only that she is prevented from being arbitrarily or untimely affected by impurity problems but also that she acquires methods of safe controls socially useful for defending people from unforeseen dangers. To reach exact knowledge of one's time is a step forward in personal status and general order.

From this it is evident that, at the anthropological level, impurity is better explained with the help of the rule of 'seeing the blood' than with that of 'remaining in the impure state'. The work of elaborating and reinforcing the temporal context of Leviticus influenced human

22. The whole tractate of *Zavim* offers a good example.

awareness in an original manner. Constructing scrupulous rules and therefore giving official visibility to the menstrual blood, the rabbis encouraged the objectivization of impurity. Overtly discernible uncleanness became a remedy against uncertainty, danger, suspicion. In other words, the rabbinic structure of thinking gives rise to a satisfying way of conceptualizing social status and relations (not simply the human condition) as a central component of the created universe.

A Crucial Knowledge: The 'Date' of Menstruation

The learned knowledge of the menstruant has a sociological importance. During menses, the rabbinic rule of 'watching the blood' seems to be able to activate functional cooperation. As one might expect, the inspections of the menstruant are secret, but the results are revealed and communicated. There is no sense in classifying symptoms if they are destined to remain unknown. With the practical aim of conjugal abstinence during menstruation days, the wife is not limited to the duties of 'remaining' or of 'seeing'. She also has the role of giving punctual information on her state of impurity. All rules of mutual references between husband and wife may be changed. Two different categories of persons and two different degrees of capacity face each other. Strikingly, control and order come from the arcane knowledge and verbal communication of the unclean woman. Any judgment on menses is actually formulated and transmitted not through the husband, the head of the family, but by somebody else, a legal dependent or minor, the wife.[23] The husband is simply informed by the person who 'saw the blood'. He depends on his wife's accuracy and ability to fulfil her duties. There is no doubt that this has a structural meaning. Speaking of the blood, a prerogative of the menstruant, becomes the way of giving value and validity to the law of Leviticus.

To see the blood and to give information on the flow is not enough. Once the menstruant knows her cycles, she becomes the guardian of her biological life, of the data hidden in her body. Following their characteristic way of thinking, the rabbis believe that the menstruant must preserve the precious memory of her cycles and of their beginnings. She is invited to fix a 'date'. This permits her to become a

23. A. Fehribach, 'Between Text and Context: Scripture, Society and the Role of Womens Formative Judaism', in P.J. Haas (ed.), *Recovering the Role of Women: Power and Authority in Rabbinic Jewish Society* (Atlanta: Scholars Press, 1992), pp. 39-60, see pp. 49-52.

regular woman and to depend on 'her time' (*M. Niddah* 1.1). In late rabbinic literature (*b. Yev.* 65a) a regular period or 'date' of menstruation (וסת) is said to be established after three consecutive menstrual cycles.[24]

It is useful to treat the 'date' not as a purely routine accomplishment. The need to calculate and to memorize it reveals a highly structured system that intends to secure order and reliability. Standardizing a calculated beginning of the menstruation, the sages safeguard the woman in particular. Once the 'date' is known, cautious restrictions may be reduced within the family and the community. Following a day of onset, everyone may know in advance when the woman's impurity begins, and thus the possibility of retrospective dangers may be excluded. Any doubt over her uncleanness may be reasonably excluded until the date of menses. On the other hand, to fix a 'date' for the woman actually corresponds to making a conscious act, much more involving than that of seeing or of speaking of blood flow.[25] When she takes note of the 'day of menstruation' she is supposed to adapt herself to, adhere to and support a cultural world[26] for the common good. Matching overall needs, this results in eligibility for marriage, for family position.

It is incontestable that the 'date' has some obscure aspects. First, what is critical is that the regular cycle (וסת) in any case varies according to the personal time and knowledge of the menstruant. As any other person, the woman is vulnerable and defective and her conclusions may bring about incorrect effects. Secondly, even if the 'date' is correctly based on three consecutive menses, it remains an artificial and conventional device. All this, however, does not mean the artifice is not convenient and convincing. The concept of וסת may automatically activate rules and behaviours and become the intellectual instrument that institutes the socio-cultural controllability of what is not controllable. To have a 'date' for a woman chiefly means to be in a simplified social situation, to be able to play an easier role.

24. A trimester is not only needed to fix a 'date', but also to 'release' the woman from the 'restrictions of the established regular period' (*b. Yev.* 65a).

25. Discussing the state of doubtful uncleanness, *b. Niddah* 15a-15b implies that the rule of 'seeing' is of biblical origin. In general, the rabbinic debate does not concern the authority of the Pentateuch but only some consequences for the woman and her husband.

26. Special calculations are also needed for defining a זב (*M. Zabim* 1.1-6).

Evidently, she is liberated from her biological sphere and is assigned to a better status.

In calculating the 'date', physical symptoms other than blood may be taken into account as proof of the approach of the impure period (provided the woman experiences them regularly). In general, these symptoms are exterior or involuntary and uncontrollable manifestations of the body such as stretching, yawing, sneezing, shivering, sensations in the lower parts of her womb, non-menstrual discharges and difficulty in urinating (*M. Niddah* 9.8). This time, the regular 'date' is calculated with or without the woman's cooperation. External perceptions are put on the same level as intimate inspections. Social arrangements of the context of the woman seem to be at work and appear as rigourous and effective as her private watching.

In short, there is no doubt that humans are given a special attention in rabbinic thought. This reflects a need to make impurity more decipherable, and to free people as much as possible from fears and risks. At the very least, it transforms the collective imagination of purity into practical ways to penetrate things that govern usual social life.

Final Remarks on Rabbis' Social Imagination

What has been described above can be summarized into two main points. First, on the one hand, the time of status quo or time of waiting (marked as 'to be' by the Priestly editors) is to some degree incompatible with personal convictions or attitudes. Being determined by a supernatural plan it bears the imprint of divine perfection and also that of an arching and generalized symbolic system. On the other hand, a specific meaning of time is elaborated in the writings of the early rabbis. The sages of the Mishnah coupled the levitical command of respecting the status quo with a rule which may be summed up in three words: 'know your state'—at certain specific times regularly observe and categorize your physical conditions over time (during the day, on weekdays, each month and so on). In this sense, the 'time of seeing' may reasonably be counted among those cultural conventions that give space to identities and personalities. Whether this is because the rabbinic rule is an attempt to push beyond Leviticus or because it is simply an attempt to give 'visible' dimensions to impurity, the result is that the rabbis articulated a cultural idiom and shaped a Jewish personality.

Secondly, in representing impurity, the rabbinic writings do not treat physical matters as purely mental or symbolic frames. They imagine worldly cases and give weight to human details in a 'realistic' way. In so doing, the Mishnah gives consistent form to the intrinsic components of the Jewish person. It has been noted earlier that the rabbis' classification of the times of impurity corresponds to a victory of the social over the merely human. This means that the sages give space to their social imagination and institute a social style. The range of this social imagination is proved by the large set of conventional criteria the rabbis adopt or invoke. Most of these criteria are not imposed by biological factors or strictly personal or individual needs. I am thinking, for example, of the rule establishing that the woman has the duty to examine herself in the morning, at night and after sexual intercourse, and also of the one stating that after a number of 'established' menses she is regular. The concept of וסת, in particular, represents an interesting solution to possible underlying and predictable tensions. Similar considerations may be applied to other conventional precepts. Many rules (apart from those applied to the woman during pregnancy, nursing or in old age) are openly conjectural instruments: sometimes the kind of uncleanness of a menstruant varies according to the age of the girl or, at childbirth, the length of the mother's labour.[27] All these injunctions have the result not only of guiding individuals but also of strengthening or aggregating society. It is because the rabbinic system of times puts together and coordinates both purely theoretical cases and concrete ones, that we may say that through the sages the covenant between the Jewish people and God was given what might be called social 'implementations'.

To conclude, when the sages are rationalizing and accommodating disparate aims and interests, they do not appear deeply influenced by scriptures. Moving from a theoretical level or envisaging quotidian topics, the sages give foundation and consistency to a 'project' which is autonomous from the scriptural writings. Their central ideas are

27. The sages hypothesize the extraordinary case of a girl one day or ten days old. Both may become impure by blood flow, but the former is seen as a regular woman, the latter as an irregular one (*M. Niddah* 5.3). During birthgiving, another example, impurity may be calculated on the length of a woman's labour (*M. Niddah* 4.4) or in the conjugal field, woman's impurity may be precisely detected on the basis of the time passed since her intercourse: 'If [the blood is] found on her after an amount of time [following marital relations], they are impure due to doubt. What is after [an amount of time]? So that she may descend from the bed and wipe her surface' (*M. Niddah* 2.3).

revealed by the fact the Mishnah is interested in priests and scribes but chiefly in 'householders' and in their universe.[28] All this may be proved by the interior order of themes, the social nature of its component parts, the ethnographic milieu contained in the Mishnah[29] that actually give plausibility to and prove the strength of the sages' social imagination and experience. I cannot comment on these features here. What is certain is that through the use of original and homogeneous cultural instruments the Mishnah unambiguously reveals how deeply the rabbis are concerned to organize their 'world', to maintain their identity[30] and to establish their Jewish style of social life. In this sense, the speculations of the sages are anthropologically interesting and attractive. They are significant precisely because they provide access to a specific logical system and contemporarily they give evidence that the rabbis 'looked in the scriptures for meanings less at variance with their experience'.[31]

28. Neusner, *Judaism*.

29. A. Destro, *Antropologia del Giudaismo antico* (Bologna: CISEC, 1992), pp. 20-27.

30. Fehribach, 'Between Text and Context', p. 57; S. Stern, *Jewish Identity in Early Rabbinic Writings* (Leiden: Brill, 1994), pp. 51-52.

31. Douglas, *In the Wilderness*, p. 40.

Discussion

Douglas: I would like to say something fundamental to Adriana. Does what you say not confirm my idea that rabbis really misunderstood Leviticus: they really got it desperately wrong? My interest is in finding out why the text can be read so differently from the way it has always been read. If you compare 11 to 15 you see that women's menstruation, bloody childbirth and so on are mentioned there, but the context is so meticulously balanced between the sexes that it cannot sensibly be read, unless the rabbis did it this way, as a discussion of women. So that when the woman gives birth, immediately you have the male child and female child, so male and female balance out at the very beginning of ch. 12. Then, when there is a question of bodily emissions, the woman's menstruation is balanced against the men's emissions of semen, so women are never discussed by themselves. It is always one gender against the other gender and then what they have in common; for instance, they could all get leprosy. When they go to great lengths to think about women especially as impure, it seems to me to be a misdirection of what Leviticus was talking about. So you are bound to misread the idea that the woman has more time to look after her baby when it is a female than she has when it is a male. The male is taken away from her and dedicated to God because he is male, after 8 days, but she keeps her baby for 14 days. Seclusion in Africa and many other societies, is simply a period of being restricted from ordinary occupations.

Destro: I believe the laws were determined by social needs, so probably they are much more strict, with some kind of regulation on duties that the wife was supposed to perform. What I understand from reading the Mishnah is that the preoccupation of the rabbis is to simplify the situation while they are giving much more regulation. They are aiming, for instance, from the very beginning of *Niddah* to shorten times of impurity. The rule of fixing sufficient time for a regular woman is similarly dictated by the need to simplify her position as far as her menstruation is concerned. She may have a regular cycle, and thus is in a position to be considered pure and accessible in the family, as regards the husband and so on. On the one hand, there is an increase of regulations, but on the other hand I perceive a concern on the part of the rabbis to introduce mechanical ways of solving problems so that everybody knows in advance how to manage her impurity, and relate one to another.

Segal: I think that the distinction between defilement and sin is an ancient accomplishment, not a modern one and that modern religions including Judaism and Christianity are responsible for the elimination of defilement, and the failure to preserve a distinction between defilement and sin. This is because what modern Judaism and Christianity alike have, and ancient religion does not, is the assumption that God is all-powerful and more just, and that given that broad assumption, nothing happens simply by chance, nothing happens accidentally, everything that happens is intentional and everything that happens is fair. There is no room for what Evans-Pritchard found so frustrating, namely, something to take the place of what we would call chance. One of the factors involved in the failure (not success) of modern religion to retain the distinction between defilement and sin, is this highfalutin set of characterisations of God which does not allow for a case of mere defilement vis-à-vis sin. The other, more philosophical, fact is almost ironically the Cartesian differentiation between mind and body, or between soul and body, which on the one hand separates body from soul and in that sense allows for physical defilement, but on the other hand so reduces body to a passive effect of mind as not to allow for pure bodily defilement. That I see as the modern abasing rather than erecting of what I think is a wonderful ancient distinction.

Douglas: In order to come out of the realm of your own preferences and speculation, we have to engage on the question of who accuses whom and when. This is about accusation, and how society is run on the basis of these intellectual ideas. I agree with what you started by saying, which is that most religions round the world, as anthropologists find them, outside the Jewish and Christian traditions but certainly not outside the Greek tradition, have a separate field of defilement. As it works, it is a focus for accusations. You accuse people of it. So how we do without such accusations today is that we have the law courts, I suppose. In order to join me and talk about the same thing, you have to do this Evans Pritchard thing and say what was the grip of accusations that was there before and has gone, and how else do they handle it.

Segal: Modern religion handles what science would characterize as chance by introducing God as involved in it, in other words, by dissolving this concept of defilement vis-à-vis sin.

Douglas: You can talk about all sorts of intellectual things, but I am really talking about accusations and living with an idea. I am talking about how they managed to live with this idea of defilement. You could accuse people of being defiled. Otherwise I agree with you but I would like to hear an example.

Segal: Susan Sondheim is writing a book saying that cancer should not be blamed on persons and more recently that AIDS should not be blamed on persons, and this, to me, is responding to the legacy of modern religion that is seeing it as something that simply alas befalls people, that they did not incur because they had done wrong and for which they are being punished. It is, for me, an example of a response by modern science, not by modern religion, to something that is the work of modern religion. She would not have needed to write that kind of book if she had lived in an ancient period.

Harrington: You said that there is a conflict between God's concern for the afflicted and the exclusion of lepers and the mutilated from the sanctuary. I do not think there is such a great conflict. God excludes the mutilated only from officiating as priests, so they are no more excluded from his service than the ordinary Israelites.

Douglas: There is a possibility of demotion in that a priest can be accused of leprosy or accused of having any kind of blemish that other people inflict him with—he does not have to have been born with it. It can be very ambiguous whether it counts as a blemish or not. But it nonetheless is an opportunity for him to be accused or demoted. It was a way of controlling priests, or it could be used as an interfactional weapon by one priest against another.

Harrington: But of course ordinary Israelites were just as much excluded from officiating as a priest with a blemish. My other point is about lcprosy. You said it was representative of the afflicted class. I don't agree because lepers are viewed in the Bible as sinners, whereas those afflicted with other diseases are not.

Douglas: You cannot find in Leviticus anything about lepers having caught their leprosy from sin.

Harrington: I think you can. In the rest of the Bible you certainly can, and in the Cave 4 text from Qumran it is clear the leper is a sinner. In the rabbinic literature the understanding is that the leper got that way because of sin. I think you can say that in Leviticus it is connected with sin because first of all, it is only the leper that is healed that comes under the control of the Leviticus law. How he gets healed is not discussed because only a miracle can heal him, because he got that way because of a curse from God. Then he comes under the control of the priests who officiate in his purification and he has to bring at least four different kinds of sacrifices. It is really serious. It is not like menstruation or sexual intercourse, or easily purified. I was interested in what you said about social control in the Leviticus laws. But Leviticus does not control leprosy. The leper only comes under the control of the Levitical laws after he is healed and his leprosy is gone. The law of purification does not control the initial problem of the leprosy.

Douglas: I can see that there is a case for picking little bits from here and there in the rest of the Bible which gives the general idea that leprosy is the result of sin. But it is not explicit at all in Leviticus. In Numbers where it says, 'Put the lepers outside the camp', it sounds like a terribly harsh thing to do to lepers. My thought on that was that many societies put lepers outside the camp. There is this thing about contagion being spontaneous and leprosy is thought to be much more contagious than it actually medically is. Also, leprosy has these cycles of cures and then it starts again, so that you might constantly want to know whether you might let the leper back or not.

Rogerson: The Deut. 19.21 version of talion does not use the word תחת, but the preposition ב and therefore an interesting question is what sort of ב is it? If it is *beth pretii* 'the ב of price', then does that link in with what you [Jackson] said at the beginning about the Deuteronomic version, that it can be redeemable by payment?

Jackson: If one took the formula out of its context, then on purely linguistic grounds the answer would be yes. I would compare, for example, in Exod. 22.2-3: 'Then he shall be sold for his theft. It is not actually for his theft but for the stolen animal. But we have to understand the formula in the context in which it now appears. Whatever its origins, it has become mandatory.

Douglas: I was wondering about the dating. At the beginning you suggested a development in Exodus, and you talk about something as being applicable 'in this period'. Later you said 'by now' talion had become institutionalized, referring to Deuteronomy. Does Deuteronomy then come in as a kind of insertion in Numbers? What sort of dating are you thinking of? When I was comparing Kings, which is supposed to be so much later than the Mosaic books, according to the structure of the book, I was thinking that it was edited by priests in the sixth century and so is later in that sense.

Jackson: I would not want to be dogmatic on actual dating. The main claim that I would be making is that there is a plausible development from less institutionalized to more institutionalized forms of regulation which corresponds to a division between the understanding of talion in the Covenant Code, and the later sources. The question of the relative dating of Deuteronomy and the priestly sources in respect of this is not something which I could conclusively answer. I think one has to look at those few areas where we have sources in all three, for example on homicides or slaves. One does not necessarily come to the same conclusions in each. Then one can evaluate these in terms of the presuppositions and intertextualities that you find there and you can come to views as to relative chronology. But I am not in a position to make claims to absolute chronology.

'But if it is a Girl she is Unclean for Twice Seven Days...' The Riddle of Leviticus 12.5

Jonathan Magonet

Since rabbis regularly preach on the weekly portion of the Torah, some passages are inevitably less popular than others. But the one that is most often described as a 'rabbi-killer' is the double section from Leviticus, תזריע־מצרע (Lev. 12.1–15.33) with its concentration on ritual 'uncleanness', after childbirth and in connection with various mysterious skin diseases. (In the case of the latter, rabbinic tradition offers a little help. 'Leprosy' is seen as a punishment for slandering someone [see Num. 12], so with a little *legerdemain* one can move onto the subject of gossip and there is always plenty of local congregational material to preach about).

It happened that my daughter's batmitzvah portion began with Leviticus 12, and in studying it with her I was forced to look more closely at this particular chapter. The problem of the negative associations of the word translated as 'impure' or 'unclean' was relatively easy to explain as a ritual rather than a moral, or moralistic, concept. But what does one make of the double period of 'uncleanness' after the birth of a female child?

Looking into the standard commentaries was not much help. Reference is made to the theory that the vaginal discharge, lochia, continues for a longer period after the birth of a girl than after the birth of a boy, so that this observation might have occasioned the necessity for doubling the period. However the medical proof apparently suggests a slightly longer period but nowhere near twice as long as this text would require.[1] Various suggestions about the supposed inferior status

1. G.J. Wenham, *The Book of Leviticus* (NICOT; Grand Rapids: Eerdmans, 1979), p. 188.

of women in Israelite society[2] are open to debate in general terms, and would anyway have little relevance in such a matter. In fact, quite the converse could be argued—the ability to pollute being a measure of one's relative power, at least in some kind of ritual context. One solution that is quite attractive is that since the baby girl who has been born is a potential mother, this might require a double purification rite—but since the baby's own childbearing is long in the future, such a suggestion must remain only speculative.

Inevitably such a question addressed to a particular text leads one to other related texts in the search for possible clarification. Since v. 1 specifically compares the state of the woman to that of a menstruant it is inevitable that consideration be given to the laws relating to this matter in Leviticus 15. However in examining this chapter yet another puzzle emerges, but one that is also related to a variant time scale between males and females. So it became important to consider this before returning to the original topic.

The Strange Case of the Menstruating Man

From Lev. 15.16 we learn that when a man has a seminal emission he must wash his flesh and that he is ritually unclean till evening. This is the exact male equivalent to the ritual uncleanness that affects a woman who is menstruating and is thus affected for seven days. However, whereas if a man has intercourse with a woman then both of them are affected and are ritually unclean till the evening (Lev. 15.18), if a man has intercourse with a woman who is menstruating, her *Niddah* affects him and he too is unclean for seven days like her (Lev. 15.24).

The commentators discuss this passage in connection with the punishment mentioned in Lev. 20.18, although the text here seems quite neutral on the matter. Nevertheless, the question remains as to why a seven day period is evoked since if anyone merely touches her they are only unclean till the evening (Lev. 15.19). Presumably the answer lies in the difference between merely touching and sexual intercourse, but before I can suggest what that may be, something more about ch. 15 as a whole needs to be examined.

2. J. Milgrom, *Leviticus 1–16* (AB, 3; Garden City, NY: Doubleday, 1991), p. 750.

Wenham analysed the concentric structure of this chapter:[3]

1	Introduction		
2–18	Male discharges		
		2–12	Long term
		13–15	Cleansed by sacrifice
		16–17	Transient
		18	Intercourse
19–30	Female discharges		
		19–23	Transient (Menstruation)
		24	and intercourse
		25–27	Long term
		28–30	Cleansed by sacrifice
31	Purpose of law		
32-33	Summary		

He writes:

> The balance and symmetry of the arrangement is striking. Two types of discharge, long-term and transient, are distinguished. Since they can affect both sexes, that gives four main cases. It should also be noted that the discharges of women are discussed in the reverse order to those of men. This gives an overall chiastic pattern (AB-BA). Chiasmus is regularly used in Hebrew to bring out the unity of a double-sided event. It is a most appropriate device to employ in these particular laws, focusing as they do on the unity of mankind in two sexes. Form and content here complement each other to express the idea that 'God created man in his own image... male and female created he them' (Gen. 1.27). The unity and interdependence of the sexes finds its most profound expression in the act of sexual intercourse, and very fittingly this is discussed in v. 18, the midpoint of the literary structure (Wenham, *Leviticus*, p. 217).

Whitekettle further refines this structure by emphasizing the distinction here between functional and dysfunctional discharges ranged around the central verse.[4] The passage is concerned with the ideal physiological functioning of the reproductive system.

		Physiological Integrity	*Systemic Function*
A	vv. 2b-15	Abnormal	Abnormal
B	16-17	Typical	Dysfunctional
C	18	Normal	Normal

3. Wenham, *Leviticus*, p. 216.

4. R. Whitekettle, 'Leviticus 15.18 Reconsidered: Chiasm, Spatial Structure and the Body', *JSOT* 49 (1991), pp. 31-45, see p. 38.

B´	19-24	Typical	Dysfunctional
A´	25-30	Abnormal	Abnormal

Thus AA´—indicate 'physiological settings which are clearly pathological' (p. 38).

BB´—Non-pathological conditions: 'that is they are not life threatening or degenerative. They cannot, therefore, be called physiologically "abnormal". On the other hand, the setting is not the chapter's ideal of sexual intercourse... Section B is systemically dysfunctional because the discharge, though typical, cannot bring about reproduction'.[5]

C—'as the fulcrum of the chapter, portrays sexual physiology in its fully functional setting.'[6]

Focusing on the difference between physiological and pathological discharges and the centrality of intercourse in this chapter is very helpful, but both need to be further examined.

In discussing the variety of conditions that lead to ritual uncleanness, commentators have tended to dismiss the relevance of any hygienic motive.[7] But this is on the basis of lumping together this chapter with others where ritual uncleanness is incurred and finding no consistent overall pattern. In this chapter alone, it is evident, as illustrated above, that it distinguishes between physiological and pathological discharges and that it does so through a number of indices.

First, the passage carefully distinguishes two kinds of pathological discharges (v. 3). Irrespective of the precise difference between them, this fact alone witnesses to a series of empirical observations and the presumption of a medical interest in the condition. Secondly, considering the overt concerns with ritual matters in this and related chapters, it is significant that neither seminal emission (15.16-17) nor menstruation (15.19-23) requires a sacrifice to 'atone' for them,[8] whereas the pathological discharges do so require (15.13-15, 28-30).

Thirdly, with one exception that I shall discuss, a differentiation is made between the degree of contamination caused by the 'physiological' and the 'pathological' conditions. The latter effectively apply a condition of quarantine on the one who is ill. It is spelled out most clearly in the case of the man with a discharge: The bed he lies on and the seat he sits on are contaminated—whoever comes in contact with them is

5. Whitekettle, 'Leviticus 15.18', p. 38.
6. Whitekettle, 'Leviticus 15.18', p. 38.
7. See, for example, Wenham, *Leviticus*, p. 222.
8. Wenham, *Leviticus*, p. 220.

'unclean till evening', must launder their clothes and bathe in water (vv. 4-6). The identical conditions apply to whoever touches the flesh of the man (v. 7) or on whom the man spits (v. 8). Any saddle on which he sits is likewise contaminated and anyone who touches anything that was under him is 'unclean till evening', must wash their clothes and bathe in water (vv. 9-10). Verses 4-6 and 9-10 concentrate on the environment that his presence contaminates, and themselves surround, literally as well as metaphorically, the central verse that deals with direct contact with him. The additional instruction about how to dispose of utensils, of earthenware or wood, that he has used (v. 12) can only reinforce the impression that here is a description of the precautions to be taken by those caring for someone who is recognizably ill and whose illness might be passed on to others.

The description of the pathological condition of a woman (v. 25) similarly distinguishes two conditions, one independent of, and one associated with, her menstrual period. This provides a symmetry with the distinction made about the conditions affecting the man, but also points to empirical observations. The description of how to deal with the contamination she causes is much shorter (v. 26): whoever comes in contact with her is also 'unclean till evening', must launder their clothes and bathe in water (v. 27). It would therefore be nice to assume that here too a clear distinction is made between a physiological and pathological condition, but for the fact that these same requirements, of laundering clothes and washing in water, are cited with regards to her menstruation (vv. 21-22).

Nevertheless there are some problems with the passage about the menstruating woman. It is evident that those objects that come into direct contact with someone with a physiological discharge are rendered unclean (the clothes of a man, v. 17; the bed or seat of a menstruant woman, v. 20). But with regards to a menstruant woman there are two 'versions' of what happens to someone who comes into contact with her bedding or seat. According to vv. 21-22 there is the more stringent requirement (otherwise needed for contact with the man with a discharge, vv. 5-6) of laundering clothing and washing in water. But according to v. 24 he is simply 'unclean till evening'. Since one of these versions seems to be redundant, it is possible that the original 'physiological' version simply included vv. 19-20 and 23, and that vv. 21-22 were subsequently added on analogy with the requirements for the man with a discharge.[9] As noted above, the requirements for a woman with a discharge are curiously truncated, referring only to the menstrual state (v. 26) for clarification. Since v. 27 briefly notes that whoever touches the things on which she lies or sits must launder clothes and wash in water, it may be that a later editor saw fit to insert the details contained in vv. 21 and 22, borrowed from the description of the man with a discharge, into the list of conditions affecting a menstruant woman.[10]

I am always reluctant to posit a 'careless editor', or even a later editor with a particular purpose, but given the physiology/pathology distinction that underpins the chapter as a whole and the redundancy of either vv. 21-22 or v. 23, I am inclined to suggest such an scenario.

Moreover, this view is strengthened by the fact that according to v. 19, whoever touches her is unclean till the evening—with no mention of the need to wash clothes or bathe in water. Levine asserts that

> Although the formulation is not explicit in every case, it is clear from the context that when any one of these impurities occurs, the requirement is to bathe and launder one's clothing. This is explicitly stated in verses 21-22 but not in verses 20 and 23.[11]

But I would agree with Milgrom[12] who notes that the phrase 'shall be impure until evening' always assumes that this is to be accompanied by bathing. But also suggests on v. 19 that it does not imply 'laundering'.

> This clause also implies that touching a menstruant generates less impurity than touching a *zav*, which requires laundering (v. 7). But this flatly contradicts the following verses (21-22) where laundering is required. For how could touching the menstruant's bedding or seat, a second remove from the menstruant, be more contaminating than touching her directly? (Milgrom, *Leviticus 1–16*, p. 935).

He dismisses attempts to suggest that laundering must be assumed

9. The fact that the syntax of v. 23 is unusual may, paradoxically, reinforce the view that, as the more difficult text, it is the original one.

10. Why someone should have done so is open to speculation. One possible reason is precisely because of the punishment detailed in Lev. 20.18 (with the warning in 18.19) and the perceived need to place even more stringent barriers around a menstruating woman to make such an act less likely.

11. B.A. Levine, *Leviticus* (JPS Torah Commentary; Philadelphia: Jewish Publication Society of America, 1989), p. 97.

12. Milgrom, *Leviticus 1–16*, p. 919.

and offers his own solution.[13] But I would prefer to assume that the distinction between physiological and pathological states also originally held good here, and that it was only at a later stage that the additional conditions were laid on the menstruant woman as well.

Incidentally Milgrom notes that there is no prohibition barring the menstruant from touching anyone which can only mean that her hands do not transmit uncleanness.[14] But nothing is said about the hands of a man with an emission causing uncleanness either, which would reinforce the view that they are viewed as similar 'physiological' conditions.

Fourthly it must be noted that the man cured of his discharge, the woman cured from her discharge and the woman recovered from childbirth (who cannot afford a lamb—12.8) bring an identical offering of two pigeons or two doves to the priest, one for a sin-offering and one for a burnt-offering, for the priest to atone for them (15.15, 30). Surely there is a symmetry here between these life-threatening situations that have been overcome, as opposed to regular physiological conditions that do not require such a ritual act.

Let us now return to the question which started the analysis of this chapter. Why is it that following intercourse a woman, like the man, is unclean till evening, but that following intercourse with a woman who is menstruant a man is unclean like her for seven days? First, following the discussion above, nothing is said about him having to launder his clothes—which would seem to confirm the view of menstruation as a physiological condition and therefore requiring less stringent ministrations. Secondly the man, like the woman (v. 20), causes uncleanness to the things on which he lies (v. 24). Surely the implication is clear here—that 'normal intercourse' effectively changes the woman into the same 'state' as the man for that day, namely 'impure till the evening' and that intercourse with a woman who is menstruant changes a man into a 'menstruant' as well for those same seven days. The symmetry is quite exact.

Why should this be the case? Perhaps because the writers of Leviticus took quite literally the view expressed in Gen. 2.24:

> Therefore a man shall leave his father and his mother and cleave to his wife and they shall be one flesh.

13. Milgrom, *Leviticus 1–16*, p. 936.
14. Milgrom, *Leviticus 1–16*, p. 936.

That is to say that the act of intercourse creates a single entity, 'one flesh', and both are affected equally by the status of uncleanness of the other.

If this is the case then we could predict that, for example, a distinction will be made in the area of forbidden sexual unions between those of an adulterous nature, where this 'one flesh' is directly affected and those, like some cases of incest, where adultery is not involved. It is interesting that ch. 18 of Leviticus that deals with these issues refers specifically to the prohibition of approaching כל שאר בשרו where בשר stands for close family. However it is in ch. 20 that the specific punishments are described. Verse 10 specifies that if a man commits adultery with the wife of a man, of his neighbour, they shall both incur the death penalty. The same applies to a man who has intercourse with his father's wife (v. 11), his daughter-in-law (v. 12), his aunt (v. 20)—all cases where adultery takes place. Conversely when a man has intercourse with his sister the death penalty is not invoked, rather both are to be 'cut off' from the community and he 'bears his sin' (v. 17).[15] (The same penalty of 'cutting off' applies to a man who sleeps with a menstruant, v. 18.) Similar is the case of intercourse with the (unmarried) daughter of one's father or mother—both 'bear their sin' (v. 19).

This would seem to confirm the hypothesis that sexual union is seen, at least within circles concerned with 'cleanness' and 'uncleanness', as creating a single entity, 'one flesh', both parts of which are equally affected.

The Case of the Menstruating Baby

After this long excursus, I return to my starting point, the question as to why a woman is considered to be 'unclean' for twice as long after the birth of a daughter as after the birth of a son. Drawing on the discussion above, there is a possible analogy here in that if any entity can be considered to be a 'single flesh' made up of two separate persons, it is a mother bearing a child. It may not be pressing the point too far to note that the child leaves through precisely the path whereby the initial union was made. What follows is purely speculative but builds on the assumption of an empirical knowledge of physiology

15. The location of this ruling is particularly significant. In ch. 18 it is the third item listed, coming, for example, before 'daughter-in-law'. The sequence there would appear to be related to the degree of consanguinity. In ch. 20 it comes after the 'daughter-in-law' because the classification is based on the severity of the penalty.

and pathology among those who formulated the laws of 'cleanness' and 'uncleanness'.

There is a phenomenon that sometimes affects a new-born girl following the withdrawal of the maternal hormones—namely vaginal bleeding. I consulted a Professor of Obstetrics and Gynaecology, the author of several textbooks on the subject, who confirmed that perhaps one in ten baby girls may bleed in this way, and even if no blood appears there may well be a discharge. He added that it is one of the first things told to midwives so that they do not become overly concerned when it happens. (Maternal hormones can also cause temporary breast development in babies of either sex and even lactation, leading to the superstition that this is 'witch's milk'). It is therefore altogether possible that with the birth of a baby girl we have the equivalent of two 'women', each with an actual or potential vaginal discharge, to be accounted for. Since this uncleanness has to be ritually dealt with and the baby cannot do so, the mother with whom the child was formerly united and from whom she has emerged, symbolically bears the uncleanness so that the period is doubled.[16] Thus we are dealing with simple mathematical logic, two generators of uncleanness require two periods of purification.

This solution has the merit of taking seriously both the acknowledged medical information available in the ancient Near East and the presumption of a logical system underlying the Priestly regulations. It also helps reinforce the view that where matters of ritual uncleanness are concerned the logic of the system should first be sought before looking for social or moralizing reasons to explain a particular discrepancy.

16. It is interesting in this connection that the standard term for blood in these passages in Leviticus is in the plural. In Ezek. 16.6, the baby girl is described as 'wallowing in your bloods', using the standard plural form. However when later in the chapter describing her wantonness in her youth, the singular form (v. 22) is used.

HOLINESS AND PURITY: THE HOLY PEOPLE IN LEVITICUS AND EZRA–NEHEMIAH

Hyam Maccoby

I greatly welcome the ground-breaking work of Mary Douglas on the structure of Leviticus, and in particular her demonstration of the centrality of the moral precepts of ch. 19. Her work shows refreshing independence of the main body of scholarship on Leviticus, which, as she points out, retains a traditional theological bias. I shall offer a demurral, however, to that part of her argument, relating to Ezra–Nehemiah, where she has followed in general the mainstream view.

The purity provisions of Leviticus mark out a priestly people that is separated from the rest of humanity, holy. The essence of holiness is separation. But it is by no means the only kind of separation. The holiness separation of Leviticus must be distinguished from other kinds of separation: for example, aristocracy, pariah-status, Brahminism, ethnic exclusivism, racism, or simple negation of all the rest of humanity.

Exodus 19.5-6 says: 'And now if you listen to my voice and keep my covenant, then you shall be a special treasure (סגלה) for me from all the nations, for mine is all the earth. And you shall be to me a kingdom of priests and a holy nation.' This both affirms the specialness of Israel and also God's concern for the rest of humanity. He stresses that he is the God of all humanity, but at the same time elects Israel to a priestly role.

Leviticus re-affirms this role for Israel, but links the specialness to the observance of purity rules in particular:

> I am the Lord your God which have separated you from other peoples. Ye shall therefore put difference between clean beasts and unclean and between unclean fowls and clean... and ye shall be holy unto me: for I the Lord am holy, and have severed you from other people that ye should be mine (Lev. 20.24-25).

Here 'holiness' is specifically linked to separation. Again it is stressed that God is the God of all peoples, but Israel has been separated for a special role. This is a corrective to another formulation (Lev. 11.45) which might have been misunderstood to mean that God has abandoned interest in all other nations: 'For I am the Lord that bringeth you up out of the land of Egypt to be your God: ye shall therefore be holy, for I am holy.' The holiness of Israel means that Israel shares in the holiness of God, so that Israel in its land functions like priests in a Temple where God's presence rests; or, if the royal metaphor is adopted, like courtiers in the palace which is the special residence of the King. Thus all the purity regulations may be likened to the special procedure and vestments of priests or courtiers—a kind of etiquette or protocol of Temple or palace.

Such separation, however, may be criticized as a form of religious élitism or aristocracy. If it could also be shown that the purity laws that mark out the holy people also include a concern for purity of descent, then that is not far from what would be called nowadays 'racism'. Of course, strictly speaking, this term is anachronistic, for the ancient world knew nothing of the concept of 'race', which is a modern biological term. But a genetically based religious elite, claiming purity of descent from Abraham, Isaac and Jacob, and banning marriages which would impair this purity of descent would be the nearest ancient analogue to modern racism. The common occurrence of the expression 'the Chosen Race' rather than 'the Chosen People' shows a perception of the Jewish doctrine of election as racist. Moreover, even biblical scholars are not too careful about choice of expression in this matter. The New English Bible translates the crucial expression זרע הקדש (Ezra 9.2) as 'holy race', a translation also adopted by Jacob M. Myers in the Anchor Bible.[1] Myers also remarks, 'The maintenance of the true relationship between Yahweh and his people could be achieved only through purity of race'.[2]

Another, and preferable, way of putting the matter would be to talk in terms of 'exclusivism'. By 'exclusivism', I mean the setting up of a club with strictly-applied rules of membership based on family connections. Racism would thus be one kind of exclusivism, in which 'family' is biologically defined. Religious exclusivism would be another variety, and would be particularly objectionable if outsiders are excluded from salvation. Mary Douglas has argued that Leviticus is

1. J.M. Myers, *Ezra: Nehemiah* (AB; Garden City, NY: Doubleday, 1965).
2. Myers, *Ezra: Nehemiah*, p. 77.

not exclusivist, because it does not mention any ban on intermarriage with non-Israelites.[3] Deuteronomy, on the other hand, is exclusivist because it does contain such a ban. Ezra–Nehemiah champions the Deuteronomic ban in an extreme form, and should be seen as in conflict with Leviticus. The biblical books of Ruth and Jonah, which show a non-exclusivist stance, should be regarded as on the side of Leviticus and against Ezra–Nehemiah. I shall argue that there is, in fact, no conflict between Leviticus and Deuteronomy, or between Leviticus and Ezra–Nehemiah, and that all of them are non-exclusivist, yet uphold the concept of a separate, holy priest-nation.

A statement often quoted as in contrast with Jewish exclusivism is that of Paul (Gal. 3.28): 'There is neither Jew nor Greek, there is neither bond nor free, there is neither male nor female: for ye are all one in Christ Jesus.' Is this actually more inclusivist than Judaism? For after all Paul does not intend to say that there is no difference between Christian and non-Christian. If he means that all people are accepted into the Christian Church without discrimination, the same was certainly true of the Judaism of his time, which accepted proselytes without discrimination. What then is the difference between Paul and Judaism? There is a difference, which depends on the Jewish concept of the priest-nation.

The concept of a holy nation is not exclusivist because it is open to anyone to join. There is one law for the 'stranger' and for the native-born, as is repeatedly stated not only in Leviticus, but also in Deuteronomy.[4] Moreover, apart from legal passages, the narrative makes clear that the holy nation is open to recruits. When the Israelites leave Egypt, they are accompanied by a 'mixed multitude' of Egyptians, who become part of the nation. Moses invites Jethro to join, offering him an honoured position, a story that foreshadows the later honoured role of the Rechabites, Jethro's descendants.[5] The Canaanite tribe of the Gibeonites is accepted, and so are the Kenites. Even Uriah the Hittite gives evidence of Israelite hospitality to entrants into the covenant.

This in no way contradicts the equally emphatic ban on

3. M. Douglas, 'The Stranger in the Bible', *Archives européennes de sociologie*, 15 (1994), pp. 283-98.

4. Exod. 12.49; Lev. 19.33, 34; 24.22; Num. 9.14, 15.15, 16, 29; Deut. 10.18, 19; 26.11, 29.11.

5. See H. Maccoby, *The Sacred Executioner* (London: Thames & Hudson, 1992), pp. 60-63.

intermarriage. For it is made clear that the ban applies to unconverted marriage partners. It is explained that such marriages would result in the breakdown of Israelite monotheism and the adoption of idolatry. 'Neither shalt thou make marriages with them, nor his daughter shalt thou take unto thy son. For they will turn away thy son from following me, that they may serve other gods' (Deut. 7.3-4). I find it hard to accept that this ban on intermarriage is confined to the authors of the Deuteronomic literature. After all, the most dramatic warning against the combined lure of sex and idolatry is in Numbers 25, a passage which is part of the P document. Here the 'whoredoms with the daughters of Moab' are immediately associated with idolatry: '. . . they called the people unto the sacrifices of their gods, and the people did eat and bowed down to their gods.' It is quite correct that there is no explicit ban against intermarriage in Leviticus, but I would suggest that it is perilous to conclude from this silence that the authors of Leviticus had no objection to intermarriage. The omission could well be because the agenda of Leviticus does not include such a topic. Leviticus does not contain any injunction against murder either, but one would not draw any conclusion from this.

Since Leviticus gives so many injunctions that can only be observed through cooperation between husband, wife and the rest of the family, it would seem impossible to live the life of a holy people if marriage were permitted with those who do not observe these injunctions. In particular, the presence of idols among the holy people would be an inevitable result of intermarriage with idolaters, and Lev. 26.1 forbids the presence of such idols within the community.

But the point that I mainly wish to make is that the ban on intermarriage does not constitute exclusivism, so long as outsiders are permitted to join the community through conversion, taking the status of 'stranger' (גר), a status often forgotten in a generation or two through intermarriage within the community.[6] The ban on intermarriage with outsiders is motivated by a desire to preserve the religion, not by any

6. There is clearly some inconsistency in P in its remarks about the status of the גר. In some texts, he is regarded as fully integrated into the Israelite community and its law (e.g. Lev. 24.22); in others, he remains an alien and is subject to different laws (e.g. Lev. 25.47). This may reflect a tension between two attitudes to the גר. Or it may be that, as the rabbis later interpreted the matter, P knows of two different kinds of גר, one fully integrated and the other only partially integrated (in rabbinic terminology, the גר צדק and the גר תושב).

prejudice against outsiders per se, much less by a desire to preserve the genetic or racial purity of the community. Despite Paul's pronouncement about 'neither Jew nor Greek, neither bond nor free, neither male nor female', the Christian Church was in no way deterred from enacting laws prohibiting marriages between Christians and non-Christians (Cyprian, Tertullian, Council of Elvira, Constantine, Councils of Laodicea, Hippo, Orléans, Toledo, Rome, Gratian collection). Indeed Paul himself (2 Cor. 6.14) pronounced such a prohibition: 'Be ye not unequally yoked together with unbelievers' (he declined to break up existing marriages, 1 Cor. 7.12, in the hope that conversion would result; if such a marriage broke up, however, he declared the marriage to be void). The reason is that to have a Church consisting of both Christians and non-Christians would have led to the collapse of Christianity. It is a matter of preserving a doctrine considered to be uniquely true. Such a consideration, of course, does not exist in the case of polytheistic religion, where there is no objection to importing new gods, and husband and wife can happily worship different gods.

The question of exclusivism or elitism or racism may be illuminated by considering the reasons given for the election of the holy community to its special position. If the reason is some excellence already inhering in the selected group, then this is exclusivism. For example, in the type of exclusivism called 'racism', the race in question is indeed regarded as superior because of its natural endowments of mind, spirit and body. The election of the Israelites as a holy people is decidedly not of this type. They are never praised as cleverer, more virtuous or more beautiful than other peoples. On the contrary, they are constantly reminded of their shortcomings: they are a 'stiff-necked people' who have tried God's patience almost to breaking-point. It is true that they are told that their election has something to do with their descent from Abraham, Isaac and Jacob, to whom God gave a promise; but this is used as a stick to beat them with, rather than as a matter of aristocratic pride, since they are assured that on their own merits they would never have been elected and that only God's promise to the patriarchs prevents him from jettisoning them (e.g. Exod. 32.10-13; Num. 14.11-19; Deut. 9.4-6).

The Israelites become a holy people not because they are any better than the other peoples of the world, but because they have been elected, through no merit of their own, for a dedicated, priestly role. There is an important corollary: that the other peoples of the world are not rendered inferior to the Israelites simply because the Israelites practise a programme of purity suitable to their priestly function. Israelites are to refrain from certain foods and practise certain ablutions; if they fail to do so, they make themselves unclean. But non-Israelites, who do not observe these purity rules, are not thereby made unclean. Since they are not bound by purity-rules, and are permitted to ignore them, they are outside the purity system altogether. It is nowhere said, for example, that an Israelite becomes unclean through touching a non-Israelite, as in Brahminism. Rabbinic law makes this matter explicit: the purity-laws do not apply to non-Jews, and therefore only Jews can ever become unclean. Even a corpse does not convey impurity to a non-Jew (see Maimonides, MT *Tum'at Met* 1.13, based on *b. Nazir* 61b).[7] Thus the biblical purity-laws, do not, as has often been said, divide the world into the domain of the pure and the outside wastes of impurity in which the Gentiles dwell. On the contrary, they divide only the Israelite community into those in a state of purity and those in a state of impurity, a functional division which decides which Israelites, at any particular time, are eligible to perform sacrifices, enter holy areas or eat holy food.

Only at a rabbinic stage was the concept of impurity applied to Gentiles, and then only as a professedly non-biblical precaution against intermarriage with idolaters (*Maim.* MT, *Tum. Met* 1.14, based on *b. Niddah* 34a).[8] Another rabbinic enactment (*b. Shabbat* 14b) imposed impurity on Gentile lands, or earth from Gentile lands.[9]

7. The exception is that a Gentile corpse does convey impurity, but to Jews only. This exception is based on Num. 31.19, where anyone who 'hath touched any slain' (i.e. Midianites killed in battle) required purification.

8. G. Alon, *Jews, Judaism and the Classical World* (Jerusalem: Magnes Press, 1977), pp.146-89, argues against the common view that the impurity of Gentiles stems from the close of the period of the Second Temple, when the Eighteen Decrees were enacted (*m. Šabbat* 1.4). He acknowledges, however, that the impurity of Gentiles 'is not enjoined in the Torah'. He argues that it is 'one of the early Halakhot, current among the people a long time before the destruction of the Temple', but that it had fallen into disuse and was 're-established' by the Eighteen Decrees. The motivation of the enactment, he argues, was to guard against idolatry. For the present argument, it is sufficient that Alon confirms that the impurity of Gentiles is rabbinic, not biblical.

9. Alon, *Jews, Judaism and the Classical World*, pp. 184-86, argues that the reason given for this in rabbinic sources (that the land may possibly be contaminated by corpses) is incorrect, and the enactment originally 'stemmed from the uncleanness

The rabbis, despite their own enactment, always fully acknowledged that in the Bible, purity and impurity applied only to Israelites. For example, all the generations before the giving of the Torah on Sinai knew nothing of purity laws; this included the Patriarchs. When non-Israelite nations, whether before or after Sinai, are accused of immorality, breaches of purity laws are never mentioned; examples are the generation of the Flood, the inhabitants of Sodom, the Canaanites and the inhabitants of Nineveh in Jonah. In the P narrative of the Flood, Noah includes unclean animals in the Ark. Although even to know the distinction between clean and unclean animals at this point is, even in the P scheme, an anachronism, the intention is to assert that unclean animals have their due place in the world as the food of Gentiles and therefore had to be preserved.

Since the special purity laws given to the Israelites are to mark them out for a priestly role, the Gentiles who do not observe these laws are not excluded from salvation, but on the contrary are in the same position as all the world in pre-Sinaitic times. The rabbis made this explicit by their two-covenant theory: the Noachide covenant for all peoples for all time, and the Sinaitic covenant for Israelites.[10] But something like this is plain enough in the Bible itself. The inhabitants of Sodom are condemned for their sins of violence, not because they eat forbidden foods. They could have repented and been accepted. When the people of Nineveh do repent, it is not suggested that they become Torah-observing Israelites. They can become reconciled with God without that. If any Gentile individuals feel called to a priestly role, they can join the priestly people, Israel, as proselytes, thereby changing their nationality, since the priestly people is also a nation. But no-one is obliged to make this great change, since salvation does not depend on it.[11] Here is the real difference between Judaism and Paul's doctrine of 'neither Jew nor Greek, neither free nor bond, neither male

of the Gentile status, which was regarded as spreading and involving non-Jewish territory'. Again, Alon acknowledges that the enactment is not biblical.

10. See H. Maccoby, *Early Rabbinic Writings* (Cambridge: Cambridge University Press, 1988), pp. 144-47.

11. A corollary is that, in the last resort, observance of ritual purity laws is less important than morality even for Jews. The prophets, the priests and the rabbis are at one in this. For the rabbis, ritual purity is less important than even ordinary hygiene, since the latter involves the moral duty of preserving life. See H. Maccoby, "Neusner and the Red Cow', *JSJ* 21.1 (1989), pp. 60-75; and *idem*, 'The Washing of Cups', *JSNT* 14 (1982), pp. 3-15.

nor female'. Paul says that all can be Christians, just as Judaism says that no-one is excluded from being a Jew. But Paul, with his doctrine of unique salvation through Christ, says that all *must* be Christians. Christians do not mark themselves out from humankind by purity laws, and are therefore felt to be less exclusive than Jews. But this is because the Christian Church is envisaged as co-extensive with the whole of humanity, and this leads to another kind of exclusivism—the exclusion of non-Christians from salvation.

Yet the difficulty is that in Ezra–Nehemiah, there seems to be an attitude of extreme exclusivism quite different from the biblical and rabbinic doctrine which I have outlined. It is no wonder that Ezra–Nehemiah figures so extensively in discussions of alleged Jewish exclusivism, for example in Max Weber's theory of Judaism as the expression of a self-imposed status as a 'pariah people'.[12] I shall argue, however, that Ezra–Nehemiah has been misunderstood. I shall discuss the aspect of alleged exclusivism, but without entering into chronological matters. Whether, for example, Ezra came before or after Nehemiah is irrelevant to this discussion, as is also the question of the date of composition of Ezra–Nehemiah.

The first apparently exclusivist episode is the rejection of those who wished to participate in the building of the Temple (Ezra 4). These are called 'adversaries', but their overture is peaceable enough: ' Let us build with you: for we seek your God, as ye do; and we do sacrifice unto him since the days of Esar-haddon king of Assur, which brought us up hither' (Ezra 4.2). Zerubbabel and Yeshua, however, reply, 'Ye have nothing to do with us to build an house unto our God'. Upon this,

12. M. Weber, *The Sociology of Religion* (London: Methuen, 1965 [1922]), p.108. Weber was, of course, influenced unconsciously by the prevalent evolutionary theory according to which Judaism degenerated into legalism at the time of Ezra, the prophetic spirit finding its continuance in apocalypticism and finally Christianity. A characteristic expression of this scheme is the following:

> The great prophets of our period are not apocalyptists; but we can see ritual beginning to take a place beside morality that was never allowed by the prophets before the exile; and when the affirmation is made that ritual of itself commends us to God, the door opens to all the racial pride of men who rejoice to have Abraham to their father; and the axe, once wielded by the prophets, must then, in hands no less stern, destroy the work of their mistaken and short-sighted successors' (W.F. Lofthouse, *Israel after Exile* [Oxford: Clarendon Press, 1928], p. 49).

This religious polemic is by no means dead today in the world of scholarship, and is endemic in textbooks for schools and theological colleges.

the rejected ones do indeed become adversaries. Why this apparently churlish rejection of people who wish to join in the worship of God?

Also apparently exclusivist is the rejection and expulsion of the wives (Ezra 9). The princes come to Ezra, saying,

> The people of Israel, and the priests, and the Levites, have not separated themselves from the people of the lands, doing according to their abominations, even of the Canaanites, the Hittites, the Perizzites, the Jebusites, the Ammonites, the Moabites, the Egyptians and the Amorites. For they have taken of their daughters for themselves, and for their sons: so that the holy seed have mingled themselves with the people of those lands: yea, the hand of the princes and rulers hath been chief in this trespass.

Upon this Ezra rends his garments and makes a long speech of reproof, reminding the people about the prohibition against marrying Canaanites. Then Ezra, at a great assembly, orders that all the 'strange wives' and their offspring should be sent away, and this is done. The question arises: 'Why does it apparently not occur to Ezra that the "strange wives" might be willing to be converted to Judaism?' Must we conclude, as many have done, that Ezra did not believe in the concept of conversion, because he thought it would be a contamination of the 'holy seed' to accept converts? The expression 'holy seed', found nowhere else in the Bible (except in a doubtful reading in Isa. 6.13), is thought to encapsulate an exclusivist, even racist, doctrine of the holy people.

The question of intermarriage is taken up again in Nehemiah 13. I shall take the three passages (Ezra 4, Ezra 9 and Nehemiah 13) in turn. The earliest incident, in the time of Zerubbabel, is surely connected with the polemic of 2 Kings 17 against the syncretic religion developed by the 'people of the land'. These were forced immigrants transported to Samaria from far lands by the Assyrians in their policy of mass transfers of population. These immigrants had developed a form of religion in which the worship of the native god Yahweh, as they saw him, was combined with that of the gods of their previous homes. The authors of 2 Kings denounce this syncretism as not the true religion of Israel. That these are the people indicated is shown by the words: 'We seek your God as ye do and we do sacrifice unto him since the days of Esar-haddon king of Assur, which brought us up hither' (Ezra 4.2). The syncretists are rejected with the words, 'Ye have nothing to do with us to build an house unto our God'; but it is remarkable that no explanation is given for this rejection. There is a reticence here, as elsewhere in Ezra, about the theological point at issue between the returnees and the 'people of the land' (sometimes called 'the people of the lands'), and this reticence requires some explanation. Yet it is surely beyond doubt that the theological issue was monotheism versus syncretism, and this is why the 'people of the land' were rejected as fellow-religionists, not out of sheer exclusivism or disdain for people of doubtful genetic descent.[13] There is here an important religious schism, far more fundamental than later conflicts with Samaritans, Sadducees, Dead Sea sectarians and Karaites, and similar conflicts and schisms in the Christian Church. It should not be trivialized as a matter of uncleanness, or of religious pedigree, or of petty heresy-hunting. It is the continuation of the embattled strictures against syncretism made by the Prophets (e.g. Jer. 7).

The second incident, Ezra 9, should be interpreted in the light of the first incident. The text tells us that Ezra was dismayed because alliances had taken place with 'the people of the lands', who are then apparently specified as 'the Canaanites, the Hittites, the Perizzites, the Jebusites, the Ammonites, the Moabites, the Egyptians, and the Amorites'. This is an impossible list for actual inhabitants of the area at this time, so it is best to understand the sentence to mean that intermarriage had taken place with the 'people of the lands' who were guilty of sins, or 'abominations', similar to those of the Canaanites of olden days. The real point is that intermarriage had taken place with the syncretists, called once more 'the people of the land' or 'lands', who, because of their polytheistic worship, were regarded by Ezra as idolaters despite the fact that they themselves regarded their worship as consistent with Judaism. If this is correct, it should again be asked why Ezra is so reticent about stating the theological point of conflict between

13. Some authors (e.g. J. Milgrom, *Leviticus 1–16* [AB, 3; Garden City, NY: Doubleday, 1991], p. 360) raise the possibility that the 'people of the land' were specifically identified with the Canaanites, who, it would appear, were ruled out from conversion by the commandment to annihilate them. Two objections to this suggestion present themselves. First, the 'people of the land' were clearly not Canaanites, but immigrants. Secondly, the commandment to annihilate the Canaanites was not taken literally, since many Israelites were descended from Canaanites (including groups among the returnees). The rabbis (Lev. R. 17.6), influenced by biblical evidence (e.g. Rahab, Uriah the Hittite, the Canaanites employed by Solomon on the work of the Temple), concluded that Canaanites were accepted as converts, and, therefore, that the annihilation-commandment applied only to those refusing conversion (or refusing a third option of emigrating from the land unconverted).

monotheism and syncretism in the plain terms used in 2 Kings 17.

'The people of the land' presented a problem of intermarriage different from any experienced before, for this was the first time that an established syncretist movement had offered amalgamation. These were people who presented themselves as enthusiastic worshippers of the God of Judaism, only too happy to help with building a Temple for him. The claim of 'the people of the land' was in fact that they were Jews, and the tone of the polemic of 2 Kings 17 shows that this was a matter of controversy, a dangerous claim that needed to be considered seriously. Intermarriage with the syncretists had taken place because their claim to be Jews had been widely accepted before the arrival of Ezra and Nehemiah, even by priests. Previously, the problem of intermarriage had been simple. Idolaters were banned as marriage partners unless they gave up idolatry, left their families, and undertook to adopt Judaism. Syncretism had been an internal problem, concerning individuals. But this syncretist body, asking for amalgamation, was problematic, and an authoritative ruling about it was needed. Ezra's decision was unhesitating, for he realized that if these 'Jews' were permanently accepted, the monotheism of Judaism would have been fatally compromised. Wives from a syncretic background could not be converted because they claimed to be Jews already. To accept them as they were would have meant to accept their parent families too as valid worshippers, although they worshipped idols along with the God of Judaism. A true convert to Judaism left his or her family behind, changing identity, and being born again. These would-be Jews, however, wished to retain their identity and their old family links. The Jewish people would be redefined to include a substantial population of practising polytheists. The result would have been the transformation of Judaism into a form of syncretic polytheism in which the Jewish God was worshipped as a member of a pantheon. Ezra's decision was at a watershed in the history of Judaism, when the future of monotheism was at stake. It was a matter of deep principle, not of ethnic exclusivism, to reject marital links with the 'people of the land'.

I am not saying that the issue of syncretism has been ignored by commentators, but that insufficient weight has been given to it. Myers, for example, does interpret Ezra 9 in terms of the battle against syncretism, saying '. . . intermarriage led to compromise and idolatry'.[14] But he then goes on to make his remarks about the alleged importance

14. Myers, *Ezra: Nehemiah*, p. 77.

of 'racial purity', a consideration that (apart from being incorrect) shows that he has not grasped how overwhelmingly important the issue of idolatry actually was. If the issue was really theological, why slide back into making it an issue of racial or ethnic purity?

My line of argument can be reinforced by considering evidence from Ezra–Nehemiah itself that is incompatible with any attitude of ethnic exclusivism. The lists given in Ezra 2.43-60 of the low-pedigree groups included in the community of returnees with Zerubbabel are very revealing about attitudes towards Israelites of non-Israelite origin. Two of these groups ('servants of Solomon' and 'Temple-servitors' or נתינים) were of Canaanite origin, while the third group (2.59-60) is simply of those who could not prove their Israelite descent. Yet all three groups formed part of the community (קהל) and were included in the definition of 'holy seed'. This latter expression, then, cannot be ethnically exclusive or racist, but simply means 'all those, whether of Israelite descent or not, who have been accepted into the Israelite community and are therefore permitted to contribute towards its genetic future'. The Mishnah (*Qiddushin* 4.1) gives an expanded version of Ezra 2, showing that it accepts that the community led by Ezra was a rag-bag of people of various ethnic origins. Given the mixed racial origins of his community, how could Ezra have held a theory of ethnic purity?

It is true that the pedigrees were carefully kept, with the result that there was a kind of loose caste-system with certain marriage restrictions between the castes (for details of these, see *m. Qiddushin* 4.1-2). But all castes were considered to belong to the holy community, and the marriage restrictions were of a kind that slowly led to integration (e.g. slaves could be freed, thereby becoming freedmen, who were not subject to marriage restrictions). Edomite and Egyptian converts were restricted to low-caste marriages for three generations, but might then marry into the upper castes. Ezra, who quotes Deuteronomy as authoritative, must have known Deut. 23.8 which permits conversion of Edomites and Egyptians; even Deut. 23.4 does not forbid acceptance of Ammonites and Moabites as converts, but only restricts for ever their marriages, after conversion, to the lower castes; a restriction which rabbinic Judaism found a way to abolish (*m. Yadayim* 4.4). I shall have something further to say about this last point when I come to the Nehemiah passage. The main point here is that the maintenance of a system of caste and pedigree within the community is quite compatible with a very liberal and hospitable attitude towards admission of outsiders into the community as a whole.

An important piece of evidence contained in the list of returnees is the group of those who 'could not shew their father's house, and their seed, whether they were of Israel' (Ezra 2.59). These are numbered among 'the whole congregation' (v. 64). Some of them must have been of proselyte descent, though some of them may have merely lost their records. The possibility that they may not be of Israelite descent at all is contemplated with equanimity, just as those priests who could not trace their priestly descent were demoted from priesthood but accepted as part of the 'congregation'.

Why, then, does Ezra give the impression that he is concerned about contamination of 'the holy seed'? That, at any rate, is the impression given by the princes who report the matter to him, saying that 'the holy seed have mingled themselves with the people of those lands'. This seems to be the language of adulteration and contamination. Ezra himself uses a different terminology, speaking of the 'abominations' of the 'people of the land' which he asserts to be comparable with the abominations of the Canaanites. But he does not specify what these abominations are. Even when he quotes from Deuteronomy the prohibition against intermarriage, he fails to include the rationale given in Deuteronomy, namely the danger of succumbing to polytheism. Instead he talks vaguely about 'abominations'.

I suggest that Ezra was indeed quite clear in his mind that the issue was one of polytheism, and that this was the 'abomination' which he wished to avoid. But there were good political reasons for not being too explicit about this in writing. Both Ezra and Nehemiah were officials of the Persian empire, and the community of the Return depended utterly on the goodwill of the Persian king. If Ezra were to say openly that all gods other than Yahweh were empty idols, and that this was his reason for rejecting the overtures of 'the people of the land', Persian royal officials reading his reports might not be too pleased.[15]

15. 'The Ezra memoirs may be isolated from chs. 8, 9 and 10, if attention is paid to the chronological data... His report, intended for the Persian authorities, extends over chs. 7 to 10 of the book of Ezra, which concerns mainly the regulation of cultic practice and suppression of mixed marriages... ' (M. Delcor, 'Jewish Literature in Hebrew and Aramaic in the Greek Era', in W.D. Davies and L. Finkelstein (eds.), *The Cambridge History of Judaism*, II [Cambridge: Cambridge University Press, 1989], pp. 342-84, see pp. 373-74).

After all, the whole imperial programme under which the Return took place was one of tolerant syncretism. He therefore had to use a language with which they would sympathise, that of pedigree and privilege. They would interpret his expressions as meaning that the Jews regarded themselves as a priestly aristocracy who could not allow their lineage to be adulterated. Ezra never explicitly says this, but he undoubtedly gives this impression to incautious readers. A parallel can be found in Josephus's reticence about Jewish opposition to idolatry, in a work that would be read by the Roman emperor or his courtiers. When Ezra refers to the 'abominations' of the Canaanites, Jewish readers would undoubtedly understand a reference to idolatry, but the word is vague enough not to alert non-Jewish readers. It is significant that the expression 'the holy seed', which is used only once and comes nearest to the language of aristocracy rather than religious concern, is put into the mouth of the 'princes' (שרים), not of Ezra himself.

It seems most unlikely that Ezra was an ethnic exclusivist. The general Jewish thought of his time was not in favour of such a concept. Zechariah wrote, 'Many nations will join themselves to the Lord on that day, and they will be my people' (Zech. 2.11). How could Ezra have ignored or flouted these words from a prophet closely associated with the Return and the rebuilding of the Temple? Zechariah envisaged whole nations being converted to Judaism, yet Ezra is represented as an ethnic exclusivist or racist who could not bear the idea of admitting outsiders to the 'holy seed'. The answer must be that Ezra did not disapprove of true converts, but only of those who retained idolatrous worship while claiming to be Jews.[16]

This conclusion prompts me to offer a solution to a puzzling problem. Ezra 10.19 speaks of the priests who had taken 'strange wives' and says, 'And they gave their hands that they would put away their wives; and being guilty, they offered a ram of the flock for their trespass.' From the Hebrew, it is clear that the sacrifice was an אשם. The problem is that from what we know of the אשם sacrifice as outlined in Leviticus, this does not seem an appropriate sacrifice here.

16. The theory that there were warring factions among the returnees, one side being exclusivist and the other universalist, is based on no textual evidence, but solely on an alleged contradiction between the universalism of Zechariah, Second Isaiah, Ruth and Jonah, and the 'exclusivism' of Ezra–Nehemiah's opposition to the 'people of the land'. If the point at issue is not exclusivism but theology, the theory collapses.

Jacob Milgrom has discussed this problem in fascinating detail.[17] He offers two alternative solutions, both of which involve the idea that Ezra invented a new concept of the 'holy seed' as equivalent in sanctity to the Temple and its appurtenances. In the first, Ezra extends Deuteronomy's prohibition against intermarriage with Canaanites to 'all exogamous marriages'. Then he concludes from Deuteronomy that 'Israel is a sanctum', and that the adulteration of the 'holy seed' is a desecration of *sancta*, for which, when inadvertent, the expiation is an אשם. The alternative explanation is that Ezra regarded only the local non-Israelites as forbidden (here Milgrom makes a distinction between 'people of the land' and 'people of the lands' which involves an emendation in Ezra 9.1). The אשם was thus necessary because of the infringement of the *ḥerem* against intermarriage with Canaanites.

My objection to this analysis is that, if it is correct, all members of the community who had taken 'strange wives' should have brought this אשם, and not just the priests. Milgrom does not comment on the fact that only the priests were required to bring the אשם. Milgrom does take the view that Leviticus regards only the priests as holy, the common people being regarded as merely potentially holy (as shown by the future tense in 'You shall sanctify yourselves and be holy', Lev. 11.44, 19.2, 20.27). But Milgrom agrees that Deuteronomy regards the whole people as holy (Deut. 7.6, 14.2, 26.19, 28.9), and that Ezra followed Deuteronomy in this. Consequently, Ezra, on Milgrom's theory, ought to have required an אשם from all.

If Ezra did invent a concept of the sinfulness of contaminating 'holy seed' by marriage with people of non-Jewish birth, this really would make him an ethnic exclusivist or racist. I suggest that there is a much simpler solution. The priests who had mistakenly regarded their wives as Jewish had allowed them to partake in the priestly food (קדשים), the portions of the sacrifices which they and their family were allowed to eat at home (Num. 18.18, *b. Zevahim* 56). For such inadvertent misuse of sacred materials, the אשם is the regular expiation (Lev. 5.15; 22.10: 22.16). This explains why only the priests were required to bring the אשם.

The rabbis, however, do not give this explanation of the אשם of Ezra 10.19, but offer a strained explanation (*b. Keritot*, 11a) based on the אשם required in Lev. 19.20 (the case of the betrothed bondmaid). They cannot give an explanation based on sacrilege (*me'ilah*), because

17. Milgrom, *Leviticus 1–16*, pp. 359-61.

they take the view (*m. Me'ilah* 1.1) that holy food that has left the Temple and entered the priest's house is no longer subject to *me'ilah*, and therefore cannot give rise to an אשם. However, as Milgrom argues,[18] this was not the teaching of P. It is therefore unlikely to have been the view of Ezra, who would consider the giving of holy food to the 'strange wives' to require an אשם as expiation for sacrilege.[19]

I now come to the third passage, that of Nehemiah 13, which comprises two incidents. The first incident, I suggest, is really very different from the Ezra incident, and is not about intermarriage with outsiders at all. It has to do with what I have earlier described as the Jewish caste-system. The incident is described in Neh. 13.1-9, and it begins with the reading of 'the book of Moses' in which it was 'found written that the Ammonite and the Moabite should not come into the congregation of God for ever'. The point here is that Ammonites and Moabites were not forbidden to be converts, but, having been converted, had to observe caste marriage restrictions, which in this case had not been observed. It is not said in relation to this incident that 'strange wives' were sent away, only that 'they separated from Israel all the mixed multitude' (ויבדילו כל ערב מישראל),[20] which means they were separated according to caste rules. The prohibition in Deuteronomy 23 against Ammonites and Moabites entering 'the congregation of the Lord' cannot mean that they were excluded from conversion, but refers, as the rabbis held, to caste restrictions on marriage. The proof of this is that the same expression is used in the same passage to refer to people wounded in the genitals and to ממזרים, and these were certainly never expelled from the community, but only subjected to marriage restrictions. (See Maimonides, *Issurei Biyah* 12.17-18, *m. Yebamot* 8.2-3, *m. Qiddushin* 4.3, *m. Yadayim* 4.4). The Mishnah (*Qiddushin* 4.3) says, 'All that are forbidden to enter the congregation may intermarry among themselves', as members of the general community.

18. Milgrom, *Leviticus 1–16*, p. 323.

19. It may even be that an אשם was required for the eating of תרומה (the priests' portion of the crop) by an unauthorised person. As Milgrom points out (*Leviticus 1–16*, p. 323), the Karaites, on the basis of plausible biblical interpretation, regarded תרומה as liable to sacrilege (*Keter Torah*, on Lev. 5.14), and this may well have been the view of Ezra.

20. This recalls the 'mixed multitude' (ערב רב) of Egyptians (Exod. 12.38). This reinforces the point that the concern here is not with outsiders, but with a caste of converts from nations with a hostile biblical record.

Later in the same chapter, however, there is another incident concerning wives from Ashdod, Ammon and Moab. Here Nehemiah takes a much more serious view, speaking of the sins of Solomon, and insisting that the 'strange wives' should be sent away. Here no reference is made to the Deuteronomic prohibition against Ammonites or Moabites 'entering the congregation of God'. The reticence employed by Ezra is still apparent, but the sins of Solomon were those of idolatry. It seems then that the outsiders in this case were syncretists, as in the previous Ezra case, not just Ammonites or Moabites who had become converted to Jewish monotheism, and who were required to observe the caste rules.[21]

My conclusion is that Ezra–Nehemiah contains no doctrine of contamination of the purity of the 'holy seed'. The unprecedented problem presented by a large outside body of syncretists claiming Jewish status had to be solved in a way that would preserve monotheism. There is no proof that Ezra disapproved of converts to Judaism,[22] and every likelihood that he approved of them, since he revered Deuteronomy and knew its injunctions about kindness to גרים. The contrast that has been drawn so often between the welcoming attitude of Leviticus and Deuteronomy to 'strangers' and the hostile attitude of Ezra–Nehemiah to 'strange wives' is beside the point. We have here two entirely different groups. The 'strangers' of Leviticus and Deuteronomy are

21. The passage about Tobiah which appears in the same chapter requires separate explanation. Tobiah is called an 'Ammonite' and even an 'Ammonite slave' (Neh. 2.10) Yet Tobiah is elsewhere mentioned (Zech. 6.10) as a Jewish aristocrat, no doubt connected with the Tobiad family famous in later times. The explanation given by V. Tcherikover ('The Hellenistic Movement in Jerusalem and Antiochus' Persecutions', in *The World History of the Jewish People*, VI [11 vols.; London: W.H. Allen, 1976]) seems convincing. Tobiah was in fact a Jewish aristocrat, a relative of the High Priest Eliashib. He was hostile to Nehemiah, who called him 'Ammonite' and 'slave' derisively, probably because he had an estate in Ammonite territory and was in servile dependence on powerful Ammonites. He is irrelevant to this discussion about intermarriage. He belonged to the group of wealthy Jewish opponents of Nehemiah.

22. It is hardly surprising that Ezra–Nehemiah does not contain explicit repetition of the Torah injunctions about kindness to the גר. The danger of oppression of the גר occurred only in a settled Israelite community, where a population of גרים arose through influx from outside countries, attracted by economic or religious motives. The community of Ezra–Nehemiah, fighting for a foothold, did not yet attract such incomers, and the injunction to be kind to the גר had no practical relevance. In later times, the issue became a live one again.

not in any way a threat to the continuance of Judaism, but on the contrary a loyal and helpless group requiring protection. The syncretists with whom Ezra had to deal were quite different: they were a powerful group (more powerful than the returnees) who threatened the existence of Judaism as a monotheistic religion.

RESPONSE TO HYAM MACCOBY'S HOLINESS AND PURITY

Robert A. Segal

Hyam Maccoby's paper raises several key issues not merely about Leviticus or the Bible generally but about Judaism itself.

1. I certainly agree with Maccoby that in Leviticus and elsewhere in the Hebrew Bible 'the essence of holiness is separation' (p. 152). I am struck by the implications, especially vis-à-vis Christianity. For separation requires the continued existence of a group from which one is separate. The whole world cannot become Israelite or Jewish in the way that, for Christians, the whole world can—and should—become Christian. Therefore even if, as Maccoby stresses, separation does not preclude *anyone's* becoming Israelite or Jewish, it does preclude *everyone's* becoming either. There cannot be a world of sheer holiness: holiness requires its opposite not just to define itself but to exist.
2. If on the one hand holiness separates Israelites from non-Israelites, on the other hand it unites Israel with God. How close to divinity does the sharing of holiness with God make Israel? How blurred does the line become between humanity and divinity, a line which Judaism, far more than Christianity, strives to maintain?
3. Maccoby's central topic is the criteria on which Israelite exclusivity is based. There are, I think, three possible factors: not only *religion* and *race*, on which Maccoby focuses, but also *nationality*. Maccoby argues that the chief, virtually sole criterion is religion rather than race. Without denying the centrality of religion, I suggest that the factor of nationality blurs the line between religion and race and thereby gives race more weight than Maccoby allows.

Against the view that Israel or Judaism defines itself racially, one might note that in the Bible non-Israelites are permitted to join the nation of Israel—for example, at the Exodus, as Maccoby himself points out. Abraham's non-Israelite servants are required to undergo circumcision and thereby to embrace Judaism. Many of Solomon's wives, to cite but one other example, are non-Israelite. Furthermore, non-Israelites in the Bible, such as Melchizedek, recognize the God of Israel. Even enemies of Israel acknowledge, though they do not worship, the God of Israel—for example, Egyptians at the time of the Exodus and the inhabitants of Jericho.

More importantly, as Maccoby emphasizes, membership in Israel scarcely absolves one of religious obligations. Simply to be born an Israelite is hardly enough. One must act accordingly. And one is judged accordingly: God does not quite excuse Israelites' failings on the grounds that they are his chosen people.

In post-biblical times, especially in the Roman period prior to Constantine, there is not only conversion but active proselytizing, which is to say among non-Israelites. If, as has commonly been suggested, Jews constituted as many as ten percent of the Roman Empire, most Jews must have come to Judaism through conversion rather than by birth. In modern times, Reform Judaism defines Judaism as a sheer religion and not also a nationality, let alone a race. A rigid divide is drawn between the private sphere of life and the public one. One is Jewish in one's religion—the private sphere—and American, English, French, or German in one's nationality—the public sphere.

There is, then, much to support Maccoby's argument for the religious rather than racial basis of Israelite or Jewish identity, but, I think, he goes too far. To begin with, descent from the patriarchs *is* biological: one is *born* Israelite or Jewish. One becomes Israelite or Jewish at the point of birth rather than, as in Christianity, at the point of baptism. Birth may not be necessary for membership in Israel or Judaism, but it is sufficient. Conversely, lapsed Israelites or Jews are still Israelites or Jews. Traditionally, Judaism has excluded dissenters or heretics from its ranks far less often than Christianity. The excommunication of Spinoza is almost unique in the history of Judaism.

Maccoby's argument that the ban on intermarriage in various passages in the Bible (e.g., Deut. 7, Ezra 9, Neh. 13; cf. 1 Kgs 11) is based on religion *rather than* race neglects the characterization of race as cultural: the association of a people with a brand of religion. After all, where intermarriage with certain peoples is banned, the ban holds forever, not merely for as long as those peoples continue to practice polytheism or idolatry. The assumption is that these peoples are ineluctably, which means naturally, polytheistic or idolatrous. Without waxing egregiously anachronistic, one might note that nineteenth-century racism equated race with culture: physical differences were a sign of cultural ones. Racism in its fullest form was never just skin-deep. The equation of 'the Canaanites, the Hittites, the Perizzites, the Jebusites, the Ammonites, the Moabites, the Egyptians, and the Amorites' (Ezra 9.1) with polytheism or idolatry may assume the same. Modern Israel's law of return, while not precluding converts (to Orthodoxy) from citizenship and while not barring non-Jews from citizenship, again gives automatic citizenship to those born Jewish.

Undeniably, nationality is different from race: one can change one's nationality but not one's race. Still, nationality is primarily biological in nature: ordinarily, one's nationality is set at birth. Because ancient Israel was not just a religious group but also a nation, and because modern Israel is far more a nation than a religious group, membership in Israel necessarily has a biological, and in that sense racial, aspect to it.

Discussion

Rendtorff: I have to confess it is very difficult to relate these two post-exilic texts, about the גר in Leviticus and the behaviour of Ezra. In principle I would agree with your approach although I found it frankly a bit apologetic. It is hard to understand the behaviour of Ezra. I liked your remark about the way he speaks about the foreign nations, quoting from Genesis 15 or the like where we have all these Canaanites, Hittites and so on, obviously as a fictional group of foreign nations, people of the land. Therefore I fully agree that we should relate Ezra's behaviour back to the earlier history of Israel and his understanding of it. Nevertheless this rigid action he takes, or at least the mood, the spirit, is totally different from the behaviour of the Israelites towards the גר in Leviticus. But in this whole field we have totally different terminology in different places. Deuteronomy does not know the term גר. Yet the whole position of the גר and the אזרח in Leviticus is different from the other one. I think we just have to admit that here within the Old Testament there are tensions that are very difficult for us to understand and solve. Finally I do not believe it is possible to interpret Jewish history, biblical and post-biblical, exclusively from the point of view of Reform Judaism. I would like to argue with you and with every non-religious Israeli, that says he is an Israeli and not a Jew, and only happens to have been born with a Jewish mother. But I don't think it will help us to solve the problem of Ezra.

Maccoby: The attitude of Leviticus to the גר is an attitude towards people who live in the land, who adopt the customs of the land, even if some of them may be full converts and some may not be. The laws apply to them; they take part in the passovers and so on. It gives the impression of an amicable ingredient of the population. The difficulty that the writer has may simply arise if or when these people might be oppressed. They might not be treated with equality. That is what the author is worried about. He is not worried that they are going to turn out to be a dissident group. He is concerned that they might not be treated well. We have in Leviticus the picture of a partially integrated group. Whereas in Ezra we get an entirely different picture of two communities facing each other with different ideas of what the worship of Yahweh implies, and this is a fraught situation which is entirely different from that of Ezra. So I do not see the difficulty in Ezra that you do. Once one allows that syncretism is the problem, then Ezra's actions do not seem to me to be incompatible with Leviticus.

Douglas: I am still not convinced. I would like to list several points. The main one is your argument from silence: the fact that Leviticus does not say something does not prove anything. I have to concede that this is a famous mistake and you are right. But you have used some arguments from silence as well, and I think you would concede that. I like your point about the nation of priests being a calling, and therefore perhaps instead of a 'chosen people' it would be better to think of a 'dedicated' people, or a 'consecrated people'. For the rest of the human race they are the priests. That is very enlightening. The idea of political discretion in deference to your Roman or Persian converts being the reason why idolatry is not mentioned; that point was very good too. But apart from that you accept Ezra as a credible witness and yet you say his dates are not important, or at least you are not going into them. To me they are very important: whether it really was written at the time it was supposed to be written or several hundred years later, in which case it would be illustrating some current issues of a later age rather than the ones that he was using at the time. For instance, you mention Zechariah as a source he could not have ignored. It sounds as though you think that the unitary non-adversarial system of priesthood could agree on something, whereas it is much more likely that it was as faction-ridden as priests ever have been. In which case, Zechariah would be somebody Ezra was not interested in because the text is messianic. He would have political views that would not be acceptable to Ezra. Also I do not see how you can ignore the political context of Samaria. Samaria, either in the fourth century or later, was always such a burning issue. It seems to me that this slippery customer, Ezra, is clearly trying to represent just the Jews who came back from exile and is not calling on the people of Israel, the whole nation. He is just talking about a small segment of the community who are inviting others to join them, and telling them, with the whole force of the Persian government, that if they do not join, they are going to lose their land and everything, and forcing people to get rid of their wives. He is taking a very violent attitude which has to be accounted for. It also seems to me that the fact that he has managed to call the people of the land those funny names from ancient disappeared tribes, ignores the fact that Numbers, Leviticus and the Priestly work are all very keen on this religion being a religion of 'Israel', that is, the sons of Jacob. All the sons of Jacob and especially the sons of Joseph are important. They have a right to inherit. Yet he seems to be trying to push them out if they come from Samaria. After all they had been brought there by an Assyrian king who is supposed to have brought huge quantities of foreigners over. Why do we not assume he just brought over Samaritans? It seems quite likely that the people he does not like, whom he calls 'the people of the land', are in fact Josephites.

Maccoby: But they identify themselves as having come from Assyria. They say right at the beginning, when they come and offer to help in building the Temple, that they have 'worshipped the Jewish God ever since we came here from a far land and were brought over by the emperor of Assyria'. So I do not see how one can deny their account of themselves which is that they identified themselves with the very people that 2 Kings 17 is talking about, the ones who are condemned there as being syncretists. It seems to me that the identification there is complete.

Douglas: So you would rather believe Ezra than the people when they say, 'We worshipped your God'?

Rendtorff: No, but I think it is very important that 2 Kings 17 clearly states that there was a group in the northern part of the country that had a certain kind of Israelite religion. It says in 2 King 17 that they actually worshipped the Jewish God. I would fully agree with this.

Maccoby: If you fully agree, then I think you ought also to agree that Ezra had a real problem of schism on his hands. It was not a question of illiberalism, that he disagreed with the doctrine of the גר, or something. He had a really vital problem, which was something that could have threatened the whole future of Judaism.

Harrington: You say that the Israelite religion was open to everyone, but of course not everybody could be priests, so there would be the possibility of second-class citizens.

Maccoby: I do not think it is a case of second-class citizens. It is like the situation in the Catholic Church, where there are monastic orders. If someone joins a monastic order, that is not a reflection on the people who do not. They are people who wish to dedicate themselves to a special life, to a special rule. The people who do not observe that rule because they are not members of that monastic order, are not denigrated as being wicked people or second-class citizens in any way.

Harrington: What if you say to the rest of the people there is no possibility that you could join a monastic order?

Maccoby: The point is that anybody can join a monastic order and similarly anybody can join the monastic order that is called Judaism.

Harrington: But not as priests.

Maccoby: There are two levels of priests: the whole nation of priests, on the one hand, and that special family of priests who are descended from Aaron.

Harrington: I mean it is a racial thing, a genealogical matter.

Maccoby: It is an aristocracy, which means you can only enter it if you belong to a certain family.

Harrington: I am more interested in the point you are making that non-Israelites are not considered subject to the purity rules. Here, I would say, following Prof. Rendtorff's ideas, that there are tensions in scripture between the גר in Leviticus and the situation after that. Following Yigael Allon, there are two tensions, maximalist and minimalist, in relationship to this issue of gentile uncleanness. So I cannot say that it was at the late rabbinic stage that impurity was applied to non-Israelites because there are a lot of little hints in that post-biblical literature that indicate continuing tension on this matter.

Maccoby: I think you are confusing things here. The point is that there was tension in relation to non-Jewish residents in Jewish land. The tension was about whether they should become full Jews or adopt some kind of status less than that. For Gentiles living outside Israel, there was no tension. They were not obliged to keep any of the purity rules at all. They were obliged to keep the basic moral rules but that is why the inhabitants of Nineveh and Sodom and all these wicked people are rebuked, not because they did not keep purity rules—nobody wanted them to do that—but because they did not keep the moral rules. The tension that you are talking about is an intra-Israelite community tension, something that happens when the Jewish or Israelite community has aliens living in its midst. Then there is tension about how far those aliens can or should be assimilated.

Harrington: But I thought you were using that as an issue to say, magnanimously, that Judaism does not even regard Gentiles as subjects to imperialize. I would say that increases the distinction.

Maccoby: Would you say that it is some kind of reflection on Catholics who do not enter a monastic order, that they are not required to keep, say, the Trappist vow of silence or the Augustinian rule?

Harrington: No, because in the Catholic system, people are not excluded by race from entering an order.

Maccoby: But no one is excluded by race from entering the Jewish people. I see no exclusion by race. You have falashas, black Jews, every kind of Jew, with no restriction by race. The observance by Jews or Israelites of purity rules such as the distinction between foods and being made impure by touching a corpse and so on, apply to Israelites as part of their 'monastic rule'. They do not apply to non-Israelites at all, who are therefore not in any way rendered unclean by not keeping these laws because the whole system of clean versus unclean, just like the Trappist vow of silence, does not apply to them. One of these people who is not obliged to keep these rules, may then decide that he would like to become a member of the nation of priests. He then goes to the Jewish rabbi or priest or whoever it is and says, 'I would like to become converted'. Then he is converted and is subject to the rules, just like anybody who wants to enter the monastic order when he feels he wants that to be his vocation. Having entered the monastic order, he is now subject to the rules.

Part III

Context and the History of the Text

A Strange Sequence of Rules: Leviticus 19.20-26

Calum Carmichael

The narrators of biblical traditions lay out the history of succeeding generations of their ancestors, Abraham, Isaac and Jacob, for example, through the history of the judges and the kings (Gen.–2 Kgs). There are two major features about their method of presentation. The narrators pay particular attention to the first time that problems occur, and they focus on matters that tend to recur from generation to generation. The reason for so much attention to origins is that beginnings set, or more accurately are seen to set, the pattern for future generations.[1]

Consider an example of how a tradition about the first sons of Jacob/Israel, namely, Joseph and his brothers (Gen. 37, 39–48), presents matters that re-appear in a later generation of Israelites, in the time of Abimelech and his brothers (Judg. 6–9). Joseph becomes a bondman in Egypt and is employed in the household of Potiphar and his wife. She seeks a sexual relationship with him. The reason why Joseph had become a bondman in an Egyptian household was because of his brothers' hostility. They had sought to slay him because of his overweening ambition. Joseph avoided death at their hands but ended up a slave in Egypt. There he takes on a dual Israelite (Hebrew)–Egyptian identity that plays a crucial role in the story. He is an Israelite (Hebrew) by birth, but he is then sold abroad where he is a Hebrew bondman, marries the daughter of an Egyptian priest and is given an Egyptian name. Later, when his brothers come to Egypt because of a famine in Canaan, a disguised Egyptian Joseph pursues vengeance against them.

In the Judges tradition motifs similar to those in the Joseph story appear. An Israelite, Gideon, has a sexual relationship with a Canaanite bondwoman in the Canaanite city of Shechem. Abimelech is the product

1. Even within a tradition, in the story of Joseph, for example, what happens in his initial dreams foreshadows what happens in his subsequent life.

of the union between them (Judg. 8.31). The issue of his dual identity, half-Israelite, half-Canaanite, dominates the tradition. Like Joseph, Abimelech shows overweening ambition and makes himself king. In doing so, unlike Joseph's brothers, he succeeds in slaughtering his many brothers with the exception of one of them, Jotham. The reason why fratricide surfaces in each generation, Joseph's and then Abimelech's, is because the same issue of dominance in a family arises. Abimelech reigns for three years but vengeance is visited upon him because of his treatment of his brothers.[2]

The story of Abimelech illustrates how, when the biblical narrators record history, they seek out patterns of similar conduct and development in succeeding generations of the nation Israel and mould their history accordingly. More readily recognized examples are the accounts of how each succeeding patriarch in the Book of Genesis has a problem in regard to which of his sons achieves the title of the firstborn; or again, how Jacob's experience of a form of servitude under Laban, has its parallel in Joseph's in Egypt, and, in due course, all of the Israelites' there.[3]

This method of writing history by harking back to what happens in a previous generation applies to the write-up of Abimelech's history in relation to Joseph's in at least four ways. First, the congruence of subject matter—rivalry for dominance among brothers, fratricide, and the dual identity of the main character—is such that coincidence alone cannot account for it. Secondly, the tradition in Judges explicitly draws a link between Gideon's era and Joseph's. Thus the Israelites, confronting oppression at the hands of the Midianites, are reminded about how God delivered them from their troubles in Egypt (Judg. 6.8-9, 13). Included in these troubles will be those of both Joseph and his brothers in Egypt. Thirdly, Gideon is a descendant not just of the patriarchs Abraham, Isaac and Jacob but specifically of Manasseh, one of the sons born to Joseph by an Egyptian woman. Fourthly, Shechem, the

2. Although his fellow Shechemites turn against him, the text is explicit about the fact that the vengeance is because of what he did to his brothers (Judg. 9.23-24).

3. The biblical procedure is but a reflection of a universal one.

> All history-writing transfers features of one event or one great personage to another, and, indeed, much history-acting is in imitation of previous occurrences. Whoever nowadays writes about Napoleon is likely to lend him some traits of Caesar, and Napoleon himself—not to mention de Gaulle—would on occasion look to that example (D. Daube, *He That Cometh* [London: Council of Christians and Jews, 1966], p. 1).

city central to Abimelech's life story and where he is made king (Judg. 9.6), is the place where his ancestor Joseph is buried (Josh. 24.32).[4] Other parallels are observable. To cite but one: a dream employing agricultural imagery about sheaves of grain bowing down to another sheaf describes Joseph's rulership over his brothers (Gen. 37.7-8). Similar agricultural imagery, this time in a fable about trees singling out one of them to reign over the others, describes Abimelech's rulership over his brothers (Judg. 9.7-21).

In looking at this example of how biblical narrators record history, my aim is to explain why the four rules in Lev. 19.20-26 occur in the seemingly haphazard sequence that they do. These rules have proved very difficult to interpret and by addressing the problem of their sequence I hope to solve many of the puzzles about them. The rules concern illicit sex with a bondwoman, fruit that is not to be eaten because it is regarded as uncircumcised, eating but not where it involves an association with blood, and a prohibition against divination and soothsaying:

20 And whosoever lieth carnally with a woman, that is a bondmaid, betrothed to an husband, and not at all redeemed, nor freedom given her; there shall be an enquiry; they shall not be put to death, because she was not free.

21 And he shall bring his trespass offering unto Yahweh, unto the door of the tabernacle of the congregation, even a ram for a trespass offering.

22 And the priest shall make an atonement for him with the ram of the trespass offering before Yahweh for his sin which he hath done; and the sin which he hath done shall be forgiven him.

23 And when ye shall come into the land, and shall have planted all manner of trees for food, then ye shall count the fruit thereof as uncircumcised; three years shall it be as uncircumcised unto you; it shall not be eaten of.

24 But in the fourth year all the fruit thereof shall be holy to praise Yahweh withal.

4. It is also the place where Joseph's other direct descendants, the Ephraimites, assemble and with the other tribes of Israel confer kingship on Jeroboam (1 Kgs 12.20). Joseph's brothers pasture their father's cattle in the fields of Shechem (Gen. 37.12-14). On the influence of Abimelech's kingship on the write-up of another fratricide who became king, Absalom, see my *The Spirit of Biblical Law* (Athens, GA: University of Georgia Press, 1996), ch. 8.

25 And in the fifth year shall ye eat of the fruit thereof, that it may yield unto you the increase thereof; I am Yahweh your God.

26 Ye shall not eat upon the blood; Neither shall ye practise divination or soothsaying.

It is clear from a cursory reading of these laws that they are narrow in scope and that it is very difficult to decipher how a lawgiver has come to set them down in the order he has. These two features alone suggest that special factors may be at work in their presentation.

To read the laws of the Bible is, I claim, to read biblical narratives through the eyes of the lawgivers.[5] The topics they set down in their laws are taken from literary traditions. Their procedure explains why the Pentateuch consists of a unique integration of law and narrative. Nineteenth-century scholars had sensed that this procedure might be at work but they did not see the implications of the one example they felt fairly certain about. I refer to their recognition that the narrative about King Solomon's reign had influenced the write-up of the law of the king in Deut. 17.14-20 with its warning that an Israelite king is not to multiply horses, wives, silver and gold.[6]

When they construct their laws the lawgivers do what the narrators of the traditions do. They delve into matters that recur in the history of the generations and they too pay special attention to origins.[7] Their

5. Mary Douglas seems to share some such view but does not spell out her reasons for it. She links the dietary rules in Lev. 11.9-19 to Gen. 1: 'The dietary laws systematically pick up the order of creation in Genesis' ('The Forbidden Animals in Leviticus', *JSOT* 59 [1993], pp. 16-18).

6. See S.R. Driver, *Deuteronomy* (ICC; Edinburgh: T. & T. Clark, 3rd edn, 1902), p. 213:

> Unless, indeed, the other alternative be adopted, and the author of Deut. 17.14-20 [law of the king] be supposed to have been influenced, as he wrote, by his recollections of the narrative of Sam. (so Budde, *Richter und Samuel*, pp. 183f.; Cornill, *Einl.* par. 17.4). As the nucleus of 1 S. 8; 10.17-27a 12 appears to be pre-Deuteronomic (L.O.T. *l.c.*), the latter alternative is not the least probable one.

7. There are modern parallels to this procedure. Many anthropologists and inquirers like Freud adhere to Emil Durkheim's approach: 'In order to gain a proper understanding of a practice or institution, a moral or legal rule, one must go back as nearly as possible to its first beginnings.' Sybil Wolfram's translation (*In-Laws and Outlaws: Kinship and Marriage in England* [New York: St Martin's, 1987], p. 171) of Durkheim's 'La Prohibition de l'inceste et ses origines', *L'Année sociologique* 1 (1897), p. 1. Sybil Wolfram cites A.R. Radcliffe-Brown's unpublished criticism of the 'conjectural history' in question, pp. 172-173, 186.

interest in the beginnings of the nation explains why the greatest number of biblical laws takes up issues and problems from traditions in the Book of Genesis.[8]

The key to the comprehension of the four rules in Lev. 19.20-26 is, I contend, that the lawgiver engages in the same process of historical reflection as the narrators. He goes back and forth between issues and problems thrown up by the two related traditions about Joseph and Abimelech. These rules exemplify, in microcosm, the editorial or redactive process that has gone into the composition of a good deal of biblical literature, specifically, the Pentateuch plus the historical literature (Gen.–2 Kgs).[9]

Illicit Sex with a Bondwoman

Lev. 19.20-22 reads:

> And whosoever lieth carnally with a woman, that is a bondmaid, betrothed to an husband, and not at all redeemed, nor freedom given her; there shall be an enquiry; they shall not be put to death, because she was not free. And he shall bring his trespass offering unto Yahweh, unto the door of the tabernacle of the congregation, even a ram for a trespass offering. And the priest shall make an atonement for him with the ram of the trespass offering before Yahweh for his sin which he hath done; and the sin which he hath done shall be forgiven him.

About this sexual rule one wants to ask: why is it so narrow in scope? It takes up an infringement by a freeman of another freeman's arrangement to marry a bondwoman who has not yet been given her freedom. Jacob Milgrom thinks the case is a marginal one.[10] Raymond Westbrook refers to it as 'the curious case of Lev. 19.20-22'.[11] I wish

8. For the prevalence of the Genesis traditions in the write-up of the rules in the Book of the Covenant (Exod. 21.2–23.19), see my *The Origins of Biblical Law* (Ithaca: Cornell University Press, 1992).

9. Commentators see the hand of the P redactor both in the narrative about Abimelech and the narrative about Joseph's family in Egypt. Judg. 8.30-32 and Gen. 46.26 contain the same phrase about those 'issuing from his loins'. On P's redactive activity in adding the Abimelech story to the Book of Judges, see G.F. Moore, *Judges* (ICC; Edinburgh: T. & T. Clark, 1895), pp. 234-35. I am going further and claiming that the P lawgiver set down rules inspired by both narratives.

10. In his comments to the *HarperCollins Study Bible* (New York: HarperCollins, 1993), p. 183; also, 'The Betrothed Slave-Girl, Lev. 19,20-22', *ZAW* 89 (1977), pp. 43-50.

11. See R. Westbrook, 'Slave and Master in Ancient Near Eastern Law',

to argue that, despite the manifest differences between the situation in the Joseph story and the situation in the rule, it is in fact Potiphar's wife's sexual encounter with the bondman Joseph that inspires the rule.

The incident involving Joseph invites legal and ethical reflection. Although Joseph is innocent in the matter, the case against him is a strong one (she has his cloak in her hands) and he is, however wrongly, convicted. Such an unjust conviction will arouse interest among legal and ethical thinkers at any time and place. One aspect of Joseph's situation that engages the biblical lawgiver's interest is in line with his intent in many of his other rules, namely, to forge an Israelite national identity.[12] As expressed in Lev. 18.3: 'After the doings of the land of Egypt, wherein ye dwelt, shall ye not do,' the lawgiver's aim is to avoid comparable deeds occurring among his own people. In this light, it is understandable that he might choose to examine an actual example of an Israelite's exposure to bad conduct on the part of an Egyptian.

In working out the relationship between a law and a narrative there is not, nor should we expect, an exact one to one correspondence between them. The lawgiver exploits the narrative to make his own legal and ethical points. As in all his rules so in this one, the (male) Levitical lawgiver addresses males. Primarily taken up with their offenses, he comes up with, I submit, a comparable male offense to that of Potiphar's wife. An additional factor would have encouraged a switch from a female to a male offense. In the ancient world in matters sexual the man does the pursuing and not the woman as in Gen. 39.7. Her initiative with Joseph, when she says to him, 'Lie with me', is, like Lot's daughters' initiative with their father (Gen. 19.32), unique in biblical material.[13] 'To lie' in the sense of 'to have sexual intercourse' is generally the man's bidding. In this light it is understandable why a lawgiver might look at a male offense that approximates Potiphar's wife's offense.

Chicago–Kent Law Review 70 (1995), pp. 16-69; *idem*, *Studies in Biblical and Cuneiform Law* (Cahiers de la Revue Biblique, 26; 1988), pp. 101-109; also 'Adultery in Ancient Near Eastern Law', *RB* 97 (1990), pp. 564-69.

12. On identity as the paramount feature of the preceding rules in Lev. 19.19, see my 'Forbidden Mixtures in Deut. xxii. 9-11 and Lev. xix. 10', *VT* 45 (1995), pp. 433-480.

13. On the outrageous way in which the slave Aesop came to be released, because of the demand of his master's wife that he pleasure her ten times in succession, see D. Daube, 'Counting', *Mnémosyne* 30 (1977), pp. 176-78.

The rule applies to an Israelite situation that mirrors the Egyptian one. In an Israelite household, or in any household for that matter, domestic servants are more likely to be bondwomen than bondmen. The same lawgiver later sets down a rule that an Israelite should not enslave a fellow Israelite (Lev. 25.39-46).[14] To him, then, an Israelite woman cannot be enslaved. It is therefore likely that the bondwoman in the rule about illicit sex is not an Israelite. Like Joseph in Egypt, she is probably a captive from abroad. The triangular set-up in the story involving Potiphar, his wife and their foreign bondman has its counterpart in the rule, namely, the foreign bondwoman, her future husband and the offending male.

The switch from a sexual violation involving a woman with a bondman in the story to a sexual violation involving a man with a bondwoman in the law requires that the lawgiver imagine the curiously complex set-up that we meet with in the law. The male–female relationship in it that is equivalent to Potiphar's wife entanglement with Joseph has to involve males from outside the household. There would be no problem for the lawgiver to exercise his judgment on if the head of household had sex with his own bondwoman. He is her owner and entitled to her services. Thus the lawgiver lays out the case depicted in the rule. A freeman is the future husband of the bondwoman and another freeman gets involved sexually with her before she is given her freedom, before she becomes the other man's wife. A violation of this legal tie is the offense the rule focuses on. Because she is still a bondwoman, not yet freed from her servitude, the offenders are not given a death sentence.[15] The Deuteronomic rule that intercourse with a betrothed woman is a capital offense appears to be recognized (Deut. 22.23-24), because of the statement that had the bondwoman been free the violation of her betrothed status would have incurred capital punishment: 'they shall not be put to death because she was not free'.

In the Levitical rule there is no penalty for the offending male—other than his conscience compelling him to make acknowledgment

14. The position was similar in ancient Rome, although there were exceptions. See W.W. Buckland, *The Roman Law of Slavery: The Condition of the Slave in Private Law from Augustus to Justinian* (Cambridge: Cambridge University Press, 1908), pp. 397-436.

15. In classical Roman law a female slave did not fall under the harsh criminal repression of irregular sex, but once freed, she did. See T. Mommsen, *Römisches Strafrecht* (Leipzig, 1899), p. 691.

before Yahweh, the Israelite God, that he is guilty of misconduct. Interpreters are puzzled by the limited concern with punishment in the rule. They wonder why there is no reference to the punishment of the bondwoman—there are unsatisfactory attempts to introduce it[16]—and why there is no concern with compensation for her owner and/or future husband.[17] Again the Joseph story proves illuminating.

A reader might think that the story concentrates solely on the punishment of the innocent Joseph. But that is to miss a most interesting aspect of the story, especially when we keep in view the lawgiver's sole interest in the offending male's conscience. Potiphar's wife, receiving no penalty for her offense against her husband, has nonetheless to reckon with her conscience. During her sexual advances to Joseph, he reminds her that sexual activity between them is 'wickedness and [a] sin against God' (Gen. 39.9). In both story and rule, then, the focus in regard to the offending seducer is solely on an offense against God, sin, and not on a deed that has earthly repercussions. In the Joseph story there is no focus on the real-life consequences of the seducer's offense, because Potiphar's wife avoids discovery.

The Joseph story may also throw light on three other matters that interpreters regularly draw attention to in the rule, namely, the issue of the bondwoman's punishment, the issue of compensation for her owner and her future husband, and the rule's puzzling reference to an inquiry. First, absent from the law is any focus on the bondwoman's wrongdoing (other than to say that as a bondwoman she is not to be put to death). Features of the story are again to be reckoned with. If the bondwoman were to be punished (short of executing her), her owner would do so as he saw fit—just as Potiphar punished Joseph. Her punishment is not for the lawgiver but for her owner to decide. Joseph's being thrown into the palace prison may have been with a

16. For example, instead of the reading 'There shall be an enquiry', the Authorized Version of 1611, following the Vulgate, reads 'She shall be scourged'.

17. So N. Micklem, *Leviticus*, IB 2, p. 98. For the attempts to understand the unique term בקרת as 'indemnity', not 'enquiry', see Raymond Westbrook's discussion, *Studies*, pp. 102-104. Westbrook's own solution is that the slave is a man's wife pledged to a creditor to pay off a debt, and it is the creditor, not some outside party, who has intercourse with her. The woman's husband can then claim his wife back from the creditor. His analysis depends on dubious philological considerations that radically alter the usual reading of the text, getting rid of one of the parties, and interpreting the law within the context of other Near Eastern legal material that suits his position.

view to his eventual execution—recall the fate of the baker (Gen. 40.22)—but, if so, it is puzzling why Potiphar did not have him executed immediately. D.B. Redford views Joseph's sentence as unsatisfactory, but does not explain why this might be so. He thinks that ordinarily someone in his situation would have been summarily executed.[18] The point is, I think, that the matter was for Potiphar himself to decide.

Secondly, the absence from the rule of any reference to compensation for the bondwoman's owner and for her future husband may be attributable to the fact that this issue is not one that arises in the Joseph story. I noted that the lawgiver brings in the outside males because without them he cannot set out a rule that has a male offense comparable to Potiphar's wife's. So focused is the lawgiver on the features of the story that he leaves aside such issues as interpreters raise about compensating the bondwoman's owner and future husband.

Thirdly, a major puzzle in the rule is its call for an inquiry. Interpreters rightly ask exactly what is to be inquired into, and does not every legal matter bring with it an inquiry? If the law were lawyers' law I would agree that it is unsatisfactory in failing to address all the issues that arise from the offense. If, however, the incident with Potiphar's wife is the dominant influence on the construction of the rule, then the failure to inquire into the truth of her accusations against Joseph stands out. I suggest that the lawgiver, aware of this major fault in the story, demands an inquiry into the alleged sexual offense hypothesized in the law.

Uncircumcised Fruit

Lev. 19.23-25 reads:

> And when ye shall come into the land, and shall have planted all manner of trees for food, then ye shall count the fruit thereof as uncircumcised; three years shall it be as uncircumcised unto you: it shall not be eaten of. But in the fourth year all the fruit thereof shall be holy to praise Yahweh withal. And in the fifth year shall ye eat of the fruit thererof, that it may yield unto you the increase thereof: I am Yahweh your God.

How do we account for the bewildering switch from the topic of wrongful sexual congress between an Israelite and a foreign

18. *A Study of the Biblical Story of Joseph* (VTSup, 20; Leiden: Brill, 1970), p. 92.

bondwoman to the topic of trees and their uncircumcised fruit? The reason is that the lawgiver turns from the story of Joseph in Egypt to a related tradition in the Book of Judges about Israel in Canaan, specifically to the tradition that begins with the sexual union between the Israelite Gideon and a Canaanite bondwoman (Judg. 8.31).[19] This lawgiver lumps together Egyptian and Canaanite influences and warns the Israelites about them (Lev. 18.3).

I have already indicated why the lawgiver might switch from the story of Joseph's presence in an Egyptian household to the story of his descendant Gideon's involvement in a Canaanite household. The lawgiver comes upon similar issues that arise in the two traditions. Gideon's sexual relationship with a bondwoman in a Shechemite household begins the saga of the son, Abimelech, who is born to them and whose story recalls Joseph's. Abimelech's reign lasts but three years. It comes to an end when his fellow Shechemites become instruments of vengeance against him, when 'God sent an evil spirit between Abimelech and the men of Shechem... that the violence done to the seventy sons of Jerubbaal [Gideon] might come and their blood be laid upon Abimelech their brother' (Judg. 9.23, 24). An incident that occurs at the beginning of this process of retribution explains the rule about uncircumcised fruit, and why it takes the form that it does. In this incident the men of Shechem bring in the grape harvest and hold a festival in the house of their god. While eating and drinking during the course of the festival the celebrants seek to influence Abimelech's fate by cursing him (Judg. 9.27).

Why, however, does the lawgiver focus on this particular aspect of the tradition about Abimelech? The key lies in a particular development which the lawgiver has been contemplating in the Joseph story. After Joseph is cast into prison for his supposed sexual offense against Potiphar's wife, the very next incident is when he interprets the dream of his fellow-prisoner, the butler. The butler dreams of a vine with three branches which blossom and produce clusters of grapes ready to harvest. He takes these new grapes and squeezes their juice into the pharaoh's cup, which he then places in the pharaoh's hand.

19. In Judg. 9.18 the woman is referred to as an אמה, a term that is synonymous with שפחה, the term for bondmaid in the rule in Lev. 19.20. B.J. Schwartz suggests that in Lev. 19.20a the unexpected selection of the term שפחה and not אמה for a 'slave-girl' is a word-play due to the fact that she is not חפש ('free'). B.J. Schwartz, 'The Slave-Girl Pericope', *Scripta Hierosolymitana* 31 (1986), p. 244.

Joseph informs the butler that the pressing of the grapes into the cup signifies that he can look forward to taking up his job again as the pharaoh's butler (Gen. 40.9-13) (unlike the baker whose dream Joseph next interprets as foreshadowing his execution). It is the link between fruit-trees and the fate of a person (when the butler's dream about vines foreshadowed his fate) that has prompted the lawgiver to turn to the similar incident in the Judges tradition about the fate of Abimelech.[20]

In the Judges tradition the men of Shechem celebrate their grape harvest: 'They went out into the field, and gathered the grapes from their vineyards and trod them, and held festival, and went out into the house of their god, and ate and drank and reviled Abimelech' (Judg. 9.27). The lawgiver, Moses, anticipating Israel's entry into the land of Canaan, calls for an Israelite harvest festival to be held in honor of the Israelite god. The rule is an ideal construction of what should take place when the Israelites first experience the new land—it is introduced by the phrase 'And when ye shall come into the land'.[21] There are three aspects of the rule that call for comment, namely, the existence of such a festival, why there is a period of time between entering the new land, planting trees, and celebrating the festival, and why the fruit is regarded as uncircumcised.

First, the rule is intended to recall the history of Israel's mixing with the Canaanites in Gideon's time, which was when Israel acquired the land. Once in Canaan the Israelites are to celebrate their own harvest festival and not the one celebrated by the Canaanites. The requirement of an Israelite festival has been prompted by the lawgiver's scrutiny of the Canaanite festival in Judg. 9.27. The term הלולים, about giving praise at the festival, only occurs in the Bible in the rule about uncircumcised fruit where Yahweh is to receive praise, and in the narrative about Abimelech where the Canaanite god receives acclamation.

Secondly, Israel's festival is to be delayed until the fourth year in the land. The fruit from their newly planted trees is to be regarded as

20. The same link will also play a crucial role in the puzzling rule that comes after the fruit trees rule, namely, not 'to eat upon the blood'.

21. Those commentators, ancient and modern, who think that the rule is geared to the actual life of the ancient Israelites miss the influence of the narrative. They try to give the rule a practical basis by suggesting that it requires that the fruit of all newly planted trees be removed for the first three years because it is not especially good fruit. See Josephus, *Ant.* 4.226; Philo, *Plant.* 95-100; *Virt.* 156. N.H. Snaith refers to the rule's 'sound agricultural principle', *Leviticus and Numbers* (Century Bible; Edinburgh: Nelson, 1967), p. 133.

uncircumcised and therefore taboo. This is to put a period of time between their entry into the land of Canaan and the harvesting of their trees. The reason for the hiatus is probably that the Canaanites subjected their harvests to their own religious rites and it was deemed important that the Israelite festival should have no association with such rites. In the story God is said to have caused the Shechemites to pursue vengeance against Abimelech, and they proceeded to do so in the context of their festival. It might have been important for the lawgiver to indicate to the recipients of his laws that, although God directed events even among the Shechemites it did not mean that God approved of such Canaanite festivities. The statement in the rule, 'I am Yahweh', makes clear that an allegiance to Yahweh is being called for, not one to a Canaanite deity in the house of the god where the Shechemite festival was held.

Thirdly, why does the rule attribute to the fruit of trees the negative feature of uncircumcision? The Canaanite context which has prompted the rule would appear to explain this attribution. The Canaanites are uncircumcised and the lawgiver's aim is to remove any association with them in Israelite life. Why, however, does uncircumcision which attaches to a person come to be attached to the product of a fruit tree? Again the Abimelech story may prove illuminating. Before Abimelech's downfall his one surviving brother Jotham communicates his opposition to Abimelech's rule by means of a fable that employs imagery about trees appointing a king over them (Judg. 9.7-21). In the fable Abimelech is compared to a tree.[22]

In the fable Abimelech is the bramble that is appointed to rule over the other trees. Unlike the fruit of the olive tree, fig tree and vines in the fable, over whom the bramble comes to rule, Abimelech represents a tree whose fruit is worthless, and whose potential for fire and hence for destruction is very real. After three years his reign does indeed come to a fiery end (Judg. 9.52-57). The particular association between the Canaanite background of Abimelech and the description of him as a worthless tree might, then, account for the odd link between the idea of uncircumcision and a fruit tree.

As a Shechemite, Abimelech would have been uncircumcised (like the Shechemites in the story of Dinah's seduction in Gen. 34). If the half-Canaanite, half-Israelite Abimelech had succeeded in becoming ruler of all Israel the threat to Israel's national identity would have

22. Joseph too is compared to a tree in Gen. 49.22.

been enormous. Although interpreters dispute the significance of the statement, the text in Judg. 9.22 states that 'Abimelech ruled over Israel three years'.[23] The Deuteronomic law about the institution of kingship warns about the threat of someone like Abimelech becoming king over Israel. By typically picking up on a tradition, namely, the one about Abimelech, it sets down the odd requirement that the Israelites should not appoint a foreigner over them who 'is not thy brother' (Deut. 17.15). It is warning against appointing someone like Abimelech, a foreigner and not a true brother, as king.[24]

The reason why the fruit cannot be touched for the first three years after Israel's entry into the land is, I am suggesting, to directly recall the threat posed by Abimelech's kingship over all Israel. His father had declined kingship for himself and his offspring, and had affirmed Yahweh's rule (Judg. 8.22). Contrary to his father's wishes, Abimelech reigned for three years and his reign was characterized as the barren rule of one useless tree ruling over other fruitful ones. The law, in effect, says that the trees newly planted in the acquired land of Canaan are to be treated as if they are barren. Their fruit cannot be touched. Eventually, in the harvest of the fourth year, the Israelites are to celebrate Yahweh, that is, affirm his providence on their behalf. Only after such affirmation can the Israelites consume the fruit. We might compare how the avoidance of leavened bread during the Passover festival is intended to recall a historical event, the haste with which the Israelites had to leave Egypt (Deut. 16.3); or how the rule about the forgotten harvest sheaf in Deut. 24.19-22 is intended to recall the first time the Israelites were delivered from famine because of Joseph's policy on behalf of the hungry in Egypt.[25]

The rule about the uncircumcised fruit raises the interesting issue of the 'deep' meaning that I attribute to it. I claim that it makes no sense to give the rule a practical meaning, as has been the standard way of reading it, namely, sound agricultural practice requires a farmer to

23. The tendency is to explain it away by claiming that he is but a local military overlord. See, for example, R.G. Boling, *Judges* (AB; Garden City, NY: Doubleday, 1975). But the text does not say this; and the issue of the Israelites wishing a king to reign over them, specifically, a member of Gideon's family, is a major feature of the traditions in Judges (Judg. 8.22, 23; 9.2, 8-15). The fable's reference to olives, figs, and vines, that is, to landed estates, also suggests that the whole of Israel is meant.

24. See my *Law and Narrative in the Bible* (Ithaca: Cornell University Press, 1985), p. 100.

25. See my *Law and Narrative*, pp. 282-88.

discard the fruit of new trees for a period of three years. For one thing, farmers will know what to do with the fruit of new trees, without needing to be told in a directive. What the standard reading of the rule fails to do is give proper significance to the weighty language used by the lawgiver, when he speaks of the Israelites entering the land, and when he describes the fruit of the first three years' crop as uncircumcised. My solution addresses the significance of the rule's language. The rule, I claim, directs historical memory to the time of Israel's entry into the land, in particular, to the involvement of Gideon with the Canaanites. The rule serves as a warning to Israelites to avoid loss of their identity, for example, by giving themselves over to someone like Abimelech who is as much Canaanite as Israelite. Its curious formulation is one indication of the richness of its background. In real life the lawgiver may well have been familiar with a customary practice whereby farmers discarded the fruit of newly planted trees, or treated it differently from the fruit of maturer ones.[26] This awareness, however, would be but a stimulus to his imagining Moses' concern with the single occasion of Israel's taking up residence in the land, when it was not just a matter of new fruit but new fruit that had negative connotations because of Canaanite influences at the time.

Eating upon the Blood
Lev. 19.26 reads:

> Ye shall not eat upon the blood.

The rule's language is cryptic. The standard translation—'You shall not eat any flesh with the blood in it'—is, I think, wrong. The rule's literal meaning militates against such a meaning. There is no reference to the animal's flesh and the preposition על ('upon') and not אם ('with') is used. The reference to eating but not to what is eaten and the reference to blood but not to its source should caution against making a direct link between the eating and the blood, as if both are thought of as being consumed together. The rule's curious formulation requires a

26. This awareness seems to underlie the rule in Code of Hammurabi 60, 'If, when a seignior gave a field to a gardener to set out an orchard, the gardener set out the orchard, he shall develop the orchard for four years; in the fifth year the owner of the orchard and the gardener shall divide equally, with the owner of the orchard receiving his preferential share.'

full explanation, not a rationalization, which in effect is what the standard translations and commentaries give.

This rule about eating follows the food rule about not eating uncircumcised fruit, so that there is a tantalizing connection of some kind between the two rules. It is tempting, but I think the temptation should be resisted, to see a link between the blood in the second rule and the notion of circumcision in the first. The way to comprehend these rules is not to use the immediate context for illumination. Rather we have to scrutinize the narrative context which has prompted the rule.

The same incident that accounts for the rule about the fruit trees also raises the issue that prompts the rule about not 'eating upon the blood'. During the vintage festival the Shechemites celebrate, they eat and drink and revile Abimelech in the house of their god (Judg. 9.27). Wine or the juice of grapes is a well established metaphor for blood. Gideon's history provides a good illustration. When he successfully routs the Midianites, the Ephraimites—who, like Gideon, are direct descendants of Joseph—are furious that they are not asked to be involved. Gideon had, however, given them the opportunity to slay the two Midianite princes, Oreb and Zeeb. In response to their outburst, Gideon asks them rhetorically, 'Is not the gleaning of the grapes of Ephraim [the two princes killed by the Ephraimites] better than the vintage of Abiezer [Gideon's rout of the Midianites]'? (Judg. 8.2). This language well conveys the link between the juice of grapes and the blood of one's enemies. Other biblical authors depict Yahweh's wrath as a wine press (Isa. 63.3; Lam. 1.15; and Rev. 14.10), that is, his wrath brings destruction on his enemies.[27]

In his rule the lawgiver has the eating and drinking of the Shechemites in focus and what he prohibits is any Israelite activity that reflects a comparable link between eating and the slaughter of an enemy. In the story, God uses these Shechemites 'to lay the blood of' Abimelech's brothers upon (על) Abimelech (Judg. 9.24). The lawgiver would approve of this activity but he does not accept what the Shechemites

27. In Gen. 49.11 the blood of grapes refers to the death of Judah's sons. See my *Women, Law, and the Genesis Traditions* (Edinburgh: Edinburgh University Press, 1979), pp. 63-64. The battle against the Midianites also provides an example of a symbolic action in which drinking water, in this instance, is associated with defeating an enemy. In a test to determine which men should proceed to battle those who drink water after the fashion of dogs are selected. Biblical dogs are ferocious.

do at their wine festival in an Israelite context, namely, eating with a view to preparing to kill an enemy.

I still have to explain, however, the rule's curious formulation and how exactly its language is to be understood. The crucial observation is that the lawgiver has also kept in focus the story of Joseph and his brothers. After all, it was his scrutiny of the Joseph story, specifically, the link between pressed grapes and the butler's fate, that got him onto the incident about the grapes and Abimelech's fate in Judges 9. The lawgiver looks at a comparable, prior incident in Joseph's life.

The juxtaposition of eating and shedding someone's blood shows up in the Joseph story for the first time in Israelite history, and it is characteristic of biblical lawgivers always to turn to the first indication of an unacceptable practice. The brothers seek to kill Joseph and then to cover up the killing by claiming that a wild beast has devoured him. The oldest brother Reuben opposes their plan and appeals to them not to shed Joseph's blood (Gen. 37.22). They however proceed to assault Joseph, strip him of his coat, and cast him into a pit. They then sit down to eat (Gen. 37.25). Their intention at this point when they are eating is still to kill him despite Reuben's opposition. Judah then comes up with an equally outrageous scheme. They should not in fact shed their brother's blood, because there is no profit in doing so; rather they should sell him to an approaching caravan of Ishmaelites. Presumably, if this caravan had not appeared they might well have proceeded to slay Joseph.

The Joseph story sets out a situation that anticipates what the Shechemites do: over a meal a group of men plan bloodshed. It is this scene in the Joseph story that prompts the rule's formulation—no eating upon the blood, that is, where the focus is the slaughter of a person. The preposition על (upon) frequently bears a hostile sense. For example, in Judg. 16.12, 'the Philistines are upon thee Samson', or in the attempt of the Shechemites to kill Abimelech they 'fortify [or stir up] the city upon him' (Judg. 9.31). As for the term דם (blood), in a Deuteronomic rule (Deut. 17.8), there is a provision about offenses 'between blood and blood' (בין־דם לדם). The reference is to persons who have been slain. The term *dam*, 'blood', by itself can therefore refer to the blood of a human victim and that is how it is to be understood in this rule: 'You shall not eat upon the blood [of a person]'. The verb to eat (אכל), by the way, frequently has the hostile sense of devouring an enemy (for example, Deut. 32.42; 2 Sam. 2.26).[28]

Contrary to the standard view I do not think that this particular Levitical rule is yet another prohibition against eating meat with the blood still part of it. The lawgiver thinks of the occasion when the brothers of Joseph sit down to eat and plot his fate. Why does he pay particular attention to this incident? These brothers are sons of Israel and, apart from the fundamental wrongness of their action, what they do too closely foreshadows the more fully developed Canaanite practice he finds in the tradition about the Shechemites. The lawgiver prohibits Canaanite practices not because anything they do is automatically to be opposed, but because anything he finds among his own Israelite group that smacks of Canaanite ways invites condemnation. The rule therefore condemns eating, after the fashion of the Shechemites, while focusing on the blood of an actual or potential victim of slaughter. Like many proverbs, the rule picks up on a pattern of conduct that recurs throughout the generations. A priestly lawgiver with his special interest in blood would understandably condemn the practice. Food rules in the Bible are intended to contribute a measure of ethical, religious and ritual distinctiveness to an Israelite's way of life.

Once the rule is understood in the way I have described, an incident in the time of King Saul takes on more significance than has been hitherto realized. In a battle against the Philistines, Saul lays an oath on his people not to eat food before he has been avenged on his enemies. After the successful rout of the Philistines the Israelites are faint from hunger, take the animals they capture as spoil, and 'slaughtered them on the ground; and... ate upon the blood' (1 Sam. 14.32). Again the translations and commentaries understand the offense to be against such rules as are found in Gen. 9.4 and Deut. 12.23, namely, eating the animals with their blood. But the text does not say this. They ate upon (על) the blood—after they had slaughtered the animals, not when they were slaughtering them. The implication is, I suggest, that the eating upon the blood, as in the rule in Lev. 19.26, refers not to the Israelites' eating blood on the occasion, but to their celebrating the slaughter of their enemies by observing the blood that flows to the ground from the slaughtered animals.

28. For על in a hostile sense, and examples of אכל in the sense of to devour an enemy, see BDB, pp. 757-58, and pp. 37-38 respectively. In English we refer to a 'young blood'.

One should not lose sight of the cryptic nature of the rule. It distorts the sense and devalues the sophistication of the lawgiver to give it the meaning, 'You shall not eat anything with its blood.' The sense is, 'You shall not celebrate killing, however justified, as in war, by festive eating'. The cryptic language serves to warn against taking the rule out of its context. It is thus crucial to underline the assumption that originally the lawgiver's scrutiny of the narrative histories produced the rules.

Divination and Soothsaying

Lev. 19.26 goes on to read:

> Neither shall ye practise divination or soothsaying.

In his move from the rule about blood to the next rule about divination we can follow exactly how the lawgiver has proceeded. The topic at issue is again vengeance, and the focus is the Joseph story, in particular, on Joseph's retribution against his brothers who, in getting rid of him, went on to use the blood of an animal to make it appear that he had died.

Recall that Joseph's dreams drive his brothers to conspire to kill him: 'And we shall see', they exclaim as he approaches them, 'What will become of his dreams' (Gen. 37.20). Dreams belong to the world of the occult and the mysterious. The brothers devise an effect, blood on Joseph's garment, to counter another effect, Joseph's dreams. Thus they use the blood of a slaughtered animal on Joseph's special garment to trick their father into believing that a wild beast has killed Joseph: 'Torn, torn is Joseph', laments Jacob (Gen. 37.17). By interpreting the cloth as containing the sign of a wild beast's activity, Jacob concludes that Joseph has died. The brothers' ruse is such that they successfully rid themselves of their enemy without suggesting that they were in any way involved. Joseph matches this make-believe when he later traps the brothers by falsely suggesting that an external agency, a divining cup, is responsible for their fate.

In formulating his rule against divination, the lawgiver notes Joseph's act of retaliation against his brothers that mirrors their specific act against him.[29] To avenge what had been done to him when they used

29. Other interpreters comment on the mirroring character of Joseph's act, for example, D. Daube, 'Rechtsgedanken in den Erzählungen des Pentateuchs', in J. Hempel and L. Rost (eds.), *Von Ugarit nach Qumran: Festschrift für Otto Eissfeldt* (Berlin: De Gruyter, 1958), p. 38. D.B. Redford states, 'By thus falsifying

his special clothing to deceive their father, Joseph tricks his brothers. He does so, significantly, by means of cloth sacks when they come to Egypt to obtain food for their family back in Canaan. When they are leaving with sacks of grain Joseph, unknown to the brothers, has his silver divining cup placed in Benjamin's sack.[30] It is a deliberate move by Joseph to accuse them of stealing not just a cup, but one that has magical properties enabling him to divine (Gen. 44.1-5).

The same term נחש *piel*, 'to divine, observe signs', is found in both the law and the story. Although it is a false claim on the part of Joseph, what is true at another and more decisive level is the unfolding reality of his dreams. The effect on the brothers of the deception with the sacks is that they tear their garments, and fall before him on the ground (Gen. 44.13, 14)—just as Joseph's dreams predicted (Gen. 37.7-10). Moreover, as part of their response to Joseph's having trapped them, Judah tells him about the fate of their brother, that is, about Joseph himself (Gen. 44.18-28). In other words, at this point in the narrative we return to the issue of blood on Joseph's garment, precisely the issue that belongs to the context out of which the preceding rule against 'eating upon the blood' was forged. The blood the brothers placed on Joseph's garment successfully deceived Jacob into believing what they claimed it signified, just as Joseph's placement of the divining cup successfully deceives the brothers into believing what Joseph claims it signifies, namely, that he has rare powers at his disposal. The lawgiver, opposed to what the brothers did with the animal's blood, is equally opposed to Joseph's conduct, his use of the divining cup to suggest that he, an Israelite, is given to divination.

I conclude by turning to a crucial aspect of my approach, how to explain the arrangement of the material that is set out in the texts. Why does the lawgiver add 'soothsaying' (ענן *polel*) to divination in his prohibition? He could have cited a number of practices such as those we find listed in a rule in Deut. 18.10, 11: one who passes children through fire, augur, soothsayer, diviner, sorcerer, one who casts spells, medium, familiar spirit and necromancer. In the narrative Joseph's divining cup is *not* available to him because of its supposed

evidence Joseph has committed the same violation as that perpetrated by his brothers with his coat!', *Story of Joseph*, p. 74.

30. So cloth again plays a role in a deception. For an illuminating discussion of the role of clothes in the Joseph story, see V.H. Matthews, 'The Anthropology of Clothing in the Joseph Narrative', *JSOT* 65 (1995), pp. 25-36.

theft by his brothers. Yet from the viewpoint of the deceived brothers Joseph 'knows' that they stole it and exactly where it is to be found. So from their stance they presumably recognize that Joseph has some means of prediction at his disposal other than the divining cup to ascertain its whereabouts. The lawgiver, setting aside the fraudulent story told to the brothers, thinks of the form of prognostication that is associated with soothsaying. This feature of the story, about another form of foretelling the future, is why he adds soothsaying to divination.

Always abreast of the history of the generations, the lawgiver will have been alert to future instances of the practices soothsaying and divination. That is why he takes seriously the incident in the Joseph narrative despite its fraudulent aspect. In the historical narratives there are two references to soothsaying. One is in the story about Abimelech in which there is a reference to the diviner's oak, אלון מעוננים (Judg. 9.37);[31] and the other is from the time of the kings, when King Manasseh resorts to soothsaying (2 Kgs 21.6). Instances of the practice of divination in the time of the kings are 2 Kgs 17.17; 21.6 (and see 1 Kgs 20.33). Just as the brothers are taken in by this Egyptian's (Joseph's) deceptions, so later Israelites are to be on guard against the deceptive practices of foreigners.

In regard to divination and soothsaying the lawgiver would have found it particularly important to underscore the falsity of Joseph's machinations. The idea that he predicted events by means of his cup or by some other comparable means could not be encouraged, because a fundamental feature of the Joseph story is that he indeed predicted events by means of his dreams, which are inspired by God. The lawgiver had to be in two minds about Joseph's dreams. On the one hand, they represent divine providence with Joseph as the agent for the rescue of his family and his people. On the other hand, they represent, on the face of it, mysteries that can be aligned with the forbidden foreign practices of divination, soothsaying and the like, against which his rules take a firm stand.

Concluding Comments

Priests are interested in mysteries, but what form these mysteries take is often far from clear. Some insight into the interests of biblical

31. On the extent of divinatory practices in the Gideon–Abimelech narrative, see Boling, *Judges*, pp. 160-61.

priests comes from the above rules and the traditions which prompted their formulation. It is surely no accident that both are often about particular ways of interpreting certain phenomena. Potiphar's wife uses Joseph's garment to have her husband interpret it as signifying Joseph's attempted rape of her. Joseph's brothers soak his garment in blood to have their father interpret it as signifying Joseph's death. The use to which wine or the juice of grapes is put determines a man's fate (the butler's and Abimelech's). Joseph's divining cup is intended to convey that he can predict events. Another form of prediction, soothsaying, suggests that such a practice can locate a stolen object. Joseph's dreams and Jotham's fable are endowed with special significance such that the future can be interpreted from them. The priestly lawgiver, then, is alert to those who, illegitimately to his mind in most instances, devise phenomena that require a particular interpretation or claim to possess special powers in interpreting other phenomena. For him, presumably, such powers are primarily the province of his priestly class.

The history that the lawgiver looks into when presenting his rule concerning the uncircumcised fruit is about Israel's struggle to settle in the land of Canaan. That is why the rule opens with the words, 'And when ye shall come into the land'. Modern scholars go wrong when they ignore such a historical notice in the text and pass over it as a mere device by which a societal rule is ascribed to Moses. Such a notice constitutes a crucial key in letting us in on the lawgiver's historical method of setting out his rules. He reacts to the history he finds in these traditions by setting down in response to it rules and practices, some of which will have existed in some form or another in his time, others of which will be purely hypothetical constructions on his part. Where his knowledge of the rules and practices that existed in his time comes from is, alas, but a matter of speculation.[32]

32. The problem I describe has its parallel in our attempts to plot how human institutions develop. Extradition, as a legal notion, influenced the religious idea that God required human communities to hand over offenders or there would be dire consequence for them—an idea that we can read about in the literary sources, for example, in the Book of Jonah and in Joshua 7 (Achan's offense), but not in any biblical legal source. The religious idea, in turn, profoundly influenced further legal thinking on the topic, for example, the rabbinic notions in *Mishnah Terumoth* 46, *Genesis Rabbah* 94 on Gen. 46.26-27. For extradition and other examples (the institution of judgeship, manumission from slavery), see D. Daube, *Appeasement or Resistance, and Other Essays on New Testament Judaism* (Berkeley: University of

Customary knowledge will be one source. A familiarity with laws and practices of other cultures is possibly another source.

The historical method of modern scholars cannot achieve the results it is designed for because the biblical lawgivers intertwine law and history. Modern historians, who are heirs to the sixteenth-century European legal humanists working initially in the area of Roman Law, attempt to reconstruct the institutions of the past in order to interpret the actions, words and thoughts of people who lived at that time.[33] Their method ran into serious problems in the study of Roman Law and it is not a method that works for the study of biblical law, because it comes up against the fundamental fictional character of all biblical law. The laws are constructed a long time after Moses and are fictionally attributed to him. Just as I would not relate a rule about the uncircumcised fruit to the actual time of the settlement in Canaan—although I cannot rule out that in historical reality some such rule did come into existence then—so, for example, I would not relate the rule about familiar spirits and mediums in Lev. 20.6 to the reign of King Manasseh, as Jacob Milgrom and other scholars do.[34] No such easy correlation between institutions in the law codes and what may have happened in the history of ancient Israel is possible. All of the biblical rules have been filtered through the historical imagination of the Deuteronomic and Priestly lawgivers. In doing so they link the laws to the history known to them in such a way that it is impossible for modern inquirers to do the kind of historical reconstruction that is so important to them today. In keeping with all ancient historiography, the biblical authors' aim is to conflate past, present and future for didactic purposes. In regard to biblical laws and history I know of no way by which modern inquirers might undo the merging of law and historical invention, the most outstanding feature of biblical legal material, and pursue historical reconstruction.

The rules I have examined appear in the Pentateuch quite separately from the narrative accounts that have prompted their formulation.

California Press, 1987), pp. 105-110. (On extradition treaties in ancient Near Eastern sources for the return of fugitive slaves, see *ANET*, pp. 531-32).

33. See the excellent introductory chapter entitled, 'The French Prelude to Modern Historiography', in J.G.A. Pocock, *The Ancient Constitution and the Feudal Law* (Cambridge; Cambridge University Press, 1957), pp. 1-29.

34. See Milgrom, *HarperCollins*, p. 184; and M. Haran, 'Behind the Scenes of History: Determining the Date of the Priestly Source', *JBL* 100 (1981), pp. 329-33.

Although it should be borne in mind that the Pentateuch consists of a curious mixture of law and narrative history, this separation nonetheless points to a difficult problem. It is not obvious that, as I claim, all of the laws have to be read as issuing from matters that arise in the narratives, although I should emphasize that some laws explicitly direct attention to some of the history, namely (and only), incidents in the life of Moses.[35]

Very little is known about how the Pentateuch came to take the form that it does, and nothing about its intended audience. One thing is certain. The Pentateuch was not intended for modern readers. When they instinctively feel that they have to make sense of the rules in the Pentateuch by reading their contents as a reflection of the social reality of the lawgiver's time and place, they are not paying sufficient attention to what the texts plainly say. Modern interpreters substitute for the Moses of the biblical texts legislators who—I simplify—respond to societal problems in their time by borrowing and modifying rules known to the broader legal culture of the ancient Near East. What these interpreters have not appreciated is that the person of Moses is so constructed that he does what even a great national lawgiver cannot do, namely, address the problems of his people centuries later and respond to them with rules and judgments. The issues and problems Moses takes up in his laws are indeed, I am arguing, those contained in the history of his people and their precise source is the narratives in the biblical records.

If we define those who committed the Pentateuch to writing as a scribal circle in a narrow sense, and if we assume that the material first circulated within it, then the members of this circle would have been familiar with the relationship between the laws and the narratives I describe. This is a reasonable assumption to make and consequently there is no need to think that the rules were in any way esoteric in character for them. I cannot emphasize enough that the meaning of the rules I lay out is their meaning at the time when they were committed to writing against the background of the narrative histories.

It is rare in the study of ancient law that we can pick up so precisely the factors that have entered into the details of the rules that we possess. More often than not, we are left guessing as to what factors

35. For example, those rules in Deut. 23.3-8 about the creation of classes within Israelite society take up incidents recounted in the narratives about the Ammonites, Edomites and Moabites. See my *Law and Narrative*, pp. 228-34.

are at work in the ancient society that produces legal records. Biblical laws are different. Because of their intimate relationships to narrative histories available to us in other parts of the Bible, we have the data that enable us to work out exactly what motivated their construction, and why they were arranged in such strange sequences.

Discussion

Sawyer: We started off with the rather naive view that this is part of a code of law. We then came to the view that it is perhaps theological discourse. We considered the idea that it might be prophecy. But this is yet another theory for what it is and I suppose the main question you leave us with, is why did the lawgiver do this at all? What was he doing it for?

Carmichael: That is straightforward. This is all about the redaction, editorial and composition of the Pentateuch. Moses is exercising his legal, ethical judgment in all these matters and the narratives themselves come in for that kind of legal and ethical judgment. It is that kind of procedure.

Sawyer: But why did he write it in the form of legislation? Why did he make this kind of commentary on the stories in Genesis and elsewhere, in the form of legislation?

Carmichael: Because the issues and problems cry out for legal and ethical judgments and it is a useful form. Much modern criminal procedure remarkably, is coming from the use of the Adam and Eve story by the canonists working out criminal procedure. The way laws come into being is not a reaction to societal problems. Rather like the composition of proverbs, they are responses to matters in these traditions.

Jackson: I wonder how far you would claim that this kind of knowledge of what they were doing was dispersed. Supposing we take the view that Judas, at the time when he took part in the Last Supper, knew that he was going to betray Jesus, would people have looked back and said לא תאכלו על הדם?

Carmichael: That is not a rule that is in the Gospels, is it?

Jackson: No, there is absolutely no reference to that in the Gospels. This is a way of asking how far and for how long this sort of knowledge would have been dispersed. Let us assume that people reading this at the time would have understood it in the way that you would. How long did it stick in the cultural tradition, so that if someone was aware of a later story, which seemed to evoke this narrative rule, would they have read it back?

Carmichael: I do not know. We know that Sirach and Jubilees have something of that going on, but I have not pursued any of these parallels in any depth. I keep an open mind about parallels in Sirach and Jubilees. I am always reluctant to swing out of one period of time into another because so much happens in the interim that one has to pay a lot of attention to that.

Douglas: If I could think of a better reason than Calum has given us for why they should have to leave their crops for five years when they go into the new land, I should be very happy, but I cannot. Why is it five years?

Carmichael: I do not want to play with numbers and say three years is because Abimelech reigned for three years. The common view of that rule is that the fruit of new trees is not all that good and no doubt there may be something in that. I just cannot imagine that an ancient lawgiver would bother to put it down as a practical rule, because everybody would know. Nonetheless, very often when these rules are set down, they have in some way to make sense to the contemporary situation. It could be that it was standard practice or it was recognized that for three years your fruit was pretty worthless.

Douglas: Do you have another reason for saying that these points absolutely cried out for correction, or is it that they have been corrected that makes you think they must have been crying out for correction? In your general thesis, why does the lawgiver do this? Did he have to, because these problems were crying out for elucidation? I wonder how you knew there were problems crying out.

Carmichael: These narratives themselves already have a religious dimension introduced into them, and one would have to characterize the religious dimension in terms of moral, ethical, legal judgment. That process is already going on in these narrative traditions and they are not just folk stories without ethical, legal reflection, so the process is very much there.

Watson: This paper is so much more central to this meeting than mine would be. I was very struck by your disbelief at his approach, and I was prompted to make some kind of response, precisely because one of our friends said to me immediately afterwards, 'It's a big joke, isn't it!' or words to that effect. I think there are at least two reasons for an unwillingness to take Calum's approach in a straightforward way, the first being the long and very different exegetical tradition. The second is a very strong belief that law develops from the conditions in a particular society and that lawmakers are responding to conditions in that society. I believe strongly that frequently that is not the case and I want to give a very striking example to illustrate this.

The general view that law emerges from society is untenable, simply because of the prevalence of legal order. In general, in most western societies at any rate, for most of the time law develops by borrowing from elsewhere, on a large scale. Usually the borrowing is not done in a thoughtful way, examining other systems and saying, 'This fits best'. One system somehow has come to be regarded as the one to borrow from. Frequently even inappropriate laws are borrowed. What I want to talk about is not about borrowing, because Calum's paper was not about borrowing. The most fruitful system of secular law in the West has been Roman private law and that developed in a very strange way which is not the same as Calum's but shows again a disconnection between law and society. In the fifth century BCE, during the early Republic, the populace was divided into a small group of patricians and a large group of plebeians, with the inevitable squabbles. The patricians had a monopoly of all offices, both governmental and priestly. The plebeians objected. It was eventually agreed that a court of law should give equality. This was the famous court of the Twelve Tables of 451 BCE, the most important single event in Roman legal history. By wonderful political skills, the patricians managed to give the college of pontiffs a monopoly of interpreting the Twelve Tables. They gave a monopoly of interpreting, each year, to one of their members. So interpretation of the law became one outstanding mark of a Roman patrician on the make, and Roman priests were part-timers in state office like many others. What was given was interpretation. All that interpretation gave rise to, among the Romans, was prestige, not appearing in court, not acting as judge, not law reform. Even when the pontiffs lost the monopoly, it still remained the mark of an aristocratic Roman to interpret the law, and you find emerging a separate class of jurists.

What makes a good jurist? A good jurist is someone regarded as a good jurist by other good jurists. They sat at home discussing, with anyone who came to ask them, points of law. Frequently, if not almost always (the sources are not clear), these are not real situations. Any situation brought to them they would discuss, and law developed primarily at Rome by the interpretation of these jurists sitting at home, sometimes giving advice, often discussing questions which almost never would arise. They took over to private law their reasoning from sacred law because their main job as pontiffs was to keep right relations between the Romans and the gods, especially the state and the gods. So there are certain arguments you cannot use. You cannot say this decision seems fair. You might say subsequently that that opinion was reached on the grounds of fairness. It was not an argument. Nor is what is better for the parties economically a sound reason, and so on. There is a limited range of legalistic argument which can be used, and nothing else. The jurists are working largely in a vacuum, with no concern, usually, for what happens at court. So far as the sources go, we have information of only one occasion when a jurist appeared in court in a lawsuit. The result is a legal system different from Calum's, different from the reflection on past events, but just as remote from daily living.

Let me give you two examples. There is a simple contract called a stipulation, a formal question and answer. The only rule you need to know about it is the stipulation, or promise of an impossibility. I am buying Calum's slave and I say in the form of a stipulation, 'Do you promise the slave is healthy?' Calum promises. What is the result? If a slave is healthy the stipulation was unnecessary because no action can arise. If the slave was unhealthy, the stipulation is void because it was a promise of an impossibility, but you can see that this is very far removed from general reality. The second example does to a limited extent involve reality. Barter had no good remedy, strangely enough.

Sale, on the other hand, had. One school of jurists, the Sabinians, tried to claim that sale and barter were the same thing. The argument for this was a text of Homer and they were refuted by the other school who also used a text of Homer to prove that the Sabinians were mistranslating the original. No mechanism appeared to resolve disputes among jurists, and like us academics, the jurists continually had differences of opinion. When Justinian in the sixth century CE decided to codify Roman law, he issued fifty decisions. These were to resolve fifty major outstanding disputes which had been existing in the classical period over three hundred years before. Any jurist, as a public servant, could have said to the emperor, 'Let's have a ruling on this. Let's settle the issue'. But they did not bother because the prestige was entirely dependent on what other jurists thought. So here is another important legal system, I think, where the law is not developing from a consideration of the present existing conditions in society. Calum's approach does not seem to me to have anything of the absurd in it or anything of the implausible. Whether it is right or not is a separate issue.

Douglas: This sounds very congenial to the anthropologists' tradition of interpreting a law and also Malinowski's interpretations of legends. I do not really see that these two examples are so remote as you make out. There are other questions that you would need to ask in order to show that this is different from what one might have expected, but anthropologists would find it quite intelligible. The changes that go on in people's heads who are contesting for power in some small secluded anteroom of actual common life, seem to be very nice.

Watson: On that basis we would be saying all sociologists of law are naive because they all claim a strong relationship between the existing law and the society in which it operates.

Douglas: Why is it remote though, to have a probability or possibility at this point which happens to be very close and why is it remote to say that barter has no remedy? Surely barter is really very difficult to identify the value or equivalence of.

Davies: I have always been interested by Calum's theories and the question which has always followed is 'How would you disprove it?'

Carmichael: All one ever does is present a hypothesis and one makes an assumption. One then presents the evidence and the only question one can ask is 'Does the hypothesis work?' I find it works with every rule in the whole of the Pentateuch. That still does not make the hypothesis correct, but at least it is out in the open in terms of the assumptions I make, the evidence I present, the consistency I am able to produce, the details I am able to work with, the linguistic problems that have never been solved, and so on. It still does not make the hypothesis correct but that is all one can do.

Jackson: A detailed version of that question would be: granted the assumption that you make, which has been generated by the accumulation of the work that you have done in this way, that all laws are explicable in this way in the Pentateuch, do you actually find that the evidence for some of them is stronger than the evidence for others? If you do, could you categorize what makes the evidence stronger in some cases than others?

Carmichael: No, I find that on every rule I can produce similar detailed connections and similar linguistic evidence.

Jackson: Have you an example standing out as being stronger or weaker than any other?

Carmichael: Not clearly in terms of the evidence I am able to produce, but that is because of not being sharp enough to produce all the evidence. The more I work, the more evidence I am able to produce.

Douglas: Can you tell us your assumptions?

Carmichael: The assumption is that the topics that have been taken up in the rules are derived from issues and problems that are found in the narratives. The question is why do we find this integration of legal material into a narrative structure? From that point of view it is not a wild hypothesis.

Maccoby: It seems to result in some very unlikely laws, for example, לא תאכלו על הדם, according to you, means, 'Do not sit down for a meal before committing murder'. What kind of a law is that?

Carmichael: The rule is a very cryptic one. That has to be recognized, and many of these rules have a proverbial character to them. 'Don't plough with an ox and an ass together (Deut. 22.10).' This one, not to eat over the blood, also has a proverbial character because these rules are intended to recall historical memory. These rules belong to a much later period of time and the whole point of them is that the people who had to understand them had to tune in to the particular historical problems and circumstances that ancient Israelites were giving them. So one has to put oneself into the position of those who first received the rules, so that they engage in the process of historical memory: just as the Passover rules are involved in the past events of the nation's history. That is true of many of these rules and that explains why some of them do have a cryptic, proverbial character. One can never generalize. On this basis, take the rule, 'Don't plough with an ox and an ass together', which I think is referring to a complaint about Jacob's rather complacent attitude about Shechem, the son of the ass, ploughing in a sexual sense, with the daughter of the ox, who is the Israelite (Gen. 34). I do not wish to generalize this rule and say that it is a prohibition against intermarriage with the Hittites, even though in another part of Deuteronomy you do find such an explicit general rule stated. The whole point of these proverbial cryptic-type laws is that they are zeroing in on a particular aspect of the history.

Jackson: I am not sure that I would endorse what Calum has said about the pervasive incredulity of the theory. I personally am selectively sympathetic to it, but I do see some of the cases more plausible than others. The underlying theoretical issue is this: the strangeness of it is that you are offering us a very unique form of symbolization, I think. If you are saying that this is the way in which the lawgiver is seeking to evoke historic memories, among the audience, of narrative elements in the cultural tradition, if you think of it in those terms, this is not the only way in which a lawgiver in this tradition uses laws in order to evoke amongst the people memories of historical aspects of the cultural tradition. There are far more direct ways of symbolization. Take the Passover, in which you are told, 'Do this'. After all, this is the basis of much of the ritual law, according to the traditional and explicit understanding of it. You are told you shall do this and that in relation to the Passover so that you shall remember that the

Lord brought you and your fathers out of Egypt. My question would be this: Does the process of symbolization that you are offering us have the same function? Is this a legitimate parallel that I am drawing and if it is, why did they need the second book?

Carmichael: I think you are making a fundamental error, namely you think that this material might have been written for later readers of the material. Presumably when these laws were written down, they were written in conjunction with handling the narrative material. I know nothing and I do not think anyone else knows anything about the purpose as to why these laws were set out. If there was an original audience, there is no way in which I can see how one can get into that subject. It has to be repeated that it is naive to think that this material was written for anybody afterwards. That it later became something called the Bible is another matter but I am not interested in discussing that. It is crucial in my scheme and I think it is much less mystifying that these rules were set down with the relative narratives in front of the people who were working on them. This seems to me a very reasonable assumption. Your position, I think, is getting in the way, because you think the material was written for you—but it is not.

INTERPRETING LEVITICUS IN THE SECOND TEMPLE PERIOD: STRUGGLING WITH AMBIGUITY

Hannah K. Harrington

The scroll of Leviticus was crucial for determining correct cultic procedures in the Second Temple at Jerusalem. However, dependence on Leviticus for the operation of the Temple, even in connection with the rest of the Pentateuch, required filling in many gaps in the system where the text does not give explicit instructions. The challenge was to fill in these gaps in accordance with Scripture. Whereas the original audience of Leviticus no doubt had traditions complementing the sacred text, Jewish groups of the late Second Temple period were divided as to proper interpretation. In this paper I will look at a sampling of ambiguous laws in Leviticus and provide interpretations from the chief Jewish denominations of this period. My aim is threefold: (1) to emphasize the vital importance of Leviticus in Second Temple Judaism; (2) to show that the ambiguous nature of Leviticus will support more than one interpretation in many cases; (3) to bring into relief the agenda of the Qumran Community and the early sages revealed in the way in which each group filled in the gaps of the text.

The Book of Leviticus is important for any study of Second Temple Judaism for two reasons. First, it was considered by all Jewish groups of this period to be sacred text, the very word of God, and thus its laws were taken seriously. Secondly, the book is about access to God through holiness, a central concept in Judaism. It is this second aspect which I would like to examine here.

Holiness in Leviticus

The term קדוש, or 'holy', is generally defined as 'set apart, separate, withdrawn from common use'.[1] Leviticus 20.26 reads, 'You shall be

1. J. Milgrom, *Leviticus 1–16* (AB, 3; Garden City, NY: Doubleday, 1991), p. 730.

holy to me; for I the LORD am holy, and have separated you from the peoples that you should be mine.' Thus, holiness in Leviticus requires an emulation of God and separation from those who are not God's people.

However, there are levels of holiness. First there is holiness which describes the character of God, who has a totally different essence than human beings. His holy house is the sanctuary, and gifts are brought to him there at his holy altar. Holiness emanates from this place because it emanates from God who lives there. The fire on the altar is a visible representation of God's presence; it originated from him and therefore is holy (Lev. 9.24).

Next, there is the holy priesthood, which is not as holy as God but which is designated קדוש in Leviticus since it is set apart for the work of the sanctuary. The priest's lifestyle is circumscribed by greater responsibility and requirements than the lay Israelite. As a primary task, Israel's priests must guard and maintain the sanctuary, providing access to God for Israel through the medium of sacrifices on the altar. The holy fire must never go out (Lev. 6.12).

Finally, God's presence depends not only on the holiness of his priests but on the relative holiness of all Israel. All Israelites are commanded to be holy (Lev. 20.26). They are to be separate from other nations both in belief and behavior. Thus, holiness is not an innate condition inherent in one's classification as a priest or Israelite. The power of the human will is essential to the creation of holiness in this world. God defines and requires holiness, but its actualization is under human control.[2]

The question Leviticus seeks to answer is: How does Israel become holy? To be sure, ethics is important to the acquisition of holiness and Leviticus contains many explicitly ethical commandments. 'Do not hold a grudge' (19.18), 'Love your neighbor as yourself' (19.18), and 'Do not withhold your employee's wages' (19.13) are all part of the acquisition of holiness according to Leviticus. Holiness clearly requires

2. Milgrom, *Leviticus 1–16*, p. 724. Note that sacrifices become holy only when the Israelites designate them as such; H. Eilberg-Schwartz claims that the Bible requires no intention in the observance of its purity and sacrificial laws, *The Human Will in Judaism: The Mishnah's Philosophy of Intention* (Atlanta: Scholars Press, 1986), pp. 101, 173, 224 n.24; cf. J. Milgrom, *Studies in Cultic Theology and Terminology* (Leiden: Brill, 1983), pp. 160-62, on the power of intention in Lev. 6.18.

godly activity within society. However, is ethics enough to ensure God's holy presence in Israel?

Surprisingly, the majority of laws in this book concern the sanctuary, its priests and matters of ritual purity. God's holy sanctuary can be violated not only by ethical sins but also by incorrect ritual procedures. Nadab and Abihu were killed by an infraction of cultic procedures. They offered 'strange fire' before the Lord (Lev. 10.1). Additionally, anyone who eats the blood of any animal is to be 'cut off' from God's people (Lev. 7.27). Anyone who eats or even touches a שלמים sacrifice, a peace or well-being offering, when he is impure (e.g. from sexual intercourse or contact with a dead body) is also cut off from God's people (Lev. 7.20). Lev. 15.31, a verse concluding the section on ritual purity, states that Israelites will die if they fail to cleanse themselves from impurity. Thus, Israel must keep God's ritual laws as meticulously as his moral law in order to ensure God's continued presence among Israel.

Finally, holiness in Leviticus is a force which actively opposes impurity. Mary Douglas, in her work on defilement, recognizes the dynamic of impurity which threatens to unleash its force on society.[3] Conversely, in Leviticus, holiness is a countering force at war with the forces of all impurity. It is the holiness of the Israelites that effects the divine presence among them and ensures success (Lev. 18.24; 20.23-26; cf. the War Camp of Deut. 23.14). It is the high degree of holiness of the high priest, effected not only by genealogy but by especially strict requirements (Lev. 21.10-15), that enables him to officiate in the presence of the divine glory (Lev. 16.2, 32; cf. Exod. 40.34-35). It is the elaborate sacrifices of the Day of Atonement as well as the confession and repentance of the people which brings God's forgiveness for all of the unintentional infractions of the previous year (Lev. 16.1-34).

With the recognition of what was at stake, the priesthood of the Second Temple had to observe correct cultic procedures and follow the sacred guidelines of Leviticus carefully. Where the text was ambiguous or did not yield sufficient information it had to be probed carefully and filled in so that the temple cult could be conducted properly. Other books of the Torah were probed in the same manner, one sometimes resolving the ambiguity of another. Often no information was

3. M. Douglas, *In the Wilderness: The Doctrine of Defilement in the Book of Numbers* (JSOTSup, 159; Sheffield: JSOT Press, 1993), pp. 22-23.

available. Here it was up to the interpreter to suggest a ruling in keeping with the principles of the Torah. It is in these 'fill-ins' of the Torah that a group's particular bias comes into sharp relief. How a group resolves textual ambiguity reveals its special perspective.[4]

Second Temple Interpreters

We have considerable information extant on the way in which two major Jewish groups in the late Second Temple era interpreted Leviticus. The first group is commonly assumed to be the predecessors of the rabbis of the Mishnah, the Pharisees. I maintain that the Pharisees are the spiritual ancestors of the rabbis because (1) the characterization in the Gospels of their beliefs and practices accords largely with the laws of the Mishnah and Tosefta[5] and (2) several arguments between the Pharisees and the Sadducees or the Boethusians, which are recorded in the Mishnah, are in fact recorded earlier in the Dead Sea Scrolls between the Qumran sectarians and their opponents.[6] The sectarians often share the views of the Sadducees or Boethusians and their opponents often share the views of the Pharisees and later rabbis.

The second group is the sect represented by the Qumran community. I do not use the terms 'sect' or 'sectarian' pejoratively but

4. D. Boyarin, *Intertextuality and the Reading of Midrash* (Bloomington: Indiana University Press, 1990), p. 8; cf. also Boyarin's identification of ambiguity in Exod. 15.22-26 regarding the Waters of Marah and its analysis in the Mekilta. Boyarin says,

> ... [T]he Mekilta is aware of true ambiguities in the biblical narrative, and that while each of the rabbinic readers it presents works towards reduction of the ambiguity, the cumulative effect of the midrash as compiled is to focus on the ambiguity and the possibilities for making meaning out of it ('Inner Biblical Ambiguity, Intertextuality and the Dialectic of Midrash: the Waters of Marah', *Prooftexts* 10 [1990], pp. 29-48).

Cf. also M. Sternberg on gaps in the biblical text, *The Poetics of Biblical Narrative* (Bloomington: Indiana University Press, 1985), pp. 186-222.

5. Both Mishnah-Tosefta and the Gospels depict the Pharisees as Jews who placed great emphasis on tithing and ritual purity, cf. Mt. 23.23-25; Mk 7.3-4; Lk. 11.38-39; *m. Dem.* 2.2-3; *m. Toh.* 4.12; *m. Kel.* 2.1; *t. Dem.* 2.2.

6. Y. Sussmann, 'The History of the Halakha and the Dead Sea Scrolls', in *Discoveries in the Judean Desert*, X (ed. E. Qimron and J. Strugnell; Oxford: Clarendon Press, 1994), pp. 187-200; E. Qimron and J. Strugnell, 'An Unpublished Halakhic Letter from Qumran', in J. Amits (ed.), *Biblical Archaeology Today* (Jerusalem: Israel Exploration Society, 1985), p. 402.

merely to identify the Qumran community as a group of Jews who, because of their particular beliefs and practices, physically seceded from the established cult and society in Jerusalem in the centuries before the turn of the era.[7]

The scrolls found at Qumran reveal a decided congruence in the area of cultic procedures and purity matters thereby justifying reference to a fairly consistent sectarian stance in these areas. This agreement is perhaps most apparent on the issue of the sanctity of Jerusalem. Several texts insist that the entire city of Jerusalem is holy (cf. 11QT 52.19; 47.4; 4QMMT B 63; CD 12.1-2). The way the scrolls propose to guard holy areas too is distinctive to the sect. The Messianic Rule and the Temple Scroll both require at least a three-day purification for impure persons before entering into the sacred assembly or the holy city, respectively (1QSa 1.25-26; 11QT 45.7-12). The Temple Scroll and 4QMMT ban the physically impaired from Jerusalem (11QT 45.12-14; 4QMMT B 42-57). This ban is echoed in the interdict on handicapped persons joining the holy war camp of the War Scroll (1QM 7.3-5). The Temple Scroll and the Damascus Document prohibit sexual intercourse within Jerusalem (11QT 45.11-12; CD 12.1-2). Also, the hides of carcasses (of both pure and impure animals) are not to be brought into Jerusalem according to both the Temple Scroll and 4QMMT (11QT 51.1-6; 4QMMT B 21-26).

Thus, since these texts agree that Jerusalem is so imbued with the holiness of the Temple that priestly laws must apply to the entire city,

7. Against the view that this community was a group of Essenes, based on Josephus' description, some scholars now consider the group to be a type of Sadducees, cf. L.H. Schiffman, 'Sacral and Non-Sacral Slaughter according to the *Temple Scroll*', in D. Dimant and L.H. Schiffman (ed.), *Time to Prepare the Way in the Wilderness* (Leiden: Brill, 1995), p. 71. If the sect is Sadducean, its members should definitely not be confused with the Hellenistic compromising Sadducees of the priestly aristocracy. As Ya'akov Sussmann suggests, perhaps these Sadducean priests seceded from the Jerusalem establishment expressly because of the laxity of their colleagues; cf. Sussmann, 'History of the Halakah', p. 199. However the sect is characterized, it is clear that its *laws* have many affinities to the Sadducean position, cf. Y. Yadin, *The Temple Scroll*, I (Jerusalem: The Israel Exploration Society, 1983), pp. 340-41; J.M. Baumgarten, 'The Pharisaic–Sadducean Controversies about Purity and the Qumran Texts', *JJS* 31 (1980) pp. 157-70; D.R. Schwartz, 'Law and Truth: On Qumran-Sadducean and Rabbinic Views of Law', in D. Dimant and U. Rappaport (ed.), *The Dead Sea Scrolls: Forty Years of Research* (Leiden: Brill, 1992), p. 229.

it is justified to speak of this unique position as a sectarian principle held by the community at Qumran.[8] This agreement is in contradistinction to the sect's opponents, who regarded Jerusalem as holy but at a much lower level than the sanctuary, a view also reflected in Tannaitic literature (*m. Kel.* 1.8; *t. Kel.* BQ 1.12; *Sifre Num.* 1[4]).

The scrolls are also in agreement that the ordinary cities of Israel had to follow stringent purity laws, although not to the degree of Jerusalem. All Israel is supposed to eat in a state of ritual purity, and drink is even more susceptible to impurity than food (11QT 49.7-12; 4Q514 ll. 4, 7-10; 4Q274 ll. 3, 5, 8; 4QMMT B 57-61; 1QS 6.16-21; *Wars* 2.137-38; 4QLeqet). Most items in an ordinary house are susceptible to impurity, including vessels of wood and stone (11QT 49.14-15; CD 12.15-18) and thus must be properly immersed after coming into contact with impure items. The scrolls, as a whole, reject the concept of *tebul yom*, held by its opponents and the later rabbis, whereby persons who have contracted a minor impurity may be allowed free access in the ordinary sphere as soon as they immerse in water. The sect did not allow such access until sundown (4Q277 ll. 5, 13; 4QMMT B 18, 75; 11QT 45.7-8; 49.19-21; 51.4-5).[9]

These cultic and purity restrictions are common to the scrolls but are in direct opposition to later rabbinic halakha. Thus, the rabbinic position regarding Temple practices may very well have been in practice in the late Second Temple period and vigorously fought by the

8. Yadin, *The Temple Scroll*, I, pp. 278-81 suggested that this view stems from Isa. 52.1 where the prophet hopes for the day when all impurity will be excluded from Jerusalem: 'Awake, awake, O Jerusalem, the holy city... for there shall no more come into you the uncircumcised and the unclean.' The Qumran sect evidently took this passage to refer to ritual as well as moral purity and so embraced stringent laws to keep impure and purifying persons out of Jerusalem, including the prohibition of sexual intercourse in the city. Yadin suggested that this text might be the source of the sect's celibate tendency. See also 2 Chron. 11.8 for another possible trace of the attitude excluding women from Jerusalem.

9. Other claims agreed upon among the Scrolls on cultic matters, against the rabbinic position, are: the giving of animal tithes and fourth year fruit to the priests (11QT 60.1-5; 4QMMT B 65-67; 4Q251, frag. 3, l. 9); the treatment of a bone as impure as a full corpse (11QT 50.4-6; 4QMMT B 76-77); the insistence that שלמים must be eaten by sundown on the day of sacrifice (11QT 20.12-13; 4QMMT B 12-14); the complaint of slaughter performed outside the 'camp' (4QMMT B 30-31; 11QT 52.13-16).

writers of the Scrolls since several of the Qumran texts refer to the same grievances.[10]

The Bible, the sectarian Dead Sea Scrolls and the Mishnah compare roughly on the issue of holy space as follows. The sectarians apply the biblical laws of the sanctuary to the whole city of Jerusalem. The rabbis limit these laws to the temple alone. Where the Torah establishes a regulation for 'the camp', the sectarians apply the law to all the cities of Israel. The rabbis apply the laws to the city of Jerusalem only.[11] The table below illustrates this comparison:

Bible	*Qumran*	*Rabbis*
Sanctuary (priests)	Temple City	Sanctuary
Camp (laity)	Ordinary City	Jerusalem

Ambiguity in Leviticus

In an effort to reveal the biases of the two major Jewish groups of the late Second Temple era discussed above, I will now examine examples of ambiguity from three major sections of Leviticus: cultic law, ritual purity and marital purity.

Cultic Law

Several ambiguities are present in the cultic laws of Leviticus. One example concerns the חטאת, or purification offering, brought by the sinner. According to Lev. 5.5, sinners must first confess the sin they have committed before presenting an offering. However, the text does not state to whom they should confess—the priest? God? themselves? The sectarians opt for the priest (CD 9.13), the rabbis allow the sinner's confession to be private and inaudible (*b. Sot.* 32b; *y. Yeb.* 8.3).[12]

According to Lev. 14.10-20, the leper brings cereal and drink offerings with his חטאת. Does this mean that all sinners should bring these accompanying offerings or just the leper? The sectarians reason that the leper brings these accompaniments because he is a sinner. Therefore,

10. L.H. Schiffman, 'Qumran and Rabbinic Halakhah', in S. Talmon (ed.), *Jewish Civilization in the Hellenistic-Roman Period* (JSPSup, 10; Sheffield: JSOT Press, 1991), pp. 138-46.

11. Yadin, *The Temple Scroll*, I, pp. 278-79; *Sifre Num.* 1[4]; *t. Kel.* BQ 1.12; cf. also *m. Kel.* 1.8-9; *b. Zeb.* 116b.

12. However, if there are injured parties, confession must be made to them, *t. Ta'an* 1.8; cf. Philo, *Spec. Leg.* 1.235.

all sinners must bring the accompaniments (11QT 25.12-15).[13] The rabbis disagree viewing the leper as a special case (*m. Men.* 9.6).

A connected matter is the usage of the hides of a slaughtered animal. If it was not slaughtered for the altar, the hide of an animal was considered part of an unclean carcass.[14] The rabbis argued that the hide was not a part of the carcass and so hides from any animal could be used to make flasks and vessels (*m. Ḥul.* 9.1). However, the Qumran community forbade the making of vessels for use in Jerusalem out of skins of animals which were not first slaughtered for the altar (11QT 47.7-18; 4QMMT B 21-22). The Temple Scroll states: 'All the purity of the Temple you shall bring in Temple skins' (11QT 47.17). This was not only the view of the sectarians but was actual practice in Jerusalem under Antiochus III according to Josephus:

> And out of reverence for the Temple he [Antiochus III] also published a proclamation throughout the entire kingdom, of which the contents were as follows, '... Nor shall anyone bring into the city the flesh of horses or of mules or of wild or tame asses... or, in general, of any animals forbidden to the Jews. Nor is it lawful to bring in their skins... or even to feed any of these animals in the city. But only the sacrificial animals known to their ancestors and necessary for the preparation of God shall they be permitted to use' (*Ant.* 12.16).

Another ambiguity concerns the fruit of trees in their fourth year. Lev. 19.24 explains that although for its first three years, one may not eat the fruit of a tree, the fruit of four-year-old trees is 'holy, an offering of praise to the LORD'. What does this mean? May the owner eat it? Must it be given to the priest? Should it be left alone? The rabbis regard this fruit as similar to the Deuteronomic tithe which the offerer brings to the sanctuary and eats there rejoicing in the presence of God (Deut. 14.26). The Qumran community however focuses on the term 'holy' which must mean, as with the holy tithe of the tithe in Numbers 18, the item belongs to the priests (4QMMT B 62; cf. Num. 18.25-32).

In fact, the sectarians greatly increase priestly sacrificial food as compared with the interpretation of the rabbis. The sect held that all butchering of sheep, goats and cattle had to be sacrificial with proper

13. Yadin, *The Temple Scroll*, I, p. 145. Indeed all burnt offerings were accompanied by cereal and drink offerings.

14. Milgrom, *Leviticus*, I, p. 681.

priestly portions taken out before the offerers could eat of them. This is clearly based on Lev. 17.3-4 which states:

> If any man of the house of Israel kills an ox or a lamb or a goat in the camp, or kills it outside the camp, and does not bring it to the door of the tent of meeting, to offer it as a gift to the LORD before the tabernacle of the LORD, bloodguilt shall be imputed to that man; he has shed blood; and that man shall be cut off from among his people.

By contrast, Deut. 12.21 concedes that when the Israelites settle in the land of Canaan they do not have to come to the sanctuary to slaughter every cow, sheep or goat they eat. Rather, if the sanctuary is too far, they may slaughter these animals in their towns. The Temple Scroll is aware of the Deuteronomic law and interprets 'too far' as more than a three-day journey from Jerusalem (11QT 52.13-15).[15] This, in effect, prefers the Leviticus text over Deuteronomy because a three-day radius from Jerusalem would include most of the towns of Israel. The rabbis, by contrast, allowed profane slaughtering (from which no priestly portions are taken) outside of Jerusalem (*Sifre Deut.* 71[134]).[16]

In addition to the amount of sacrifices to be offered, the sect also increases the portions of these animals to be given to the priests. Leviticus designates the right thigh and the breast of all Israelite שלמים for the priests (Lev. 7.33). Deuteronomy requires the shoulder, jowls and inner parts of all firstborn animals to be given to the priests (Deut. 18.3). Thus, according to the sectarians, Israelites should add the two requirements giving the following portions to the sanctuary from every offering they bring: right thigh, breast, jowls, inner parts and, as a portion for the Levites, the shoulder.[17] These laws granting greater food portions to the priests arise from differences between the texts of Leviticus and Deuteronomy which the sect resolves according to its priestly bias.

15. Schiffman too notes the motive of the writer of the Temple Scroll to make all slaughtering within a three-day radius of Jerusalem sacral. See his analysis of the sect's interpretation in 'Sacral and Non-Sacral Slaughter', pp. 76-83.

16. According to Yadin it was originally forbidden to eat non-sacrificial meat in Jerusalem in the early Second Temple era but this was later abolished, Yadin, *The Temple Scroll*, I, p. 319; *t. Nid.* 9.18; cf. *m. Ma'as. Sh.* 1.9-10.

17. See Yadin's comments on this, *The Temple Scroll*, I, p. 154. For the Levitic shoulder portion see Milgrom, 'The Shoulder for the Levites', at the end of Yadin's discussion, pp. 169-76.

Ritual Purity

In the area of ritual purity, three examples of ambiguity suffice. Unclean foods are clearly defined in Leviticus 11. However, what about the insignificant gnat? Is it too prohibited because it is a flying insect with legs? What about larvae? According to the sectarians (CD 12.11-13) even gnats and larvae must be avoided. The rabbis draw the line with these items stating that it is not necessary to strain gnats and larvae out of juices (*m. Ter.* 7.11).

Another concern was the type of cooking pots and vessels which, if contaminated by an unclean carcass, would contaminate all food within them. Lev. 11.32 states, 'And anything upon which any of them (8 creeping creatures) falls when they are dead shall be unclean, whether it is a כלי, an article, of wood or a garment or a skin or a sack, any vessel that is used for any purpose; it must be put into water'. Verse 33 adds earthenware to this list of susceptible כלים. Does this mean that only items made of wood, leather, fabric or clay are susceptible to impurity? Or are all types of כלים included and these materials just examples? The rabbis limit susceptible items to a few materials which form usable receptacles on the basis of this verse.[18] The sectarians regard even stone items to be susceptible, including stone floors (hardly usable receptacles) and stone pots (CD 12.15-18; 11QT 49.13-16; 50.16-17).

With regard to the impurity of the leper, again questions arise. In Lev. 13.45 the leper is ordered to cover his upper lip and cry, 'Impure, impure.' Verse 46 states that the leper should 'dwell alone outside the camp'. Does this mean, apart from all other lepers? Should the leper be confined? According to the Qumran sectarians the meaning of the leper's call, 'Impure, impure', is that the leper is impure even to those who are impure. Thus, they insist on the leper's solitary confinement outside the camp (11QT 46.16-18; 48.14-15; 4Q276 2). The rabbis too restrict lepers outside of city walls but evidently allow them free mobility (*m. Kel.* 1.7; *b. Zeb.* 117a; *b. Pes.* 66b-67a; *Sifre Num.* 5.2). Judging from the Gospel narratives, lepers had to stay outside of the cities but were apparently not confined (cf. Mk 1.40-45; Lk. 7.22; 17.11-19).

18. Note also that the metal items listed in Num. 31.22 are impure. A good analysis of the rabbinic position is found in J. Neusner, *Purity in Rabbinic Judaism: A Systematic Account* (Atlanta: Scholars Press, 1994), pp. 120-22.

Marital Purity

Leviticus 18 provides examples of ambiguity in the area of marital purity. Lev. 18.13 reads: 'You shall not have sexual relations with your mother's sister, for she is your mother's near kinswoman.' Thus, marriage with one's aunt was strictly forbidden. The sectarians of Qumran made the inference here that also the marriage of a man and his niece was forbidden since it is the same type of relationship (CD 5.7-11; 11QT 66.14-15). Indeed if the subject in v. 13 includes both the male and the female, the marriage of a woman and her uncle would be explicitly forbidden. However, the rabbis, who allowed and even encouraged marriage between a man and his niece, were evidently of the opinion that if the Torah wished to exclude such a marriage it would have explicitly stated so.[19]

Another ambiguity in the marital laws concerns polygamy and divorce. Lev. 18.18 reads, 'And you shall not take a woman as a rival wife to her sister, having sexual relations with her while her sister is yet alive.' The ambiguity here is regarding the intention of the law: Is the law merely forbidding a man to marry two sisters or does it mean to curb strife arising from any rival wife? According to the sect the Torah's real concern must be the rivalrous nature of women, not necessarily sisters, in a polygamous family and so polygamy was completely forbidden.

The exegetical moves here are apparent in the Temple Scroll. The author sets forth the Deuteronomic instructions for the king's lifestyle, in particular, that he should not 'multiply wives' (Deut. 17.17). However, he then reverts to Leviticus for explanation of this law and states,

> He shall not take a wife from among all the daughters of the nations, but instead take for himself a wife from his father's house from his father's family [cf. Lev. 22.13; 21.14]. He shall take no other wife apart from her because only she will be with him all the days of her life [cf. Lev. 18.18] (11QT 57.15-18).

This attitude toward polygamy is also supported by the Damascus Document which appeals to the monogamous precedents of Adam and

19. Cf. *Code of Maimonides* (trans. H. Danby; Yale Judaica Series; New Haven, CT: Yale University Press, 1954), *Laws Concerning Forbidden Intercourse* 2.14; L.H. Schiffman, 'Laws Pertaining to Women', in Dimant and Rappaport (ed.), *The Dead Sea Scrolls*, p. 227, states that like the Qumran sectarians most ancient Jewish sects banned man–niece marriages.

Noah to support its prohibition of polygamy (CD 4.20–5.1).

The sect also appears to have prohibited divorce, or at least remarriage after divorce, since the text states that a man is under obligation to his wife as long as she is alive (11QT 57.17-18). By contrast, although differing opinions existed, the rabbis allowed both polygamy and divorce based on other texts in the Torah (Deut. 21.15-17; 24.1-3) limiting Lev. 18.18 to the forbidden marriage of a man to two sisters.[20]

Conflicting Motives

From the above examples of resolutions to ambiguity in Leviticus the biases of the Qumran community and the Pharisees come into sharp relief. I will now examine these two ideologies to try to discover what motivates them. First, let me examine the position of the Qumran sectarians. Quite clearly the sect held stricter interpretations than their opponents on the subjects of cult and purity. The question I wish to raise is why? Why should any Jewish group seek to intensify the laws of the Torah at every turn? Isn't the Torah demanding enough? Why increase the already substantial requirements of the cult? Where the Torah does not make explicit demands, why is it necessary to create them?

I would suggest the answer lies in the ideological starting point of the Qumran community. The writers of the Dead Sea Scrolls were, in large part, priests.[21] The scrolls reveal a primary concern for the Zadokite genealogy of the priesthood, the correct priestly calendar, the behavior of priests in the sanctuary, the proper conduct of the cult and ritual purity and the contributions and respect accorded to priests by the people of Israel.[22]

20. The Mishnah sets the limit of wives at 18, *m. Sanh.* 2.4; cf. *t. Sanh.* 4.5.

21. See L.H. Schiffman, 'The Temple Scroll and the Systems of Jewish Law of the Second Temple Period', in G.J. Brooke (ed.), *Temple Scroll Studies* (Sheffield: JSOT Press, 1989), p. 252, who states, 'It is most likely that the sect was founded by disaffected priests who left the Jerusalem Temple after the Maccabean revolt when the Zadokite High Priests were displaced by the Hasmoneans.' See also D.R. Schwartz, 'On Two Aspects of a Priestly View of Descent at Qumran', in J.T. Barrera and L.V. Montaner (ed.), *The Madrid Qumran Congress: Proceedings of the International Congress on the Dead Sea Scrolls, Madrid*, II (Leiden: Brill, 1992), p. 158.

22. D. Dimant refers to the Qumran community as a 'temple-like' community

The chief objective of the priests, as stated above, was to ensure the sanctity of the sanctuary. The greatest threat to the sanctuary was not physical assault from outside but impurity resulting from within Israel. If God was pleased with his house, he would reside there. He would fight the people of Israel's battles for them and give them health and prosperity. If he was not pleased, he would leave Israel defenseless or worse go to war against her. In the sect's view, it was better to be safe than sorry. Mary Douglas has written, 'Purity is the enemy of change, of ambiguity and compromise.'[23] For the sectarians, purity was a weapon which could neutralize ambiguity in the Torah.[24]

The above rationale accounts for the strict attitude of the Qumran sectarians toward impurity, giving it a wide berth, as it were. However, what about the cases of stricture where the text could easily have been interpreted more leniently? Why, for example, do the scrolls maintain that the sanctity of the Temple must be extended to all of Jerusalem? Since the prophets often use impurity as a metaphor for idolatry, why did the sectarians insist on such a physical notion of impurity? Why, for example, did they wish to impose a three day wait on all purifying persons entering Jerusalem (11QT 45.11-12)?

Here I would like to suggest a converse principle. Just as impurity is a threatening force not to be underestimated by legal acrobats seeking loopholes, so also the power of sacrifices, holy gifts to the priest, and purifications is not to be underestimated. The latter items will increase God's presence, power and blessing among Israel. Sacrifices are not just an obedient response to God's laws. They are powerful. In the sect's view, the greater the gifts to God, the greater God's blessing.

which intended to recreate the level of sanctity of the priests on duty in the Temple. She refers to (1) the meals of the community conducted in priestly purity; (2) the organization of the group on the model of the holy Israelite camp in the wilderness; (3) their self-reference as 'a holy house'; and (4) their exclusion of handicapped persons from the community; '4Q Florilegium and the Idea of the Community as Temple', in A. Caquot *et al.* (ed.), *Hellenica et Judaica* (Leuven: Editions Peeters, 1986), p. 188.

23. M. Douglas, *Purity and Danger* (Harmondsworth: Penguin Books, 1970), p. 191.

24. For a good analysis of the sect's exegetical techniques, see J. Milgrom, 'The Qumran Cult: Its Exegetical Principles', in Brooke (ed.), *Temple Scroll Studies*, pp. 171-75, especially his discussion of the sect's 'homogenization' or 'equalization' of all scriptural data on a given subject, similar to the rabbis' *binyan ab* technique.

The Pharisees, on the other hand, as lay exegetes of the Torah, regard this attitude as a cover for excessive priestly authority and economic gain. For example, if every sheep, goat and cow slaughtered within three days of Jerusalem must first be a sacrifice, the priestly dinner table will be greatly over-supplied, since substantial portions of each sacrifice must be given to the priests. If all fruit in its fourth year must be given to the priests, its owners will be put under hardship only to benefit the priests. Priestly control over all of Jerusalem seemed scripturally unwarranted to the Pharisees and served only the power-hungry priests.

The Pharisees, while they did regard impurity as a threatening force which must be continually guarded against and neutralized by purification, were committed to living within the extremely diverse society, comprised of Greek or Roman rulers, Jews and foreigners, in late second Temple Jerusalem. Clearly impurity according to biblical definitions was everywhere. Non-Jews could not be expected to keep the purity laws of Leviticus. In fact, often Jews could not trust each other in this matter. The common people could not be trusted to separate tithes in purity or to keep food pure (*m. Dem.* 2.3; *t. Dem.* 2.2, 20-22).[25] So the Pharisees were confronted with the sure possibility of contamination on a daily basis. Mark tells us that they bathed every time they returned from the market (Mk 7.4). Unlike the Qumran sect, which opted to move to the desert away from this society, the Pharisees were bombarded regularly with impurity, carcasses on the roadside, funeral processions, passersby who had not bathed after sexual intercourse, and vessels containing food and possibly also an unclean insect or two. The possibilities for contamination were numerous and often unavoidable.

Additionally, if all Jerusalem must maintain the holiness of the sanctuary, as the priestly sectarians claimed, the implications for society would be astronomical. Women would not be allowed to reside there, making Jerusalem a celibate city. All visitors to the city who may have contracted even a minor impurity would have to spend at least three days outside the city before entering. This view simply was not practical.

25. A. Oppenheimer, *The ʿAm ha-ʾAretz: A Study in the Social History of the Jewish People in the Hellenistic-Roman Period* (trans. B. Levine; Leiden: Brill, 1977), pp. 61-62.

However, rather than ignoring or avoiding their social situation, the early Sages set about to enable Jews to maintain purity in such a socio-political environment. To that end, definitions of the biblical laws were limited as far and as precisely as possible. Without an intellectual framework which could accommodate both the Scripture's laws as well as the facts of life under foreign domination, the Pharisees could not retain the confidence of fulfilling Scripture's demands.

The Pharisees had a slightly different attitude to the Torah than the priestly sectarians. For the latter, authority did not have to be achieved; it was a given based on priestly genealogy.[26] As sons of Aaron, their authority came by birth. However, the Pharisees could claim their authority only by their expertise in the law. According to one tradition of the Talmud, the rabbis are said to have once been in such a fierce struggle against a particular priestly decision that they even disagreed with God and locked him out of their deliberations. At the close of their analysis of the law, God is said to have chuckled like a proud parent and agreed with them saying, 'My sons have defeated me' (*b. B. Meṣ* 59b). This attitude does not appeal to priestly genealogy or the cult for support but to the law, and it considers even God's activity to be circumscribed by the Torah and its human interpretation.

The Pharisees view holiness as powerful but not so powerful that it was inaccessible to lay Israelites. They encouraged lay participation in the festivals in the Temple courts and acknowledged the legitimacy of the Court of the Women. On festivals, they even had the sacred objects brought out into full view of the people standing in the courts or on surrounding rooftops (*m. Sukk.* 4.5).[27] The rabbinic system of impurity organizes the laws of Leviticus in such a way as to be true to the text while enabling the general Jewish population to observe its laws.

To sum up the two perspectives I would say, for the Qumran sect the primary goal was to maintain the presence of God in his sanctuary. The requirements of the Torah were not to be underestimated and ambiguity in the realm of purity and holiness had to be resolved safely. Seemingly excessive requirements were a small price to pay for security and they also provided greater opportunity to actualize more

26. D.R. Schwartz, 'Law and Truth: On Qumran-Sadducean and Rabbinic Views of Law', in Dimant and Rappaport (ed.), *The Dead Sea Scrolls*, p. 229.

27. I. Knohl, 'Post-Biblical Sectarianism and the Priestly Schools of the Pentateuch: The Issue of Popular Participation in the Temple Cult on Festivals', in *The Madrid Qumran Congress*, II, pp. 602-603, especially n.4.

of God's powerful holiness. For the Pharisees and the rabbis after them the most important goal was to enable Israel to observe the Torah. What if God was present in his sanctuary but Israel was absent? Holiness which was unattainable and inaccessible to lay Israelites was irrelevant.

Conclusions

In conclusion, what do we learn from this brief study of interpretation of Leviticus in the Second Temple Period? First, it becomes apparent that the nature of the text is often ambiguous and on many issues it can support more than one interpretation. Secondly, since Leviticus was considered a sacred guide to holiness both in cultic and non-cultic matters in the Second Temple, ambiguities in procedures had to be resolved. Thirdly, and more generally, the way in which a worship community resolves the ambiguities of Scripture reveals its own identity. A community's biases, culture and traditions often find expression between the lines of Scripture. In those places where the text is not explicit human minds must intervene. Points of ambiguity can provide the key to a group's orientation. In the above discussion, the group agenda of the priestly sectarians and the lay Pharisees came to light. Both groups vied for authority in the Second Temple and each shaped Scripture's ambiguous passages to support its own concerns. As a final note, ambiguity in Scripture is not only inevitable due to the nature of a written text, it is healthy. If every instruction on every issue was stated unambiguously in Scripture, no thought would be necessary; blind obedience would be the only requirement. As it is, the Torah provides explicit instructions on major issues setting forth the will of God in no uncertain terms. Still, the details are left to responsible, sensitive human interpreters who will not violate the text as they cautiously fill in its gaps.

Leviticus as a Cultic System in the Second Temple Period: Remarks on the Paper by Hannah K. Harrington

Philip R. Davies

My opening comment must be that I liked Hannah Harrington's paper, much as I liked her book, which she has modestly declined to cite, and which has established her high competence in the area of early Jewish cultic legislation.[1] It is a British tradition to disregard the things one agrees on and focus on the things one does not; it is also my role and my intention to initiate some lines of discussion. So it is important that I be not misunderstood as dissenting from the contents of this paper, with which, as far as it concerns the interpretation of Leviticus in the Qumran scrolls and the rabbinic literature, I find myself in agreement.

I shall concentrate, then, on some broader issues, but also on the nature of Leviticus itself. I start with the first paragraph of the paper, according to which Leviticus is an 'operations manual' for the cult of the Second Temple, and yet rather ambiguous and full of gaps which were augmented for its original audience by oral traditions and filled out by explicit exegesis on the part of later groups.

I am unhappy about taking this assumption as a starting point for examining either Leviticus itself or the Qumran and rabbinic uses of it. Why are there gaps and ambiguities? If there is an oral tradition that makes the ambiguities into a system, why is there a text of this kind at all? And if there is an established and working system, constituted by oral tradition and cultic texts, how does it come about that later groups, presumably well acquainted with the operation of the Temple cult, set about exegetically reconstituting a system from the ambiguous and fragmentary data of the text? One might rather expect the gaps to be filled from the oral traditions, from the practices well known but not explicitly referred to in Leviticus.

1. H.K. Harrington, *The Impurity Systems of Qumran and the Rabbis: Biblical Foundations* (SBLDS, 143; Atlanta: Scholars Press, 1993).

In view of this question, we need to keep an open mind about how Leviticus itself relates to actual practice, or how far it demonstrates a coherent and working system. Indeed, if *intended* as a 'working manual' it is hardly well organized as such. Possibly it is a collection of different 'manuals' (though this is not the view taken by Milgrom, who, like most scholars, sees only two sources here: P and H, although he assigns them rather differently from most). If, on the other hand, it was *used* to regulate the Temple cult, but not originally composed for that purpose, then such use needs to be demonstrated, and its original purpose needs investigating.

It is indeed hard to be certain as to what Leviticus actually *is*. Allowing the conventional allocation of material to P and H, its present form cannot be earlier than the Second Temple period (see 26.33-45). Recent efforts to date P earlier do not affect this basic premise, and in any case I do not find them convincing. Hurvitz's arguments for a pre-exilic date for P depend on the dating of Ezekiel, and what are the linguistic arguments for dating Ezekiel? I don't think it is scholarly to assume that Ezekiel must belong to the sixth century; it needs to be argued. And even if we could be confident in the belief that the Book of Ezekiel was composed during the first deportation of Judeans to Babylonia, there should be some uneasiness about precise typological classification of language, as if there were not dialects and idioms, such as we have evidence of at Qumran. It seems to me quite reasonable that a priestly tradition might conserve its own special language, whether that language has old words in it or not. This is the opinion of R. Rendtorff, which strikes me as plausible. Older terms can be used to express later formulations. How many hymns of the nineteenth century preserve seventeenth- and eighteenth-century language? Trying to date texts via discrete terms, upon which Milgrom relies quite a deal, is a rather simplistic exercise. It is surely a more secure basis for understanding Leviticus as a book to recognize that it comes into existence during the Persian period, either before or just after the building of what we call the 'Second Temple'.[2]

2. I become increasingly uncertain as to how many Judean temples there may have been in antiquity. We have no unambiguous biblical testimony to the *destruction* (as opposed to damage) of the sixth century Jerusalem Temple (see Jer 41.5, Ps. 79); no description (as opposed to mention) of the building of the first Persian period Temple; and little opportunity for archaeological reconstruction of the history of the Temple site. Certainly, it would be more accurate to call Herod's

But even if we try to date Leviticus in the early fifth century, there is then the question of whether it dictated the cult of the Second Temple. After all, we have several competing systems, not all well articulated, attested in the Jewish Scriptures: there is one in Deuteronomy, one in Chronicles, another in Ezekiel. These differ notably but not exclusively in the definition of priesthood: according to Deuteronomy, priests are Levites; according to Ezekiel, priests are sons of Zadok. Both P and Chronicles have the term 'sons of Aaron'. Of these, it is Chronicles which in the opinion of the largest number of scholars is definitely post-exilic (and its influence on the Temple Scroll in particular has recently been demonstrated fully by Swanson[3]). Any reconstruction of the Second Temple cult needs to deal with all the legal materials in the Torah and even outside.

Again, we have different calendars at Qumran and most of the scriptural cultic texts, except that in P we have a trace of the Qumran one in the Flood narrative (as Jaubert showed and VanderKam confirmed[4]). The Qumran calendar (which differs, of course, from the rabbinic calendar) is not derived from Leviticus. What the Second Temple cult calendar was during the Persian and Ptolemaic periods remains disputed. In fact, we know extremely little about the cult of this sanctuary until we begin to be able to infer data from the Scrolls, Josephus and the Mishnah, and these are all relate to the later part of the period. I think the evidence points to a plurality of systems, and either they existed consecutively, as different parties imposed their practices, or they were permitted side by side in an ecumenical Temple (which I think is entirely possible until the Hasmoneans took over), or some of them were theoretical and never put into effect. A combination of these options is not to be ruled out. A mind open to these possibilities, however, needs most definitely to be ruled in.

Relevant to the paper under discussion is the question of theory as against practice. Hannah Harrington has very deftly contrasted the

massively rebuilt sanctuary complex the 'Third Temple', though whether it was only the third to occupy that site since the foundation of Judah is open to question!

3. D.D. Swanson, *The Temple Scroll and the Bible: The Methodology of 11QT* (STDJ, 14; Leiden: Brill, 1995).

4. A. Jaubert, 'Le Calendrier des Jubilés et de la secte de Qumrân: Ses origines bibliques', *VT* 3 (1953), pp. 250-64; J.C. VanderKam, 'The Origin, Character and Early History of the 364-day Calendar: A Re-Assessment of Jaubert's Hypotheses', *CBQ* 41 (1979), pp. 390-411.

situations of 'Qumranites' and rabbis regarding the sanctuary. The writers of the Qumran scrolls developed their legislation out of what seems to have been a situation of voluntary or enforced self-exclusion from full participation in the Jerusalem cult, while the majority of critical scholars of the Mishnah will agree that there is much in it that betrays a utopian system retrojected into the past. Thus the Mishnah's description of the Sanhedrin or its prescriptions for capital punishment (both in the tractate *Sanhedrin)* is hardly to be accepted as historical practice. But is the case any different for Deuteronomy's runaway slave who is not to be returned to the owner (Deut. 23.15), or for the exemptions from warfare (Deut. 20.5-8, unless they are designed to stimulate the economy by encouraging building and planting! But would every fearful man be exempt?)?

Biblical laws, too, are likely to contain strongly utopian, impractical and thus unhistorical legal stipulations. Certainly they also contain real practices, but such practices are gathered into systems that may themselves be driven not by a concern to reproduce practice but a desire to create a legal system commensurate with philosophical or religious principles. The specificity of legal formulation may tempt even critical scholars to a 'realistic' interpretation, rather as genealogies have done in the past, until social anthropology clarified their function. What evidence do we have, then, that Leviticus was conceived as a record of what took place, or even what was expected to be enforced? If it *was* actually enforced, when, and why and by whom? (Certainly not by Levites, for they are mentioned twice only, in Lev. 23).

Another line of discussion, where I am in some agreement with Hannah Harrington, is that in the *Damascus Document* we have a picture of a sect trying to apply scriptural laws, and especially from Leviticus, to its own lifestyle. What Neusner has said about the Mishnah, important and useful as it has been in clarifying Mishnaic origins, needs to be developed and modified. In the Qumran scrolls there is evidence of a process of developing laws for community life that starts from 'scriptural' (I use the term without closer definition) writings. Whether exegesis is the right word, legal reasoning is, in any case, what we can call 'exegetical' when it proceeds either from precedent or statute, and so 'exegetical' activity does not have to imply a rigid concept of 'Scripture'. Neusner's contention that the Mishnah originated with a loose relationship to Scripture and was later brought more into line with Torah via the literary genres of Midrash and Talmud, which is fully and ingeniously argued, can be reversed when applied to the Qumran corpus. I would defend the use of the term 'halakhah' for the laws in CD, and suggest that they are consciously derived from 'Scripture', as if the Damascus sect, in seeking an ever more rigid definition of itself as the true 'Israel' determined to apply the Law of Moses, the constitution of 'Judaism' to its own organization. The contrast between this explicitly sectarian development and the purpose of the far from sectarian Mishnah adequately accounts for the differences in the Qumranic and rabbinic treatments of Mosaic law.

We now have to turn to the nature of the relationship, historically, between Leviticus and the two communities, Qumranic and rabbinic, that developed purity systems from it. What distance is there between these two points? I agree with Hannah Harrington that, from the point of view of the 'interpreting' and 'systematizing' communities, Leviticus presented itself as an authoritative revealed law of divine origin. But, as my first query implied, it may have come as a textual 'system' and not an historical one. It is construed, at least in the Qumran writings, not as authorized *practice* (for in any case these writers were more opposed to existing practice than respectful of it) but as authorized *text*. The Mosaic law, for these communities, is something that applied in reality only before the 'exile', and even then was regularly contravened. It is construed as an ideal system which hitherto has not been followed—hence the very need for the sect, who alone will be the true Israel by virtue of turning that ideal into reality for the first time ever since Moses!

But from the perspective of a modern historian of Judaism, there is no place for an authoritative text to burst at a moment of revelation into the affairs of humans. Just as the Talmud treats the Mishnah as law from Sinai, and generations of Talmudic scholars have treated the Talmud as the law of God, so the historian knows that these documents in their turn are the products of human history, and often themselves reflections on earlier documents. The topic of this symposium is Leviticus itself. What is it, how and why was it designed? In what context do we best understand its production? I would like to suggest as my final contribution to this debate (and fortunately I have no space to *defend* this view at any length!) that the historian may see in the production of both Leviticus (and other priestly legislation for that matter) and also the Qumran scrolls the literary outcome of a continuous priestly movement developing over several centuries (not too many) a culture of holiness, inspired by traditional priestly categories of thought and practice, but also by theories and ideals. When I say 'continuous', however, I do not imply 'normative' or 'homogeneous'. I would imagine the matter of purity theory to be an occasion for serious disagreement, even sectarian opposition (as of course turned out to be the case: as well as the Qumran authors, Sadducees and Pharisees disagreed on these matters—if only we could all agree about the identity of the parties in 4QMMT). In particular, I wonder whether there any hints of sectarian or proto-sectarian language in Leviticus itself. I am interested in the reference Hannah Harrington makes to Leviticus 18:18, taking a woman as a rival wife to her sister.' I wonder if 'sister' (and, indeed, 'brother') does not mean fellow member of a group, and indeed whether 'neighbour' (רע, עמית) in Leviticus always means simply 'Israelite', or a fellow member of a group *within* 'Israel'.[5] What is the difference between saying 'do not sleep with your brother's wife', 'do not sleep with anyone's wife', and 'do not sleep with your neighbour's wife'. All three formulations occur in Leviticus: are they really synonymous? In CD we have a clearly sectarian connotation to the word 'brother' (6.21; 7.2); could the same be true of the book from which these CD texts were derived, Leviticus?

5. The relevant references include Lev. 19.17: 'You shall not hate your brother in your heart: you should certainly rebuke your neighbour, so as not to bring guilt upon him'; Lev. 21.2-3 '... except for his close relatives, that is, for his mother, and for his father, and for his son, and for his daughter, and for his brother, likewise for an unbetrothed sister... ' (where 'brother' certainly means family member); Lev. 25.25: 'If your brother has become poor, and sold off some of his possessions, then let his next of kin come and redeem what his brother sold.' Here 'brother' has an obviously extended sense—'member of extended family', as also in Lev. 25.35-36, 'And if your brother has become poor, and dependent on you [?] then you shall support him: with the status of a גר or a settler he shall live with you. Take no interest from him, or profit from him: but fear your God and let your brother may live with you.'; Lev. 25.39-41, 'And if your brother who lives with you has become poor, and sold himself to you; you shall not compel him to serve as a slave... then they and their children shall return to their own family (משפחת).' (is this really extended family? Or does 'brother' mean *any* Israelite?; Lev. 25.47-48: 'And if a גר or settler should become rich by you, and your brother becomes dependent [?] on them and sells himself to a גר among you, or the גר's family... they shall have the right of redemption'. The question of a 'sectarian' meaning to 'neighbour' in Lev. 19.17 has already been raised by H.-P. Mathys, *Liebe deinen Nächsten wie dich selbst: Untersuchung zum alttestamentlichen Gebot der Nächstenliebe (Lev 19,18)* (OBO, 71; Freiburg: Universitätsverlag, 1986).

In other words, have we in Leviticus a text that belongs to a particular tradition of priestly theorizing which leads directly to the Qumran documents? I am aware that this suggestion brings me towards the assertion of Milgrom that H and the Qumran texts are indistinguishable in respect of purity legislation.

But let me pursue this thesis a bit further. It is acknowledged that the sectarian laws included within CD have been developed from Leviticus, more precisely the 'Holiness Code' (chs. 17–26) among other sources; but the connections extend beyond purity laws: the Leviticus ideology of a desolate land enjoying its sabbaths is also the ideology of CD whose writers see themselves in an ongoing internal exile, with a desolate land, with the ultimate deliverance marked by a progression of sabbaths.[6] Is this fundamental ideological tenet the result of reinterpretation on the part of the Damascus sect, or does it represent a continuum? Maybe lack of access to the Temple, for whatever reason, drove some to form a sect and intensify the cult of holiness. But perhaps Leviticus, or possibly the 'Holiness Code' (which may have been a separate document at some point[7]) is already on a trajectory towards the kind of sectarian formation that we see within the Qumran scrolls.

If the second of these alternatives is correct, then my next problem would be to understand the kind of social situation that generates what strikes me as a neurosis, in which all life is reduced to the category of 'holiness'. What social or economic or political or psychological motivations produce such a curious schematization? That, of course, is exactly the sort of question Mary Douglas prompts us to ask, but which I am not competent to investigate. I do not doubt, however, that we need to consider such a question rather than be content to consider Leviticus merely as an 'operations manual'. Its structural ideology is as important, if not more so, as the surface legislation that is thrown up

6. The influence of scriptural texts on the *Admonition* of CD has now been fully expounded by J.G. Campbell, *The Use of Scripture in the Damascus Document 1–8, 19–20* (BZAW, 228; Berlin: de Gruyter, 1995). There is a convenient table on p. 179. It is interesting, however, that the only part of Leviticus that Campbell is able to detect underlying CD is from the 'Holiness Code'. Was it known to the writers of CD as a separate composition?

7. The Leviticus texts from Cave 4 (edited by Tov), now published in DJD XII (ed. E. Ulrich, F.M. Cross, T. Davila, N. Jastram, J.E. Sanderson and E. Tov; Oxford: Clarendon Press, 1995) give no evidence for a separation of Lev. 1–6 from 17–26. Unfortunately no single *fragment* actually contains both the end of ch. 16 and the beginning of ch. 17.

as a result. Is this ideology of 'holiness' a class neurosis, or a general social neurosis? Is it typical of the world view of a whole society, or of a caste, or of a few dreamers?

Perhaps the drift of my remarks is towards a greater agnosticism about the complexities of the issues. The account Hannah Harrington has given I find satisfying enough regarding Qumran and the rabbis, and it would certainly be unfair of me to imply that in focusing my remarks on Leviticus itself (where she does not) I am expressing disappointment or disagreement with her excellent paper. Rather, I have used this response as a pretext to explore some of the issues that her fine treatment presupposes. I am also mindful of working in a profession which has always claimed to know too much (and grateful to be in the company of so many exceptions to this dreary rule). I would like to be able to convince myself that I have any idea as to why there is a book of Leviticus at all. Is it the product of (at the one extreme) a working Temple cult, one of whose members jotted down lists of things to be remembered? Or is it the outcome of a very peculiar individual mind, such as the writer of Ezekiel had? Does it perhaps owe something to both of these origins, or rather belong in the very large area between them? I may have my preferences, but the question is not what I think, but how I go about the business of arguing for it.

Discussion

Harrington: I do not think Leviticus can ever have had a sectarian use, such as Philip suggests it might have had at Qumran, because it is a text that is considered sacred. It was canonized and not considered sectarian, at any rate during the Second Temple period.

Davies: I am not suggesting that the people of the Dead Sea Scrolls ever considered it sectarian or that they thought they had written it. My question is how long did it take the texts to become Scriptures: three generations?

Harrington: I don't think anyone can say. But I would have thought all of Leviticus derives its laws from Scriptures. There are traditions on both sides that are not Scripture but they all take scriptural laws as their starting point. My whole thesis is that the impurity system in *Kelim* and so on in the Mishnah is derived from Scripture.

Davies: You mean that the whole pharisaic tradition of the Oral Torah is really an exegetical one?

Harrington: Yes, I disagree entirely with Neusner on that.

Carmichael: How can you account for the enormous pressure put on Hillel and the Pharisees in general around that time, who had to base their customs and traditions on Scripture (because the Sadducees were much more attuned to what was going on in Scriptures), and introduced all sorts of complicated rules borrowed from Hellenistic culture in order to cause their practices and customs to be related back to Scripture?

Harrington: I do not think they would put it like that. I think they would have said: We can try to understand it. We can legalize around it, so to speak. But this is the system we inherited. We have to deal with it. We can add in traditions. We can add in our own customs. I work in the world of Torah and I find constantly that usually the rules and explanations in the Torah are quite clearly an attempt to understand Scripture. You mentioned Deuteronomy and Leviticus. I would say Deuteronomy is more influential at Qumran than Leviticus, but on this issue of the cultic and purity laws all the texts of Pentateuch are important, but Leviticus gives me more information on the purity laws. There are so many competing systems but, for example, if we are going to have Yom Kippur, we can only have that on one day. The system has room for discussion but there are certain things that we can only have one way.

Davies: You may be right but if there is only one way of doing it, on what basis does disagreement emerge? Why do people suddenly start saying they want to do it a different way?

Harrington: Because the text is ambiguous.

Davies: But you say the system is not ambiguous. You are saying this is actually a function of the system.

Harrington: Let me give an example from the American government. There is one system, the constitution, with scope for judicial decisions. But in the final analysis, some things are only going to come down one way. You can only have one calendar, only one July fourth, for instance.

Maccoby: Differences of opinion arise. That is natural to every human committee. The problem is how do you achieve a compromise when differences of opinion arise? This is really the problem here because the Sadducees did come to a compromise with the Pharisees about the Temple. They worked together on the Temple. I agree with you about the Qumran sect being a sort of Sadducean sect. They were the Sadducees who would not compromise and that is why they withdrew into the desert, because they regarded their views about the Temple as so all-important that they could not compromise. That is why they withdrew from the Temple service altogether.

Harrington: I do not think the Qumran sect equals the Sadducees exactly. All I am saying is that there are similarities, especially with regard to their legal traditions.

Rogerson: I feel, first of all, Philip's difficulty, about how, particularly within a temple, a worshipping situation, differences are going to arise. Anthropologists will know more about this than me but one point I think that is sometimes made is that the oral tradition among priestly castes is especially tenacious because one generation teaches the next how to do it all and that is passed down. I think back to when I was first ordained as a priest in the Anglican Church, and was taught how to say Mass or celebrate Communion and I think of all the curious things I was told. You can imagine that if there was a priesthood in the Second Temple (and we know so little about it), one could argue that there is a very tenacious thing there and I feel that difficulty with Philip. How could differences arise in such a situation? Perhaps one has to look among other things for what little we know about historical interruptions. Philip mentioned the Hasmonaeans: that was a break, then the thing was restored. Who was in charge when things were restored? You then begin to get arguments about the legitimacy of the priesthood. This could be the beginning of your disagreements. Or alternatively, one might be so dreadfully old-fashioned as to think that individual people might be important, and perhaps a charismatic figure such as the מרה צדק comes along and feels, through some sort of revelation from God, that things are not right, and that you need to withdraw from the traditional system. That could be another possible explanation.

Harrington: What if we have to take account of a lay faction? What I see in the Hasmonaean period is evidence of a priest/lay problem. The priestly system may be the one that has continued, but now there is discussion because the priests are seeming to encroach too much on the laity and there should be more power given to lay Israel. That is what I see as the problem, when you read in the Temple Scroll things like 'You know what it should be but you are not doing it right. . . '

Maccoby: Could I just comment that there is this priest–lay dispute in the Mishnah. The rabbis have a very strong anti-priest bias: for example, they say, 'A learned bastard takes precedence over an ignorant high priest.' That runs through the whole rabbinic movement. The limitation of the privileges and authority of the people ties in with the question of the exegesis of Scripture as well, because the rabbis were the lay teachers, taking the side of the people rather than the priesthood. They would pay attention to the folk traditions of the people more than the priests would, the Sadducees or the Qumran sect. For example, the ceremony of the water-drawing at Sukkot is not in Scripture at all but the rabbis insisted that it was important. It was really a folk rain-making ceremony which arose among the people. This is part of what is meant by the oral torah, standing for the folk traditions of the people. I would suggest that it is not just a Second Temple phenomenon but goes back to much earlier times, where you get the lay prophets opposing the priesthood and the rabbis seeing themselves as the heirs of the prophets. They spoke of Moses as 'our rabbi', משה רבנו. Just as the prophets were a counter-force against the priesthood, so the rabbis saw themselves as a counter-force against the priesthood.

Davies: But some of the prophets were priests.

Maccoby: Of course, just as some of the rabbis were priests. Anybody could be a rabbi, just as anybody could be a priest. But if he was a priest rabbi, his authority derived from his rabbi hat, not his priest hat. Similarly with a prophet. A prophet could be a priest, but he did not derive his authority as a prophet from being a priest.

Carmichael: You have to interpret every text in its historical context. To go to the Mishnah and Isaiah and make these kinds of comparisons is not all that satisfactory because many centuries intervene. The Mishnaic bias against priests is solely to do with the pharisaic antagonism against the Sadducees, alongside their exclusivity. You say the contrast is between priest and lay. A very important category that emerges in the Talmudic period is the category of the stranger where the stranger equals the non-priest. That becomes a very important concept in a great deal of the discussion, but more often than not it is in the context of the Pharisees hitting out at the Sadducees' claims for exclusivity.

Harrington: I am not saying that all rabbinic literature represents an actual functioning system. But definitely what is said about the Second

Temple refers to something that was in working order. Then we have the Qumran sect also from the time of the Second Temple and we are talking in that case about actual practices in the Second Temple. Some of this of course is idealized construction. The Temple Scroll is an ideal construction. But it is related to the fact there is still a Temple in working order in Jerusalem. They did not have control over that Temple, situated out there in the desert. So in the Temple Scroll they make an ideal construction of how they would like it to be when they get back in power. I am not saying the Temple was actually functioning as they describe it, though there are other texts in which they say 'You are doing it this way and you should be doing it this other way'. It is like the later rabbis in the Talmud talking from memory. It is impossible to say precisely what is actual practice and what is not.

Davies: The problem of using the Second Temple as your primary model is that it implies some kind of continuity. We know that the temple was taken over, for example, by the Hasmonaeans. The cult might not have been continuously practised by the same people. When did the sons of Zadok start taking over? What about the priestly terminology? Are the sons of Zadok and the sons of Aaron terminology for the same thing or do they represent different priestly dynasties?

Sawyer: I am surprised Ben Sira has not been mentioned yet as a contemporary Second Temple period text. Do you have any comment on it in relation to what you have been saying about Temple practice in that period?

Harrington: I don't think there is much evidence of priestly influence there.

Johnstone: Could I make a brief comment on Jerusalem as a sex-free zone. It seems to me very interesting that the Chronicler seems to have that idea as well. Solomon removed Pharaoh's daughter from the city of David to a house which he built for her and he said, 'A woman of mine shall not live in the house of David, King of Israel, for these are holy things (קדש המה) which have come unto them, namely they are of the Lord' (2 Chron. 8.11). This kind of text raises the question of how sectarian is the Chronicler?

THE USE OF LEVITICUS IN CHRONICLES

William Johnstone

Some years ago, I suggested that Leviticus supplies the Chronicler with his central theme: guilt and atonement.[1] Israel's guilt, according to the Chronicler, consists in מעל (conventionally, 'unfaithfulness' [NRSV]); for an exposition of מעל , we have to turn to Lev. 5.14-26. But there מעל is not only defined; it is placed within the context of the אשם (conventionally 'guilt offering' [NRSV]), and it is the אשם which opens the possibility of atonement for מעל.

In the interim, the massive commentary on Chronicles by Sara Japhet has appeared, which is surely destined to be a major point of reference in Chronicles study for years to come.[2] In her commentary, Japhet maintains that the connection between Chronicles and Leviticus on this point is merely verbal; the usage is entirely different in the two works. She writes: 'The root [מעל], which is used mainly in a limited technical meaning in the Priestly literature... takes on a very general meaning in Chronicles, covering the whole range of man's sins against God...'[3] It is perhaps, then, apposite within the context of this

1. 'Guilt and Atonement: The Theme of 1 and 2 Chronicles', in J.D. Martin and P.R. Davies (eds.) *A Word in Season* (W. McKane Festschrift; JSOTSup, 42; Sheffield: JSOT Press, 1986), pp. 113-38.

2. S. Japhet, *I & II Chronicles* (OTL; London: SCM Press, 1993). This work has to be read in tandem (as Japhet herself explicitly states in *I & II Chronicles*, p. 43) with her earlier work, *The Ideology of the Book of Chronicles and its Place in Biblical Thought* (Beiträge zur Erforschung des Alten Testaments und des antiken Judentums, 9; Bern: Peter Lang, 1989 [original Hebrew 1977]). These works provide a compendium of discussion of all manner of issues that is as impressive as it is invaluable, and I have gone on record in praise of the latter ('Which is the Best Commentary? 11: The Chronicler's Work', *ExpTim* 102, 1990–91, pp. 6-11). They are, nonetheless, seriously flawed, I believe, in overall conception.

3. Japhet, *I & II Chronicles*, pp. 229-30 in connection with 1 Chron. 10.13. She does not discuss Lev. 5 in *Ideology*, though the point is referred to on p. 202, n.10:

colloquium to reconsider the question whether there is or is not a connection between Leviticus and Chronicles on this point and, if possible, to defend and develop my view in conversation with Japhet's work.

Now, whether or not the connection between Chronicles and Leviticus through מעל can be maintained, I must insist on the centrality of the concept for Chronicles.[4] The distribution and use of מעל in Chronicles is striking:

1. It binds together the genealogies of Israel in 1 Chron. 2.1–9.1, where it occurs three times in the relatively rare narrative sections or evaluative comments, and each of these times is at an absolutely critical moment in Israel's history:

(a) 1 Chron. 2.7, at the moment when Israel first sets foot in the land, Achar of Judah is guilty of מעל, by stealing some of the spoils of Jericho dedicated as חרם to the LORD;
(b) 1 Chron. 5.25, to account for the loss of the settlements of Reuben, Gad and Half-Manasseh on the East Bank;
(c) 1 Chron. 9.1, to account for the final loss of the land by Judah in the Exile.

On East Bank and on West, from first to last, Israel has been guilty of מעל, and it is מעל that accounts for Israel's forfeiture of the land and exile.

2. This theme, having been enunciated in the genealogies, is expounded at length in the narrative section of the work, where the root occurs a further 14 times.[5] The use and distribution in the narrative section is equally significant, in my view, to that in the genealogies:

(a) Despite the extensive parallels in the narrative section to Samuel/Kings, מעל only occurs in material peculiar to Chronicles and may, thus, be legitimately regarded as diagnostic of his view.
(b) The distribution in the narrative section is particularly interesting: it accounts for the death of Saul (1 Chron. 10.13-14);

'Regarding Priestly language, it must be noted that the meaning of a phrase when used in Chronicles may not correspond to its original technical definition. The correspondence is one of literary form rather than content.'

4. The point is not pursued by Japhet; she does not annotate the word, for example, on its first occurrence in I.2.7 (*I & II Chronicles*, pp. 75-76).

5. 1 Chron. 10.13(2x); 2 Chron. 12.2; 26.16, 18; 28.19 (2x), 22; 29.6, 19; 30.7; 33.19; 36.14 (2x). The root occurs 64x in HB.

it then leaps over the reigns of David and Solomon (1 Chron. 11–2 Chron. 9) without mention but reappears in Rehoboam (2 Chron. 12.2), whence it continues its deadly path until it culminates in the Fall of Jerusalem in 2 Chron. 36.14).

3. The omission of מעל in the account of David and Solomon is to be explained by the fact that they approximate to the Chronicler's ideal of monarchy. But only 'approximate' in the case of David. The hinge event in the Chronicler's presentation of David's reign is David's census of the people in 1 Chronicles 21, where David incurs guilt (אשמה, v. 3). The explanation for the heinousness of the crime of counting the people the Chronicler gives in 1 Chron. 27.23: it is to count the people of God who, he had promised, would be as many as the stars in the heavens.

Incidentally, the topic of David's census in 1 Chronicles 21 gives me an opportunity to state the obvious, that Chronicles is presupposing much more material in the Pentateuch than Leviticus, as the use of genealogies in 1 Chronicles 1–9 from Genesis and Exodus (and Joshua and Nehemiah) already shows. 1 Chronicles 21 itself provides two examples of the use of Exodus. (a) I suspect that behind the outrage at David's census lies, in part, the legislation on the muster of the people (root פקד), in Exod. 30.11-16: there *is* a way to muster the people which already involves atonement (cf. the variations on the root פקד, 1 Chron. 21.5-6, plus eighteen further times in Chron.). (b) Another very striking feature of 1 Chronicles 21 is the use of the Passover motif of the משחית, the 'destroyer', of Exod. 12.13, 23, only this time turned in a 'negative passover' against Israel itself (v. 12). This motif is then quite widely used in Chronicles (e.g., in the Egyptian invasion in the time of Rehoboam, 2 Chron. 12.2-12). But all that is another story.

To resume: the term מעל does not occur in Chronicles under David and Solomon. But David's census provides opportunity for the use of the term 'guilt' (אשמה, 1 Chron. 21.3), which, of course, immediately relates the discussion again to מעל in Lev. 5.14-26. For it is precisely the so-called guilt-offering, אשמה (better, I think, 'reparation offering'), which provides the mechanism for dealing with מעל. Thus the immediate outcome of David's אשמה is the building of the altar of sacrifice on the threshing-floor of Ornan (1 Chron. 22.1). At the place where guilt is incurred, there, up to a point at any rate—for David's status is catastrophically changed from now on—the means of atonement is provided.

Admittedly, there are differences in the use of מעל in Chronicles from that in the immediate legislation in Leviticus, as I earlier acknowledged.[6] There are at least three such differences:

1. In the Leviticus legislation on the 'guilt offering', the מעל is inadvertent; in Chronicles it is deliberate. Chronicles is, indeed, at pains to develop the theme of the consciousness of Israel of their guilt because of the ministry of the prophets.[7] The prophetic ministry is two-fold:

(a) the prophets have recorded in writing an unbroken Midrash on the reigns of the kings of Judah in every generation down to the reign of Jehoiakim[8] (by 'Midrash' is meant here a critical account of events from a theological perspective);

(b) the prophetic word (not always spoken through those officially designated prophets but through those who are prophetic in function[9]) has been communicated to every generation virtually without fail.

6. Johnstone, 'Guilt and Atonement', p. 124.

7. It is this continuous and cumulative raising of consciousness through the generations to bring to repentance and in order to display the long-suffering patience of God that has been the function of the prophets, rather than merely 'warning' delivered *seriatim* to each generation, as on Japhet's argument (*Ideology*, pp. 176-91; the gaps in the series provide her, therefore, with some problems, p. 190, n.561).

8. I am assuming that, though there are some eight varieties in the terms used for the record of the reigns of the kings of Judah, they all refer to essentially the same enterprise. This is twice termed 'midrash'—'the commentary of the prophet Iddo' on Abijah (2 Chron. 13.22) and 'the commentary on the book of the kings' for Joash (2 Chron. 24.27).

9. Sometimes it is very generally stated (Ahaziah in 2 Chron. 22.7; Manasseh in 2 Chron. 33.10, 18). Most typically it is the prophets themselves (Shemaiah to Rehoboam; Oded to Asa; Micaiah ben Imlah and Jehu ben Hanani to Jehoshaphat; Elijah to Jehoram; Zechariah ben Jehoiada, among others unnamed, to Joash; an anonymous prophet to Amaziah; Isaiah to Hezekiah; Huldah to Josiah; Jeremiah to Zedekiah). But sometimes it is the priests (to Uzziah), occasionally the kings themselves (Abijah, Hezekiah). Sometimes it has been a non-Judaean prophet (Oded to Ahaz), sometimes even a foreign king, who has been not only God's instrument of punishment but even his spokesman (Neco to Josiah). Only very occasionally is no such intervention recorded (Jotham, and, naturally, in the light of the Chronicler's view of when the exile begins [see below], Jehoahaz, Jehoiakim and Jehoiachin).

2. Leviticus legislates for the מעל of the individual; in Chronicles the unfaithfulness is corporate and compounded generation by generation.

3. In Leviticus the unfaithfulness consists, in the main, in the defrauding of God in 'holy things', offerings in kind (such as are listed in Num. 18[10]). These are the tokens of the consecration of the whole of life. In Chronicles the defrauding of God consists not merely in the tokens but in that very totality of life.

At first sight at least, these differences between the uses of מעל in Leviticus and in Chronicles may, indeed, support the contention of Sara Japhet, quoted above: 'The root... used mainly in a limited technical meaning in the Priestly literature... takes on a very general meaning in Chron.'. I should like to maintain that, nonetheless, the use of מעל in Leviticus remains fundamental to the Chronicler's work. The reason for so arguing comes from two passages in Leviticus itself:

1. Leviticus itself broadens the applicability of מעל in 5.14-26, beyond the 'limited technical meaning' (the immediate reference to fraud in 'holy things'): specifically in v. 17, where it is extended to failure in 'any one of all the commandments of the LORD' (though there the trespass remains inadvertent).
2. More tellingly, Leviticus itself broadens the applicability of its own category of מעל in precisely the same way, it seems to me, as that in which Chronicles uses it. This broadening is to be found in Lev. 26.40,[11] precisely at the end of the Holiness Code, which encompasses all life, in the promise of blessing and the threat of curse which constitute the inducements to lead the holy life. It is not a matter of isolated verbal coincidence. The conceptual framework is the same: for example, the necessity for 'humbling oneself', acknowledging that one is in the wrong, before there is any possibility of atonement (כנע, Lev. 26.41, cf. 2 Chron. 7.14; 12.6-7).

The point being made in Leviticus 26 is that there *is* no possibility of atonement for Israel because of its מעל, at least not immediately.

10. The importance of 'holy things' is well recognized in Leviticus, for example, Lev. 22.1-16. The stress there on appropriate handling is matched in 2 Chron. 31. But—again—there is no need to tie up every connection between Chronicles and the Pentateuch with Leviticus alone.

11. A passage not noted by Japhet in *Ideology*, and skirted on pp. 1075-76 of *I & II Chronicles*.

The legislation for the individual guilty of inadvertent defrauding of God in the tokens of sanctity cannot possibly apply in the case of Israel guilty of national, deliberate fraud in every aspect of life, compounded over the generations. Nor can the penalty exacted on the individual guilty of deliberate fraud, like Achar, apply—the death of the defrauder and the destruction of his whole family and possessions (Jos. 7.25): the death penalty would simply wipe out Israel (cf. 2 Chron. 12.7). What, then, is the alternative to the death penalty? The only alternative is forfeiture of the land. And for what purpose? So that the land can recover from the rapacity of Israel, in *not* repaying its tithes and other holy offerings in kind, and thus be regenerated.

That there is a deliberate exploitation by Chronicles of this sense of מעל developed by Leviticus itself is, I think, evident. The wording of part of the peroration of Chronicles, 2 Chron. 36.21, picks up the words of the peroration of the Holiness Code in Lev. 26.34 (cf. v. 43): 'until the land gets satisfaction for its sabbaths'; the *hophal* infinitive in the phrase 'during all the days of its being devastated' occurs in HB only in 2 Chron. 36.21 and Lev. 26.34-35, 43, even down to its anomalous form with suffix, הָשַּׁמָּה.[12]

Why should Japhet be resistant to such observations? Her resistance derives, I believe, from her interpretation of the Chronicler's view of Israel's relation to the land. In her view, Israel's relation to the land is a matter of continuity from beginning to end.[13] Much of her interpretation of Chronicles hangs on this point:

1. In the genealogies, the Chronicler traces Israel's origins back to Adam. By passing any doctrine of election or covenant, the Chronicler presents Israel's relation with God as a priori, simply a given which requires no justification.[14]
2. Similarly, because the narrative section begins with the monarchy, omitting exodus and conquest, the Chronicler regards Israel's settlement in the land as continuous since Jacob.[15]
3. Equally, at the other end of Israel's history, the exile is

12. The reference to 'the word of the LORD through the mouth of Jeremiah', with which 2 Chron. 36.21 begins, has a different function (see below).

13. Japhet, *Ideology*, p. 363

14. It is 'an integral part of Creation'; Japhet, *Ideology*, p. 199.

15. 'The tie with the land is an undisturbed continuity'; Japhet, *I & II Chronicles*, p. 47.

consistently played down by the Chronicler. This is so in terms of the sheer space he devotes to it: in place of the 57 verses of 2 Kgs 23.31–25.30, Chronicles offers only 23 (2 Chron. 36.1-23). The exile of 587 affects in truth only Jerusalem, not Judah.[16]

4. If there is no significant exile, then there can be no significant return; therefore, Chronicles can have no eschatology.[17]
5. The picture is static and continuous, not cumulative. The Chronicler's work is a series of vignettes of ancient Israel, presented generation by generation, each treated in its own right. There is no inherited, compounded sin; retribution takes place in the generation that has merited it.[18]

Let me give a couple of brief quotations from Japhet, in summary:

> Chronicles presents a different view of history [from the standard presentation in other post-exilic writings]: the dimensions of the Babylonian conquest and exile are reduced considerably, the people's settlement in the land is portrayed as an uninterrupted continuum... The bond between the people and the land, like the bond between the people and its god, is described as something continuous and abiding. This bond cannot be associated with a particular moment in history, for it has existed since the beginning of time.[19]
>
> There is only one complete captivity in the book of Chronicles [namely, the East Bank]... Chronicles takes the account of Israel's exile and destruction and associates these disastrous events with the tribes who lived east of the Jordan... With respect to the land west of the Jordan, in both the northern and southern kingdoms, the effects of enemy invasions are minimized. Foreign armies come and go, but the people's presence in the land continues uninterrupted.[20]

Now this is not the place for a full-scale review of Japhet's work.[21] I

16. Japhet, *Ideology*, pp. 364-73.
17. Japhet, *Ideology*, pp. 493-504.
18. Japhet, *Ideology*, pp. 162-63.
19. Japhet, *Ideology*, p.386; 'axiomatic', p. 393.
20. Japhet, *Ideology*, pp. 372-73.
21. On the alleged absence of conquest narrative, one might reply that the conquest is indeed cited (2 Chron. 20.7, 11; cf. 1 Chron. 5.25; 16.18; 2 Chron. 33.9). One might as well argue that since the 'event' of Moses at Sinai is made little of (Moses is mentioned 21 times, Horeb occurs but once [2 Chron. 5.10] and Sinai never), Chronicles has a radically different view of revelation and of the tradition of Torah; a position that Japhet—rightly—does not adopt (e.g., *Ideology*, p. 497). In

have space only for a comment or two on her interpretation of the Chronicler's work on the exile:

1. The space the Chronicler allots to the exile (23 vv. as opposed to 57) may be given an entirely different interpretation, again related to material from Leviticus, this time Leviticus 25, as I shall hope to show in a moment.
2. 2 Chron. 36.20 makes the explicit statement: 'He [Nebuchadnezzar] carried off into captivity in Babylon those who survived the sword.' Japhet seeks to tone down the statement by saying that it is modelled on material on Jehoiachin borrowed from 2 Kgs 24.15-16[22] and is, therefore, limited to Jerusalem. But the Chronicler has already made his selection of the 2 Kings 24 material on Jehoiachin in 2 Chron. 36.9-10; he has abandoned any close following of the Kings text at 2 Chron. 36.13aβ, and is hardly going to revert to an earlier section of it at v. 20. One cannot be expected to elevate the Chronicler's alleged editorial techniques above the plain sense of the text. The Chronicler is fully capable of making himself clear.
3. Her contention that 'there is only one complete captivity in the book of Chronicles'—that of the East Bank tribes—is based on a similarly complex redactional argument. The material on the exile of the East Bank tribes in 1 Chron. 5.25-26 absorbs the material in 2 Kgs 17 on the exile of the North, so as to apply now only to the East Bank and no longer to the North, thus producing but one exile.[23]
4. I find Japhet's interpretation of 2 Chron. 36.15-16 equally unacceptable. The text runs:

> Now the LORD, the God of their fathers had sent by the hand of his messengers, at earliest opportunity and persistently... But they were ridiculing the messengers of God, rejecting his

Chronicles, David figures as new Moses and Solomon as new Joshua (cf. the encouragement of David to Solomon as of Moses to Joshua, 'Be strong and of a good courage', 1 Chron. 22.13). The upshot is that the whole of Israel's past is presupposed, whether overtly mentioned or tacitly implied.

22. So, rather than 2 Kgs 25.15-16 as stated by Japhet, as the reference to the verb ויגל makes clear (*I & II Chronicles*, p. 1074; cf. *Ideology*, p. 368)

23. Japhet, *I & II Chronicles*, pp. 141-42.

> words and mocking his prophets, until the anger of the LORD was provoked to the point that there was no more healing.

In line with her view that there is no inherited guilt in Chronicles,[24] Japhet relates these verses exclusively to the reign of Zedekiah.[25] But surely the verses are most naturally understood in terms of a long process of events: Zedekiah is not alone in his culpability, but marks the climax of an age-long process.[26]

If such counter-arguments hold, then the Chronicler's argument is entirely different from Japhet's interpretation. There is only one unconditional element in the whole of Chronicles and that is enunciated in the first word in 1 Chron. 1.1: the existence of a relationship between God and humanity expressed in exemplary and instrumental terms in Israel. Israel's relation to the land is conditional (as Leviticus holds; cf. Solomon's prayer, 2 Chronicles 6, e.g., vv. 36-39), just as the monarchy is conditional (cf. the exposition of the apparently unconditional promise to David, 1 Chron. 17.14, in totally conditional terms in 1 Chron. 22.11-13; 28.7).

Let me give, finally, an example of the consequences of following the view I am advocating, that concepts derived from Leviticus are functional in the Chronicler's argument. This is the question of the over-all chronology with which Chronicles is operating—which takes us back again to Japhet's argument about the alleged insignificance of the exile.

It is clear that the Chronicler is working with a chronology of ten generations from Adam, the first father of humanity, to Noah, the second (1 Chron. 1.1-4). There are a further ten generations from Shem to Abraham, the father of a host of nations (1 Chron. 1.24-27). But what of the ensuing generations? Here I acknowledge the stimulus

24. Japhet, *Ideology*, p. 197: 'each king's account is settled with his death. A new unblemished and neutral chapter, freed from the influence of the past, opens with the accession of the succeeding king.'

25. Japhet, *Ideology*, p. 163: 'Only Zedekiah and his generation are responsible for the disaster that occurred in his time'; cf. pp. 188-89.

26. See 2 Chron. 29.6; 30.7 for the point made again specifically in terms of the history of מעל precisely as the Chronicler does here (v. 14). Other examples of continuity can be given; for example, the pernicious influence of the house of Ahab through four generations, from Jehoshaphat to the death of Athaliah (2 Chron. 18-23).

of a citation which Japhet makes from *Exodus Rabbah* 15.26:

> The moon begins to shine on the first of Nisan and goes on shining till the fifteenth day, when her disc becomes full; from the fifteenth till the thirtieth day, her light wanes, till on the thirtieth it is not seen at all. With Israel, too, there were fifteen generations from Abraham to Solomon. When Solomon appeared, the moon's disc was full...'[27]

Japhet is happy to endorse that statement so far: the fifteen generations from Abraham to Solomon. That the Chronicler has indeed fifteen generations from Abraham to Solomon through the descent of David is clear.[28] But, naturally, given that she does not believe in an exile when Israel was completely on the wane, Japhet does not follow up the implications of the second part of the quotation, the demise of the monarchy. The text in Exodus Rabbah actually begins, 'Even before God brought Israel out of Egypt, He intimated to them that royalty would last for them only until the end of thirty generations.'[29]

At first sight it does not seem that fifteen generations after Solomon to the exile fits the Chronicler's presentation. In 2 Chronicles 10–36 nineteen kings are listed (from Rehoboam to Zedekiah). But suppose we follow the lead of Midrash *Exodus Rabbah* and look at the fifteenth-king in the sequence from Rehoboam to Zedekiah, what do we find? We have reached the end of the reign of Josiah. Is it possible that the Midrash is correctly reflecting the chronology intended by the Chronicler?

There are a number of indications which suggest that the Chronicler does indeed regard the exile as beginning with the death of Josiah:[30]

1. The paragraph marker, *pᵉtûḥā'*, marking the end of the presentation of the reign of Josiah and the opening of the next section, is placed at the end of 2 Chron. 35.24 (I believe the paragraph markers of MT to be the absolute base-line in

27. Japhet, *Ideology*, p. 75, n.203.

28. The fifteen are Abraham, Isaac, Jacob, Judah, Perez, Hezron, Ram, Amminadab, Nahshon, Salma, Boaz, Obed, Jesse, David, Solomon (1 Chron. 1.34; 2.1, 4-5, 9-15; 3.5).

29. H. Freedman and M. Simon (eds.), *The Midrash Rabbah*, II (with introduction by I. Epstein; London: Soncino Press, 1977). The footnote at 'Josiah' reads 'Joash' by error.

30. That is, far from Chronicles underplaying the exile because of the Chronicler's drastic reduction of the coverage of it, as Japhet argues (*I & II Chronicles*, pp. 106-107), Chronicles actually extends the exile to begin in 609!

the interpretation of HB).[31] This results in the rearrangement of the last three elements of the standard framework of seven elements within which the reigns of the kings are normally set (5, the record of the rest of the deeds; 6, the burial in Jerusalem; 7, the succession of the son). Element 6, the burial of Josiah in Jerusalem, is moved out of position and marks the end of the presentation on Josiah. Josiah is the last of the Davidic line to die in Jerusalem (the Chronicler has deliberately changed the text of 2 Kgs 23.29-30 so that Josiah is not killed at Megiddo, but dies in Jerusalem).

2. All the succeeding kings are puppets of foreign powers; foreign dominion has begun.
3. Not only so; all these kings are removed from Jerusalem and disappear in exile. For this purpose the Chronicler invents an exile for Jehoiakim (2 Chron. 36.6).
4. The positioning of the paragraph marker throws into prominence the work of the prophet Jeremiah. The whole of these final paragraphs in 2 Chron. 35.25–36.23 is now held together by the words of Jeremiah—his lament over the death of Josiah with which they begin (2 Chron. 35.25), his unavailing presence under the last king Zedekiah (2 Chron. 36.12), and the edict of Cyrus as fulfilment of Jeremiah's prophecy of seventy years for the duration of the exile (2 Chron. 36.22).
5. All this argument would hold, even if crude arithmetic did not support it. But it should be acknowledged that seventy years from the edict of Cyrus, conventionally dated 538, takes us close enough to the death of Josiah, conventionally dated to 609.

And so to return to the question of the Chronicler's chronology. If, in his view, the exile takes place in the sixteenth generation after Solomon, the exilic generation, held together by the prophecy of Jeremiah (2 Chron. 36.21) is the fiftieth generation from Adam (10 + 10 + 15 + 16 = 51, less one because Abraham is double-counted).

If that is so, then there is another interconnection between Chronicles and Leviticus, this time the legislation, again in the Holiness Code, on the Jubilee (Lev. 25.8-24). This passage is enormously suggestive for

31. Contrast Japhet, who takes the section on Josiah as extending from 2 Chron. 35.1–36.1 (*I & II Chronicles*, pp. 1038-59).

the eschatological character of Chronicles. The exilic generation is the time of Jubilee, of the proclamation of eschatological return to the land.

Let me give but two examples of the use of the vocabulary of Jubilee in Chronicles:

1. Lev. 25.13: בשנת היובל הזאת תשבו איש אל־אחזתו. In 1 Chron. 9.2, the ideal of all Israel's possession of the land is stated in terms of 'dwelling in their holding' (היושבים...באחזתם). 1 Chron. 9.2 is strategically positioned: it comes immediately after the explanation for the forfeiture of the land in 1 Chron. 9.1 (and before the account of the ideal population of Jerusalem in 1 Chron. 9.3-34). This becomes the point of reference for the restoration of the ideal under Hezekiah—or the nearest approximation to the ideal Israel is to be capable of achieving under the later monarchy—in 2 Chron. 31.1: וישובו כל־בני ישראל איש לאחזתו.
2. The fundamental principle of tenure of the land is enunciated in Lev. 25.23: הארץ לא תמכר לצמתת כי־לי הארץ כי־גרים ותושבים אתם עמדי. That last phrase in echoed in David's farewell prayer in 1 Chron. 29.15: כי־גרים אנחנו לפניך ותושבים ככל־אבתינו.[32]

I should further point out that there is, it seems to me, verbal interconnection between the proclamation of Cyrus's edict at the end of 2 Chronicles and the proclamation of the Jubilee in Leviticus 25. The formulation of 2 Chron. 36.22, 'He [Cyrus] *sent* proclamation *throughout all* his dominion' (העביר...בכל)—which are 'all the kingdoms of the world' (v. 23)—echoes the formulation of Lev. 25.9: 'You will *send* proclamation by trumpet blast *throughout all* your land (העביר...בכל)'.[33]

32. The connection is not noted by Japhet, *Ideology*, p. 340, n. 262; p. 416, n.58, where it is related to Ps. 39.13.

33. It is taking the discussion too far afield to open the issue of the role of the foreign nations in Chronicles, raised by the edict of Cyrus to all the kingdoms of the world. Once again I find myself completely at odds with Japhet (e.g., 'Chronicles contains no reference to the nations in their own right, nor does it show any interest in reforming the world' [*Ideology*, p. 53]). The point of the Chronicler's beginning his history with Adam is not connected with any 'a priori ' relationship with God, independent of election (another aspect of the alleged 'autochthonous' character of Israel), as shown by tracing Israel's origins back to primaeval beginnings (cf. *Ideology*, pp. 117, 123). It is, rather, in my view, to prepare a setting for Israel amid

What, then, is Chronicles? Not for the purpose of historiography (again I am at odds with Japhet[34]), but for the purpose of theology it weaves a tale of Israel's past on a highly eclectic use of already 'canonical' texts, using the Levitical concept of מעל as dominant theme. What else can one call it but a 'Midrash' on a theme of Leviticus?[35]

the nations of humanity, within three 'coaxial pyramids' at the apex of which stand Adam, Noah and Abraham, respectively (cf. the very significant alteration Chronicles makes to his underlying text with the addition of Adam in 2 Chron. 6.18). What happens in Israel then has an immediate bearing on the nations of the world, whether in ideal achieved under David as Yahweh's vice-regent on earth (1 Chron. 29.30), or in exile and hope of return, as here.

34. For example, Japhet, *I & II Chronicles*, pp. 31-34.

35. Here I happily adopt Japhet's definition of 'Midrash' (writing on 1 Chron. 5.1-2): 'Its midrashic features are, first of all, the fact that the passage is formed as an interpretation of a given text. A citation is followed by an interpretation... Secondly, this interpretation introduces a new theological concept' (*I & II Chronicles*, p. 131).

מעל IN LEVITICUS 5.14-19 AND OTHER SOURCES: RESPONSE TO WILLIAM JOHNSTONE

Philip J. Budd

Professor Johnstone's paper helpfully raises a number of interesting questions. The focus of my response is the word מעל, its meaning in Leviticus 5.14-19, and its use in some other biblical texts.

The word has caused translators problems. In at least two instances renderings appear to have become less precise—thus RSV's 'commits a breach of faith' becomes 'commit a trespass' (NRSV), and JB's 'guilty of fraud' becomes 'is unfaithful' (NJB).

To 'act unfaithfully, treacherously' is the meaning highlighted by Brown, Driver and Briggs,[1] and though this undoubtedly works in many contexts it raises some obvious problems in Leviticus. Can a faithless or treacherous action really be שגגה—'unintentional'?

The suggestion that in Lev. 5.15 a relatively narrow or specific meaning is intended seems, given the overall context, very probable. The suggestion that v. 17 (where מעל does not in fact occur) is giving it a wider, more general frame of reference, comparable to that in the Holiness Code at 26.40, is of interest, but requires more caution.

Among the commentators there has been debate about the relationship of vv. 17-19 to the neighbouring guilt (or reparation) offering passages. A difficulty in distinguishing the circumstances in mind here from those which call for a sin (or purification) offering in ch. 4 has been the main problem. Martin Noth saw vv. 17-19 as a 'secondary insertion', placed here because the offering, as in vv. 14-16, is a ram, but in reality offering modifications and new rules for the sin offering in ch. 4.[2] If we were to accept this approach, the meaning in v. 17 would still be technical or specific.

In point of fact I think that view of vv. 17-19 mistaken. The stress in

1. BDB, p. 591.

2. M. Noth, *Leviticus* (trans. J.E. Anderson; OTL; London: SCM Press, 1965 [1962]), p. 48.

4.14, 23, 28 is on errors which become known or are made known. This offering (5.17, 19), by contrast, may be seen as precautionary, for a situation where an error is suspected or feared (this view is shared by a range of commentators including Chapman and Streane, Snaith, Levine, and Milgrom).[3] Milgrom in particular draws attention to widespread anxieties of this kind in the ancient Near East at large. There is a precautionary burnt offering (though not with מעל) in Job 1.5, offered by Job on behalf of his children. Milgrom's preference for 'sacrilege' as a translation for מעל receives support, I think, from the following section (5.20-26) where the offences are not inadvertent, and seem in the first instance to be against the neighbour; the מעל nevertheless is specifically 'against' Yahweh.

The point would therefore be that vv. 14-16 legislate for inadvertent misappropriation or misuse (Levine[4]) of holy things, or some inadvertent failure to render what Yahweh requires, some dues perhaps inadvertently neglected, or, as Hartley suggests,[5] eating some meat not known to be consecrated. That the error has become known must of course be assumed, since restitution is specified (v. 16).

In vv. 17-19 the distinctive 'without knowing' would therefore signify precaution, contingency, suspicion, or fear about possible inadvertent error, and for this the ram without restitution is sufficient, at least for so long as the situation remains not 'known'. The suspected or feared offences might be with regard to the 'holy things', as in vv. 14-16, or judging by the reference to 'commandments' which 'ought not to be done' (v. 17), they could also be those for which a sin offering is appropriate once it has become 'known' (cf. the occurrence of 'commandments' and the reference to 'things not to be done' in 4.2). In any event, whatever precise shade of meaning is adopted, the application in v. 17 remains technical and specific, rather than wide and general.

There is a reference to infringement of Yahweh's 'commandments'

3. A.T. Chapman and A.W. Streane, *The Book of Leviticus* (The Cambridge Bible; Cambridge: Cambridge University Press, 1914); N.H. Snaith, *Leviticus and Numbers* (NCB; London: Nelson, 1967); B.A. Levine, *Leviticus* (JPS Torah Commentary; Philadelphia: Jewish Publication Society of America, 1989); J. Milgrom, *Leviticus 1-16* (AB, 3; Garden City, NY: Doubleday, 1991).

4. B.A. Levine, *Leviticus* (JPS Torah Commentary; Philadelphia: Jewish Publication Society of America, 1989), p. 30.

5. J.E. Hartley, *Leviticus* (WBC; Dallas: Word Books, 1992), p. 81

in v. 17, and in a Deuteronomistic context this would be suggestive of a wide frame of reference, but in Leviticus, outside the Holiness Code and the very last verse (27.34), the meaning of מצוה remains rather limited and specific. It relates only to offences for which sin offerings are appropriate (4.2, 13, 22, 27).

My remaining points are only brief observations about מעל in other contexts; they provide some textual data on which others may wish to comment. It is certainly the case that Chronicles, in its use of מעל, is concerned not with inadvertent but with wilful sin, and that it has strong generalizing or totalizing tendencies. 'Faithlessness' or 'unfaithfulness' seem to be the favoured renderings in NRSV. There is also however an interest in the specific מעל of kings. There is an 'unfaithfulness' of Saul (1 Chron. 10.13), of Ahaz (2 Chron. 28.19-22), and of Manasseh (2 Chron. 33.19). In one instance (2 Chron. 26.16, 18), in relation to the sin of Uzziah, it takes on a quite specific (technical?) sense. Following NRSV translations he was 'false' (מעל) to Yahweh in making his incense offering, and in v. 18 Azariah the priest says to him 'you have done wrong (מעל). . . '

It is also worth noting that wilful מעל occurs with some frequency in Ezekiel, and it does so in the generalizing totalizing way which is familiar in Chronicles and in Lev. 26.40. Ezek. 14.13 speaks of a whole land 'acting faithlessly, and 18.24 of the 'treachery' (מעל) of those whose whole way of life had previously been righteous, but which has now become wicked. The מעל ('treachery') of a particular king is cited in 17.20. The treacherous ancestor motif, found in Lev. 26.40, 2 Chron. 29.6; 30.7, also surfaces in Ezek. 20.27. Affinities between Ezekiel and the Holiness Code have long been recognised of course, even if explanations are as elusive as ever. Caution must be exercised in tracing directions of influence, and much will depend on whether Holiness perspectives are seen as a later or earlier element in the editing of Leviticus. In either event, however, the Chronicler(s) may owe something to the world of Ezekiel and the Holiness Code.

My last observation has to do with Joshua 22, where מעל occurs four times, in connection with the altar built by the Transjordanian tribes. This interesting incident embodies alleged מעל, which in the event is declared to be inadvertent in that it was not intended, and which is therefore not מעל. The congregation has interpreted the action as wilful מעל ('treachery'—NRSV) (v. 16), citing Achan's מעל ('break faith'—NRSV) in Joshua 7 (v. 20). The Transjordanian tribes reply that the action was not taken in rebellion (מרד) or in מעל ('breach of faith'—NRSV) against Yahweh (v. 22). Since Phinehas is finally persuaded (v. 31) that what has happened was not מעל ('treachery'—NRSV) no further action is required and no disaster ensues. In short, disposition and intention are the critical factors.

That is also true of Lev. 5.14-19 where unintentional neglect of obligations to the sanctuary has taken place (vv. 14-16), and where well intentioned fears about the possibility of such neglect seem to be present (vv. 17-19). In short, there is further confirmation in this study of the fact that serious ethical and pastoral concern is integral to the priestly preoccupation with purity and offerings.

Discussion

Sawyer: מעל was one of the examples I quoted in my paper earlier as a technical term. As soon as it is contained in the overall work, where מעל in ch. 26 has a general usage and the language moves on in the direction that we find in Chronicles, chronologically, then it does not have that technical meaning any more and it is very difficult to find that technical meaning consistently used. Looking at the text which William discussed to begin with in Leviticus 5, מעל is always defined by something else. So מעל could be completely general there and then it says וחטאה בשגגה to explain that the type of מעל referred to here is an involuntary sin. The next time it is defined by another term as well, וכחש בעמיתו to explain that here it is about deceiving. You could almost say that the term is used in a general sense here, and is defined by the other terms. It does not actually say there that מעל is a specific term for sacrilege. In each case, the sacrilege is expressed by other words in the same context. So the general translations that you start with, which refer to faithlessness or the like, are not incompatible with a technical one, but the general meaning of the term is the one that is now uppermost in the other texts of Leviticus, Chronicles and other non-technical passages where it is used.

Jackson: The two passages which you are comparing, 15–16 on one hand and 20–22 on the other, as you rightly say, both begin with a kind of general מעל formula and then go on to an elaborate set of property offences. I think you can argue that מעל is superfluous from a definitional point of view in the second but not in the first. In the first, for it to be superfluous, you have to interpret the חטא בשגגה as meaning, 'and sins inadvertently in taking something'. The verb חטא cannot bear the sense of 'taking' as well as 'sinning'. Otherwise, where do you find the taking? Is it in the preposition מן, in the חטא or, as most likely, I think, in the מעל? This is certainly the view that the rabbis took, because there is a whole tractate of the Mishnah called *Meʿilah*, usually translated 'sacrilege'. It deals exclusively with this kind of offence, taking holy things and so on. But it does not include the offences which are referred to in the second passage.

Sawyer: That seems to me a very nice example of how the technical sense surfaces again later in the oral torah. Meanwhile, in the written torah, it seems the non-technical sense predominates as most of the older translations take it. That would confirm William's thesis that the connection between the technical senses does not come into it. It is the general non-technical sense in Leviticus and Chronicles that is uppermost.

Maccoby: I would like to take up an implication of what you just said, John. The assumption that we start off with a technical meaning for מעל and then expand it into a broader sense, is not necessarily correct. That kind of evolutionary approach may perhaps be the other way round: you start off with a general meaning and narrow it down to a technical meaning. In physics, for example, the word 'force', which originally had a very general meaning, is given a special, narrow, technical meaning.

Sawyer: This would be the case if the Priestly source were later than H. Then the argument would be that the technical sense appears in the Priestly context, that is to say, the first chapters of Leviticus, whereas in the Holiness Code it does not. The dating of these two sources would then be crucial. It could be the other way round but it seems unlikely. In principle I agree it could go both ways, but not perhaps in this case. Whether ch. 26 is earlier or later than ch. 5, it has the overall effect of confirming that the main meaning of the term is general and not technical or specific.

Maccoby: William's very ingenious system of generations was very interesting but I have just one little objection. You seem to change the definition of a generation halfway through. A generation that has come between say Adam and Seth is different from a list of kings. A king may reign just for a couple of years, which is hardly a generation.

Johnstone: I am just following the rabbinic tradition in Midrash Rabbah of thirty generations from Abraham to Josiah.

Davies: Two very minor points. On the definition of Midrash at the end of your paper, I wondered whether it is not related to the parallel Greek term ἱστορία ('inquiry'). There may be a connection between the two. They are more or less contemporary usages. My other thought concerns what may be a pure coincidence, but on your very ingenious and very plausible definition of the Chronicler's view of the exile, as beginning with the death of Josiah, is it an accident that the first king after the death of Josiah is called Jehoahaz (2 Chron. 36.1)? Is this a deliberate play on the words אחז and אחזה ('land-possession')?

Johnstone: It is not beyond the bounds of possibility, though I must say I think the Chronicler is sometimes stuck with historical data.

Sawyer: Could I mention one more term that I think occurs mostly, if not exclusively in Chronicles and Leviticus? I was thinking of יובל in the sense of 'jubilee'. I think that is another connection between the two books.

LEVITICUS IN MARK: JESUS' ATTITUDE TO THE LAW*

Alan Watson

Mark is for me the most tightly constructed of the Synoptic Gospels. This is very clear with regard to legal episodes. Not on that account would I regard it as closest to early historical tradition—the construction could be the result of art, and, indeed, we have the witness of Papias (Eusebius *Historia Ecclesiae* 3.39) that matters were not set down in order in Mark.[1] But Mark's closeness to tradition is brought out by details or episodes that appear in Mark and also in Matthew and/or Luke, and that are relevant in Mark but not in Matthew/Luke. It might be easy to maintain that in Mark these details were artificially constructed and inserted into the tradition, but it would be difficult to believe that they existed irrelevantly previously in a Mark/Matthew/ Luke tradition, and were retained, still irrelevantly, in the later Matthew/Luke but were made relevant in Mark. It is simpler to hold that the details were taken over in Matthew/Luke from Mark, but that their full significance in Mark was overlooked. I find the relevancy of legal episodes in Mark—a relevancy that is weaker in Matthew and Luke—among the most persuasive arguments for the proposition that Mark was the earliest of the Gospels. I admit that the argument by itself is not conclusive.

At the outset certain themes should be made explicit. Jesus is in the mould of Hebrew prophets, especially Isaiah. But unlike Isaiah his stock

* This paper derives from three books of mine, and especially from the third: *Jesus and the Jews: The Pharisaic Tradition in John* (Athens, GA: University of Georgia Press, 1995); *The Trial of Jesus* (Athens, GA, 1995); *Jesus and the Law* (Athens, GA: University of Georgia Press, 1996). Further argumentation and bibliography will be found by looking up the texts cited here in the books' Indices of Texts.

1. R.M. Grant emphasizes 'that Mark has imposed a certain measure of arrangement upon his material'. R.M. Grant, *A Historical Introduction to the New Testament* (London: Collins, 1963), pp. 123-26.

in trade is miracle working. The Markan Jesus has no very obvious specific spiritual message. Hence it is inconceivable that his mission was also to the Gentiles. For Mark, Jesus is justified, and his authority confirmed, by the Resurrection. So convinced is Mark of this that the Resurrection is even underplayed. The Markan Jesus is the messiah. But this messiah does not challenge the domination of Rome. Indeed, as a messiah, Jesus' behavior is distinctly odd. He goes out of his way to infuriate institutional authorities—above all the Pharisees, but subsequently also the Sadducees—by showing contempt for those commands of God that otherwise had no obvious ethical relevance: observance of the sabbath, ritual cleanliness, and sacrifices in the Temple. His attitude here is reminiscent of Isaiah, but in Jesus' time it is precisely the observance of these commands that would indicate that, despite everything, Jews were (in religion) independent of the Romans. And there is in Mark no corresponding emphasis on Jesus teaching obedience to those of God's commands that have a moral basis. Jesus has set himself out to be a troublemaker—but to his fellow-Jews. All the more infuriating when they are dominated by the enemy Romans, and need a messiah.

Thus, Mark's Jesus is the messiah who does good works through his miracles. He sets himself up against the institutional Jewish religious leaders but, curiously for the messiah, not against the Romans. If one does not accept the Resurrection, Jesus becomes a much more comprehensible person as a rather confused and confusing cult leader.

The common dissatisfaction with Mark and my own stance are not paradoxical. If one is a Christian who fails to notice the strength of Mark's structure one has a real problem. Why was the Gospel written? What is the meaning for Mark of Jesus' message? Why does he not overthrow the Romans? For the evangelist that presumably was to come. A later generation sought to resolve part of the problem by creating a new version of the messiah.

What must not be overlooked in Mark is the progression in the episodes involving law. The episodes tend to occur in groups, with the group introducing a new stage. In Mark ch. 1, as it now is, there are four distinct episodes concerned with law, and they have interconnections. On the sabbath Jesus cured a man possessed of an unclean spirit (1.21-27). This he did in public. He did it by words alone; thus without breaching the prohibition against working on the sabbath. Immediately thereafter, so still on the sabbath, he cured Simon's mother-in-law by a laying on of hands (1.29-31). Thus, he breached the prohibition on sabbath working. But this he did in private, inside a house in the presence only of his disciples. 'When evening came, after sunset' people brought their sick to be cured (1.32). The repetition only in Mark—evening had come and the sun had set—emphasizes that the sabbath had ended. So although the people had seen him cure without working, the idea of respect for the sabbath is depicted as so strong that people waited until it ended before they approached him. Later in the chapter he cured the leper by a laying on of hands (1.40-44). So, he made himself unclean (Lev. 13.45-46): unnecessarily, because we have already been shown that his words were sufficient. This laying on of hands was in private otherwise he would not have commanded the leper to tell no one. Still, he also told the leper to show himself to the priest and make the offerings commanded by Moses.

The episodes contrast public and private healings: in fact the order is public, private, public, private. In the private healings Mark shows Jesus as regarding himself as beyond the law: he worked on the sabbath, he made himself unclean. But Mark also shows Jesus as far from confrontational. In the first public healing, on a sabbath, Jesus cured without working: in the second it is emphasized that the sabbath was over. Again, though Jesus made himself unnecessarily unclean he ordered the cured leper to follow the law.

These four legal episodes all concern a miracle, specifically of healing. They recur in Matthew to some extent (8.14-17; 8.2-4) and in Luke (4.33-36; 4.38-39; 5.12-14) but the structure is lost.

With what now appears as ch. 2, Mark moves to a new stage. There are again four episodes—four is not significant—involving law, and they are treated as a unit. They have a five-fold common structure: (1) Jesus or his disciples behave in a surprising way. (2) This prompts a question from Pharisees or scribes. (3) Jesus replies in a way that silences the questioners. (4) The Pharisees or scribes are not represented as obviously being hostile. (5) Each episode concerns a specific event.

In one respect the first episode in ch. 2 is transitional. Like all four episodes in ch. 1 it involves a miracle whereas none of the other three in ch. 2 does. Still, it differs in a most significant way from those in ch. 1. Jesus is shown as confrontational. This is Jesus' first brush with the authorities and it was he, not they, who brought it on (2.1-12). Jesus said to the paralytic, 'Your sins are forgiven', words that had to be offensive as implying that the speaker knew God's mind. Scribes who were present thought (but, significantly for Mark, did not say), that Jesus was 'blaspheming'. Jesus rounded on them. The scribes were not seeking to trap him. And Jesus used an argument that would not satisfy them. He asked rhetorically whether it was easier to say 'Your sins are forgiven' or 'Take up your mat and go home'. But that was not the issue. The issue was the offensiveness of Jesus' first verbal formulation.

The other three episodes in ch. 2 have further elements in common that distinguish them from the first: in all three the question is expressed and, perhaps strangely, it is not addressed to the actor. The second episode was Jesus' eating with tax collectors and sinners (2.15-17), which was considered improper for the pious. The scribes of the Pharisees asked his disciples why he did so, a question not necessarily hostile but seeking his motivation. Jesus' reply was again confrontational. His 'I have come to call not the righteous but sinners' implies that he had no business with Pharisees, who are thus excluded from his mission.

The third episode involves the question to Jesus why his disciples did not fast (2.18-20). Fasting twice a week had become a mark of piety, but was not obligatory.

The fourth episode (2.23-28) has the Pharisees ask Jesus why his disciples plucked grain (worked) on the sabbath, which was unlawful. Jesus' reply was not to the point and would not be persuasive to the Pharisees. Scripture (Exod. 16.25-26) forbade reaping on the sabbath, and by interpretation plucking grain was reaping. The rule being based on scriptural law was thus *halakah*. Jesus' legalistic response was that there was a precedent: David and his companions ate the consecrated bread. But this behavior was not a rule but an example, a matter of religious importance which did not affect the law. It was thus *haggadah* which could not prevail over *halakah*. Besides, the precedent was not in point: it did not concern a breach of the sabbath; and what was permitted to David need not have been permitted to others.

This second group of four episodes differs in other ways from the first group. They all have Jesus using language that indicates he believed he was someone very special. More importantly, they now have the Pharisees following Jesus about to discover what kind of a person he is.

The legal episode at the beginning of chapter 3 (3.1-6), the curing of the withered hand on the sabbath, marks an ending and a beginning. It is connected with the episodes in ch. 2: the Pharisees were still watching Jesus, Jesus is still the one who began the confrontation, and he again used an inappropriate argument about law. But the episode marks a new phase: the Pharisees watched him *with hostility* and then they plotted to kill him. They had decided he was not like them and could not be co-opted.

Jesus was being watched to see whether he would cure a withered hand on the sabbath. He asked 'Is it lawful to do good or harm on the sabbath, to save life or to kill?' The question was palpably unfair. There was no prohibition on doing good on the sabbath, only on working. Even more to the point, it was lawful to work on the sabbath in order to save life.

The other episode in this chapter is relevant for the tightness of Mark's structure and his understanding of law in a different way (3.19-35). People were saying that Jesus had gone mad and his family came to restrain him, as was proper under Jewish (and other) law. When he was told that his mother, brothers and sisters were looking for him, he neatly replied that 'Whoever does the will of God is my brother, sister and mother'. He thus denied that his blood relatives had legal authority over him. The legal point that gives the episode its meaning is lost in Matthew (12.46-50).

There are two legal episodes in ch. 5 and surprisingly they are intertwined (as they also are in Mt. 9.18-25 and Lk. 8.40-56). Such intertwining of episodes occurs nowhere else in the Gospels.

Jairus, a leader of the synagogue, begged Jesus to lay hands on his little daughter who was at the point of death (5.23). Jesus went with him and a large crowd followed (5.24-34). Now the second episode intrudes. A woman who had been haemorrhaging for twelve years touched his robe believing if she did so she would be healed. She was cured, and when Jesus asked who had touched him she told him *the whole truth* 'in fear and trembling'. Then Mark reverts to Jairus' daughter. Before Jesus reached the house he was told she was dead (5.35). Inside, he claimed she was only asleep, told her to rise, touched her, and she did rise (5.39-43).

What these episodes have in common is that in both Jesus is rendered unclean by contact with a woman. For the structure of Mark we should notice that there is again a marked escalation. The haemorrhaging woman, by touching Jesus, made him unclean according to Scripture (Lev. 15.19-30, especially 15.25), and this uncleanliness lasted until evening (Lev. 15.19). That is why the woman was terrified by what she had done; a point not noted in Matthew although it is in Luke (8.47). Jesus, by touching the dead girl made himself unclean for seven days (Num. 19.11). The escalation is not just that in the second episode the period of uncleanliness is longer, it is also that in the first it was the woman who made Jesus unclean, in the second it was Jesus who made himself unclean. But the fact of uncleanliness is not mentioned for either episode. Mark, by intertwining the stories, is making the point that Jesus was unconcerned about ritual purity. It must be emphasized that the importance of ritual purity was established expressly by God, not simply by Pharisaic interpretation.

At the beginning of Mark's ch. 7 Jesus is asked by the Pharisees and scribes why, contrary to tradition, his disciples ate without washing their hands. Jesus took this as an opportunity to attack the Pharisees quite unjustifiably. He accused them of abandoning the commandment of God and holding to human tradition (7.6-13). He illustrated with a contrast between God's command to honor father and mother on the one hand and Corban—improperly understood as an offering to God—on the other, which would deny its use for parental support. But the strictness of the necessity for keeping an oath was not enjoined by Pharisaic tradition but by a commandment of God set out in Deut. 23.21-23, Leviticus 27 and Num. 30.2. In fact, the Pharisees actually tempered the inviolability of oaths (*M. Ned.* 2.3). It should be noted in passing that for the Pharisees there would be no difference between Scripture and their interpretation of it.

Subsequently in the same chapter (7.14-19) Jesus declared that no food makes one unclean. The pronouncement was made with an absence of clarity, and only privately did he expand on his meaning to the disciples. Jesus thus again pronounced against the express commandment of God in Leviticus. Indeed, God's command against unclean food is expressed in strong language: the food is 'detestable' or 'abominable' (Lev. 11.10-13). It should also be stressed that the uncleanliness of the partaker cannot be cleansed by any purificatory rite or the passage of time.

At Mk 10.2-9 Jesus in effect condemned divorce though Moses allowed it (Deut. 24.1-4). It is sometimes claimed by modern scholars that Jesus was not changing the law: after all, the argument goes,

Moses did not command divorce. The argument is false. There is a vast legal difference between a system that permits divorce, and one that forbids it. To divorce I will return.

The so-called cleansing of the Temple is told in Mk 11.15-17 in a way that is much more muted than in Jn 2.13-16. Still, Jesus' atrocity towards Pharisees, Sadducees and all observing Jews alike, shines through. Jesus threw out those buying and selling in the Temple, that is, in the Temple precincts (11.15). But the sales, as is known from John (2.14ff.), were of the sacrificial animals; cattle and sheep, and doves for the poor. The sale of such was permitted in the Temple by the Temple authorities—indeed the sale of doves was directly under their control (*M.Shek* 6.5). Only religiously clean animals could be offered for sacrifice, and apart from sales in the Temple precincts these would not be easy to find, especially by pilgrims to Jerusalem for the festival. God, moreover, had centralized worship, and sacrifice could be offered only in one place, Jerusalem (Deut. 16.5-6). Thus, Jesus was inhibiting the necessary sacrifices to God, at the one place where they were permitted and, at that, just before Passover, the holiest day of the Jewish year.

Jesus also overturned the tables of the money changers. Their function was religious or quasi-religious: to enable the Temple tax to be paid. Roman denarii with the portrait of Tiberius on the obverse, and the graven image of a false deity—Pax in the form of Tiberius' mother Livia—on the reverse could not be offered. Similar objections applied to Greek didrachms. The money changers gave unobjectionable Tyrian coinage in exchange. So Jesus was preventing the payment of the Temple tax (see *M. Shek.*).

Such are the passages in Mark that relate to Jesus and the law that is set out in Leviticus and Deuteronomy. It must be stressed that Jesus' hostility is not just to Pharisaical interpretation but to the laws of God themselves. There are six observable stages in Jesus' behavior. At stage one, Jesus thinks he is beyond the law, but he behaves with discretion and does not disclose the fact. At stage two, Jesus is confrontational, and the Pharisees follow him about to find out what kind of a person he is. At stage three, Jesus is even more confrontational and the Pharisees become hostile. At stage four Jesus displays open indifference to ritual purity. At stage five Jesus becomes still more confrontational, violently attacking the Pharisees verbally. At stage six Jesus is physically violent in obstructing the Passover sacrifice and payment of the Temple tax.

Something very odd is going on. The legal passages relate to Jesus' hostility to the prohibition of working on the sabbath, to laws of purification, to dietary restrictions, to sacrifice in the Temple, and to the payment of the Temple tax. In effect, they concern those matters that in the annual round of life show a Jew that he is a Jew. But this cannot be because Jesus wanted to assimilate Jew and Gentile. In Mark Jesus' mission is decidedly not to the Gentile. Though Mark ignores that issue, the Gospel's stance is obvious from Jesus' reaction to the Syrophoenician woman who wanted her daughter cured (7.24-30): the symbolism is obvious, the children are the Jews, Gentiles are dogs.

But what about the laws in Leviticus that have a moral content? They are ignored by Mark's Jesus, except for divorce. Jesus not only forbade divorce: he declared, 'Whoever divorces his wife and marries another commits adultery against her; and if she divorces her husband and marries another, she commits adultery' (Mk 10.11-12). So Jesus was presumably in favor of the seventh commandment that forbade adultery.

There is also the blanket condemnation of evil coming from within in Mk 7.20-23.

> And he said, 'It is what comes out of a person that defiles.[21] For it is from within, from the human heart, that evil intentions come: fornication, theft, murder,[22] adultery, avarice, wickedness, deceit, licentiousness, envy, slander, pride, folly.[23] All these evil things come from within, and they defile a person.'

But this is unspecific, and does not take us very far. And even this much was explained only privately to his disciples.

But otherwise in Mark there is nothing about Jesus' attitude to God's laws in Leviticus that might be regarded as having a moral content, such as those against incest (Lev. 18.6-18), against sacrificing offspring to Molech (Lev. 18.21), against male homosexuality (Lev. 18.22), against bestiality (Lev. 18.23), those to benefit the poor (Lev. 19.9-10), those condemning theft, fraud and lying (Lev. 19.11, 13), those against stealing, harsh dealings with poor employees and the deaf and the blind (Lev. 19.13-14), and so on. This cries out for an explanation.

Mark's Jesus has no precise and clear moral, social or spiritual message except for any that is inherent in his miracle cures. But these miracle cures may have had a different function, such as to demonstrate his powers or show that he was the Messiah. At the very least one should say there is no emphasis in Mark on a specific spiritual message from Jesus.

But then why the stress on Jesus' opposition to those commandments of God that had no obvious ethical content? The only explanation that seems plausible to me is that Jesus as the charismatic religious leader believed from the beginning of his mission that he was above or beyond these laws, that when he recognized his inevitable opposition to the institutional religious leaders, the Pharisees, he set himself up to confront them, becoming more and more hostile. Eventually, in the cleansing of the Temple, he also roused the anger of the Sadducees, and brought about his own death. (Deliberately, I think.)

One final issue should be addressed. Why was Mark written at all, with a Jesus hostile to those laws specific to Jews, and with no emphasis on an ethical or spiritual message? The answer for me is that the author accepted the Resurrection as a proven fact, from which it followed for him that Jesus was the Messiah. Nothing else was of consequence.

Discussion

Maccoby: I have some bones to pick with you on the question of when Jesus says, 'Your sins are forgiven'. You suggested that this was a very offensive remark because he suggested that he knew the mind of God. Every prophet claimed to know the mind of God. What was blasphemous about that? If he was claiming to be a prophetic figure, which I am sure he was, then I do not see that it is in any way offensive to Jews that he should claim to know the mind of God. Secondly, about the plucking of grain, that does seem to be an incident in which Jesus was breaking the law, or encouraging disciples to break the law, because as you said quite correctly, plucking grain is an offence against the law on the sabbath. I think the clue to that is in an early Jewish Christian document which explains the whole incident in terms of פקוח נפש, that is, that there was danger to life. This makes sense of the whole incident because, as you said, when Jesus cited the case of King David and the sanctities of the temple, that was irrelevant. It is irrelevant unless we are talking about a situation of danger to human life, where the law is the same for both. That is the rabbinic explanation of the whole David incident, that he had to steal the shew bread because he was in danger of starvation. Matthew does say that they were very hungry. Mark does not. I think Mark omits that because he wants to represent Jesus as flouting the sabbath because that is his picture of Jesus. If you simply put that back in, you have a perfectly intelligible incident. The disciples were actually on the run, from Herod Antipas perhaps, and were in mortal danger. So, according to Mark, Jesus quotes a very significant thing: 'The sabbath was made for man, not man for the sabbath', which is found in rabbinic literature as well, precisely in that context of 'You may break the sabbath if there is any danger to human life'.

Watson: With regard to the first point, Jesus being a prophet. This comes at a relatively early stage. After the Pharisees followed him to see what he was like, his legal replies to this point have been unsatisfactory, therefore it is less likely that he would appear to them to be a prophet. Secondly, with regard to plucking grain, you mention danger of death from starvation. If I were starving, plucking grain would not help me to live, because you cannot get all that many grains by simply plucking by hand. It does not work. Even Matthew's 'very hungry' does not imply starvation.

Maccoby: I would only pluck grain if I was starving.

Segal: If one could go beyond the case of Mark and the Gospels in general, it is very hard to come up with a consistent line on the attitude of Jesus toward the law. On the one hand, Jesus says, 'You shall not enter the kingdom unless your adherence to the law is more meticulous than that of the scribes and Pharisees.' On the other hand, no sooner does he say that than he loosens the law. Sometimes he loosens the law, sometimes he tightens it. Sometimes he loosens ritual law. Sometimes he is concerned with violation of the ritual law, like hypocrisy in the form of praying or sacrificing so that others will notice. As far as precedent goes, sometimes he invokes the Bible, and what he does seems to vary from case to case. But sometimes he invokes no authority at all. Something is to be changed just because he himself says it. Finally, I know there is the secrecy motif in Mark in particular, but I think that throughout the Gospels Jesus seems to be at pains to make himself as clear as he can be, but at other times he seems almost perversely to be trying to be as elusive as he can be. I am not questioning the progression you find in Mark, but I think read overall it is very, very hard to find a progression or indeed any kind of consistency.

Watson: Ancient historians say that if you have one account, you know what happened. If you have two, you know nothing about what happened. Here we have four separate, sometimes conflicting accounts. To me the beginning of wisdom on this is to take your stance, for whatever approach you are using, on one Gospel, being aware, though, of the differences in the others, keeping them in mind but always trying to work out what that one Gospel says. I was talking only about Mark, and for example, I agree entirely with you about secrecy and that no clear message appears in Mark, whereas it does in Matthew and Luke.

Harrington: I think you have a valid point when you say that, at least in Mark, Jesus is presented as somehow above the ritual purity laws. I thought it is also very interesting in the case of the haemorrhaging woman, that she reaches out and touches only his robe but does not actually touch him. According to rabbinic law, this particular impurity can be transmitted through clothing. But Mark does the reverse in the case of Jesus where he heals her through the robe, without touching her.

Jackson: A small point about the sabbath healing. Part of your argument was that its significance was that it did not involve touching and this would not be considered to be work. One could debate that in terms of the technical rules of the sabbath. But perhaps as relevant in this kind of context, is the fact that in one of the creation accounts, God created the whole world without touching and it most definitely is regarded as work because he rested from his work (מלאכתו) after six days. I question what would the models for work be. Would they be models of *halakah* or *haggadah*? That would seem to be an argument that this could be conceived as work.

Watson: In Luke, or it may be Matthew, Jesus again cures without touching and he is nonetheless accused by the rulers of the Synagogue. Also Josephus has a rather mixed up passage where he says 'he was not well behaved on the sabbath because he cured, but he did it without working'. I agree it is a difficult area.

BIBLIOGRAPHY

Alon, G., *Jews, Judaism and the Classical World* (Jerusalem: Magnes Press, 1977).

Andersen, F.I., and A.D. Forbes, *The Vocabulary of the Old Testament* (Rome: Pontifical Biblical Institute, 1989).

Auld, A.G., *Kings without Privilege* (Edinburgh: T. & T. Clark 1994).

—'Reading Joshua after Kings', in J. Davies, G. Harvey and W. Watson (eds.), *Words Remembered, Texts Renewed: Essays in Honour of John F.A. Sawyer* (JSOTSup, 195; Sheffield: JSOT Press, 1995), pp. 167-81.

Baskin, J., 'The Separation of Women in Rabbinic Judaism', in *Women, Religion, and Social Change* (eds. Y.Y. Haḥhad and E. Banks Findley; New York: SUNY Press, 1985), pp. 3-18.

Blackman, P., *Mishnayot* (London: Mishna Press Ltd., 1951–56).

Boyarin, D., *Carnal Israel: Reading Sex in Talmudic Culture* (Berkeley: University of California Press, 1993).

Calvez, M., 'Composer avec un danger: Approche des réponses sociales à l'Infection du VIH et au SIDA', *Institut Régional du Travail Social de Bretagne* (1989).

Carmichael, C.M., *Law and Narrative in the Bible* (Ithaca, NY: Cornell University Press, 1985).

Chapman, A.T. & A.W. Streane, *The Book of Leviticus* (The Cambridge Bible; Cambridge: Cambridge University Press, 1914).

Cohen, S., 'Menstruants and the Sacred in Judaism and Christianity', in *Women's History and Ancient History* (ed. S.B. Pomeroy; Chapel Hill: The University of North Carolina Press, 1991), pp. 273-99.

Damrosch, D., 'Leviticus', in R. Alter and F. Kermode (eds), *A Literary Guide to the Bible* (Cambridge, MA: Harvard University Press, 1987), pp. 66-77.

Delcor, M., 'Jewish Literature in Hebrew and Aramaic in the Greek Era', in *The Cambridge History of Judaism*, II: *The Hellenistic Age* (Cambridge: Cambridge University Press, 1989), pp. 342-84.

Destro, A., 'Antropologia del Giudaismo antico', Bologna, Letture CISEC (1992), n. 2, pp. 5-36.

—'La donna *niddah*: Ordine del corpo e ordine del mondo giudaico', in *idem*, *Le politiche del corpo* (Bologna: Patron, 1994), pp. 87-130.

Di Segni, R., '"Colei che non ha mai visto il sangue". Alla ricerca delle radici ebraiche dell'idea della concezione verginale di Maria', *Quaderni Storici* 75.25.3 (1990), pp. 757-89.

Douglas, M., 'Techniques of Sorcery Control in Central Africa', in J. Middleton and E.H. Winter (eds.), *Witchcraft and Sorcery in East Africa* (London: Routledge & Kegan Paul, 1963), pp. 123-42.

—*Purity and Danger: An Analysis of Pollution and Taboo* (London: Routledge & Kegan Paul, 1966).
—*Natural Symbols: Explorations in Cosmology* (London: Barrie and Jenkins, 1973).
—'Witchcraft and Leprosy: Two Strategies for Rejection', *Man* 26 (December 4, 1991), pp. 723-36.
—*In the Wilderness: The Doctrine of Defilement in the Book of Numbers* (JSOTSup, 159; Sheffield: JSOT Press, 1993).
—'The Forbidden Animals in Leviticus', JSOT 59 (1993), pp. 3-23.
—'Atonement in Leviticus', *Jewish Studies Quarterly*, 1.2 (1993), pp. 109-30.
—'The Forbidden Animals in Leviticus', *JSOT* 59 (1993), pp. 3-23.
—'The Stranger in the Bible', *Archives Européennes de Sociologie*, 33.2 (1994), pp. 283-98.
—'The Glorious Book of Numbers', *Jewish Studies Quarterly*, 1.3, pp. 193-216.
—'Poetic Structure in Leviticus', in *Pomegranates and Golden Bells: Studies in Biblical, Jewish and Near Eastern Ritual, Law and Literature in Honour of Jacob Milgrom* (ed. D.P. Wright, D.N. Freedman and A. Hurvitz; Winona Lake, IN: Eisenbrauns, 1994).
Draï, R., *Le mythe de la loi du talion: Une introduction au droit Hébraïque* (Aix-en-Provence: Editions Alinea, 1991).
Eilberg-Schwartz, H., *The Savage in Judaism* (Bloomington: Indiana University Press, 1990).
Elliger, K., *Leviticus* (HAT, 4; Tübingen: Mohr, 1966).
Fainzang, S., 'L'alcoolisme, un maladie contagieuse? Reflections anthropologiques sur l'idee de contagion', *Ethnologie Francaise: Melanges* 4.24.4 (1994), pp. 825-32.
Fehribach, A., 'Between Text and Context: Scripture, Society and the Role of Women in Formative Judaism', in *Recovering the Role of Women: Power and Authority in Rabbinic Jewish Society* (ed. Peter J. Haas; Atlanta: Scholars Press, 1992), pp. 39-60.
Fishbane, M., *The Garments of Torah: Essays in Biblical Hermeneutics* (Bloomington: Indiana University Press, 1989).
Greenstein, E.L., 'A Mind to Savage Judaism', *Judaism,* 4 (1994), pp. 101-109.
Hacking, I., *Rewriting the Soul: Multiple Personality and the Sciences of Memory* (Princeton, NJ: Princeton University Press, 1995).
Hartley, J.E., *Leviticus* (WBC, 4; Dallas; Word Books, 1992).
Houston, W., *Purity and Monotheism: Clean and Unclean Animals in Biblical Law* (JSOTSup, 106; Sheffield: JSOT Press, 1992).
Hubert, H., and M. Mauss, *Sacrifice*: *Its Nature and Functions* (trans. W.D. Halls; Chicago: University of Chicago Press, 1964 [1899]).
Jastrow, M., *A Dictionary of the Talmud* (London: Putman's Sons, 1886–1903).
Jenson, P.P., *Graded Holiness: A Key to the Priestly Perception of the World* (JSOTSup, 106; Sheffield: JSOT Press, 1992).
Jodelet, D., *Folies et representations sociales, Sociologie d'Aujourd'hui*, PUF (1989).
Knohl, I., 'The Sin Offering Law in the "Holiness School" (Numbers 15.22-31)', in G.A. Anderson and S.M. Olyan (eds.), *Priesthood and Cult in Ancient Israel* (JSOTSup, 125; Sheffield: JSOT Press, 1991), pp. 192-203.
—*The Sanctuary of Silence: The Priestly Torah and the Holiness School* (Minneapolis: Fortress Press, 1995).
Kornfeld, W., and H. Ringgren, '*qdš*', in *ThWAT* 6 (1989), pp. 1179-1204.
Lévi, I., 'Le sacrifice d'Isaac et la mort de Jésus', *Revue des Études Juives* 64 (1912), pp. 161-84.

Lévi, S., *La doctrine du sacrifice dans les Brahmanas* (Paris: Leroux, 1898).
Levine, B.A., 'Priestly Writers', *IDBSup* (1976), pp. 683-87.
—'The Epilogue to the Holiness Code: A Priestly Statement on the Destiny of Israel', in J. Neusner, B.A. Levine and E.S. Frerichs (eds.), *Judaic Perspectives on Ancient Israel* (Philadelphia: Fortress Press, 1987), pp. 9-34.
—*Leviticus* (JPS Torah Commentary; Philadelphia: Jewish Publication Society of America), 1989.
Lofthouse, W.F., *Israel after the Exile* (The Clarendon Bible; Oxford: Clarendon Press, 1928).
Maccoby, H., *The Sacred Executioner* (London: Thames & Hudson, 1982).
—'The Washing of Cups', *JSNT* 14 (1982), pp. 3-15.
—*Early Rabbinic Writings* (Cambridge: Cambridge University Press, 1988).
—'Neusner and the Red Cow', *JSJ* 21.1 (1989), pp. 60-75.
Markus, R., 'Augustine on Magic: A Neglected Semiotic Theory', *Revue des Etudes Augustiniennes* 40 (1994), pp. 375-88.
Milgrom, J., *'Did Isaiah Prophesy during the Reign of Uzziah?'*, *VT* 14 (1964), pp. 164-82.
—*Numbers* (Philadelphia: Jewish Publication Society of America, 1990).
—*Studies in Cultic Theology and Terminology* (Studies in Judaism in Late Antiquity, 36; Leiden: Brill, 1983).
—*Numbers* (JPS Torah Commentary; Philadelphia: Jewish Publication Society of America, 1989).
—*Numbers* (Philadelphia: Jewish Publication Society of America, 1990).
—*Leviticus 1–16* (AB, 3; Garden City, NY: Doubleday, 1991).
—*Leviticus: A New Translation with Introduction and Commentary* (AB, 3; Garden City, NY: Doubleday, 1991).
Murray, R., *The Cosmic Covenant* (London: Sheed & Ward, 1992).
Myers, J.M., *Ezra: Nehemiah* (AB; Garden City, NY: Doubleday, 1965).
Neusner, J., *Judaism: The Evidence of the Mishnah* (Atlanta: Scholars Press; 2nd edn, 1987).
—*Purity in Rabbinic Judaism: A Systematic Account* (Atlanta: Scholars Press, 1994).
—'Rabbinic Judaism: Its History and Hermeneutics', in *idem*, *Judaism in Late Antiquity: Historical Syntheses*, II (Leiden: Brill, 1995).
Noth, M., *Leviticus: A Commentary* (London: SCM Press, 1965 [1962]).
Paicheler, G., and A. Quemin, 'Une Intolerance diffuse: rumeurs sur les origines du Sida', *Sciences Sociales et Santé* 12.4, pp. 41-76.
Paschen, W., *Rein und Unrein* (STANT, 24; Munich: Kösel, 1970).
Pegg, M.G., 'Le corps et l'autorité: La Lèpre de Baudouin IV', *Annales, ESC* 2, March–April (1990), pp. 265-87.
Rendtorff, R., 'Two Kinds of P? Some Reflections on the Occasion of the Publication of Jacob Milgrom's Commentary on Leviticus 1–16' (JSOTSup, 106; Sheffield: JSOT Press, 1993), pp. 75-81.
Schwartz, B.J., 'Selected Chapters of the Holiness Code: A Literary Study of Leviticus 17–19' (Hebrew University of Jerusalem dissertation (1987) [Hebrew]).
Smith, M., 'Jewish Religious Life in the Persian Period', in *The Cambridge History of Judaism*, I (Cambridge: Cambridge University Press, 1984), pp. 219-78
Snaith, N.H., *Leviticus and Numbers* (NCB; London: Nelson, 1967).
Sorabji, R., *Animal Minds and Human Morals: The Origins of the Western Debate* (London: Gerald Duckworth, 1993).

Stern, S., *Jewish Identity in Early Rabbinic Writings* (Leiden: Brill, 1994).

Tcherikover, V., 'The Hellenistic Movement in Jerusalem and Antiochus' Persecutions', in *The World History of the Jewish People*, VI (1976) (London: W.H. Allen), pp. 115-46.

Weber, M., *The Sociology of Religion* (London, 1965 [1922]).

Wenham, G.J., *The Book of Leviticus* (NICOT; London & Grand Rapids: Eerdmans, 1979).

Whitekettle, R., 'Leviticus 15.18 Reconsidered: Chiasm, Spatial Structure and the Body', *JSOT* 49 (1991), pp. 31-45.

Zelcer, H., *Companion Mishnayot: Niddah* (New York: Hebrew Linear Press, 1994).

INDEXES

INDEX OF REFERENCES

OLD TESTAMENT

New Testament

OTHER ANCIENT LITERATURE

INDEX OF AUTHORS

JOURNAL FOR THE STUDY OF THE OLD TESTAMENT
SUPPLEMENT SERIES

35 G.W. Coats (ed.), *Saga, Legend, Tale, Novella, Fable: Narrative Forms in Old Testament Literature*
36 M.D. Goulder, *The Song of Fourteen Songs*
37 J.T. Butler, E.W. Conrad & B.C. Ollenburger (eds.), *Understanding the Word: Essays in Honor of Bernhard W. Anderson*
38 T.H. McAlpine, *Sleep, Divine and Human, in the Old Testament*
39 D. Jobling, *The Sense of Biblical Narrative: Structural Analyses in the Hebrew Bible, II*
40 E.R. Follis (ed.), *Directions in Biblical Hebrew Poetry*
41 B.C. Ollenburger, *Zion, the City of the Great King: A Theological Symbol of the Jerusalem Cult*
42 J.D. Martin & P.R. Davies (eds.), *A Word in Season: Essays in Honour of William McKane*
43 G.C. Heider, *The Cult of Molek: A Reassessment*
44 S.J.L. Croft, *The Identity of the Individual in the Psalms*
45 A.R. Diamond, *The Confessions of Jeremiah in Context: Scenes of Prophetic Drama*
46 B.G. Webb, *The Book of Judges: An Integrated Reading*
47 S. Soderlund, *The Greek Text of Jeremiah: A Revised Hypothesis*
48 W. Claassen (ed.), *Text and Context: Old Testament and Semitic Studies for F.C. Fensham*
49 J.D. Fowler, *Theophoric Personal Names in Ancient Hebrew: A Comparative Study*
50 M. Noth, *The Chronicler's History* (trans. H.G.M. Williamson with an Introduction)
51 P. Joyce, *Divine Initiative and Human Response in Ezekiel*
52 C.C. Broyles, *The Conflict of Faith and Experience in the Psalms: A Form-Critical and Theological Study*
53 R.N. Whybray, *The Making of the Pentateuch: A Methodological Study*
54 J. Unterman, *From Repentance to Redemption: Jeremiah's Thought in Transition*
55 T.L. Thompson, *The Origin Tradition of Ancient Israel: 1. The Literary Formation of Genesis and Exodus 1–23*
86 A. Niccacci, *The Syntax of the Verb in Classical Hebrew Prose* (trans. W.G.E. Watson)
87 D.J.A. Clines, S.E. Fowl & S.E. Porter (eds.), *The Bible in Three Dimensions: Essays in Celebration of Forty Years of Biblical Studies in the University of Sheffield*
88 R.K. Duke, *The Persuasive Appeal of the Chronicler: A Rhetorical Analysis*
89 R. Rendtorff, *The Problem of the Process of Transmission in the Pentateuch* (trans. J.J. Scullion)

90 M.F. Rooker, *Biblical Hebrew in Transition: The Language of the Book of Ezekiel*

91 F.H. Gorman Jr, *The Ideology of Ritual: Space, Time and Status in the Priestly Theology*

92 Y.T. Radday & A. Brenner (eds.), *On Humour and the Comic in the Hebrew Bible*

93 W.T. Koopmans, *Joshua 24 as Poetic Narrative*

94 D.J.A. Clines, *What Does Eve Do to Help? And Other Readerly Questions to the Old Testament*

95 R.D. Moore, *God Saves: Lessons from the Elisha Stories*

96 L.A. Turner, *Announcements of Plot in Genesis*

97 P.R. House, *The Unity of the Twelve*

98 K.L. Younger Jr, *Ancient Conquest Accounts: A Study in Ancient Near Eastern and Biblical History Writing*

99 R.N. Whybray, *Wealth and Poverty in the Book of Proverbs*

100 P.R. Davies & R.T. White (eds.), *A Tribute to Geza Vermes: Essays on Jewish and Christian Literature and History*

101 P.R. Ackroyd, *The Chronicler in his Age*

102 M. Goulder, *The Prayers of David (Psalms 51–72): Studies in the Psalter, II*

103 B.G. Wood, *The Sociology of Pottery in Ancient Palestine: The Ceramic Industry and the Diffusion of Ceramic Style in the Bronze and Iron Ages*

104 P.R. Raabe, *Psalm Structures: A Study of Psalms with Refrains*

105 P. Bovati, *Re-Establishing Justice: Legal Terms, Concepts and Procedures in the Hebrew Bible* (trans. M.J. Smith)

106 P.P. Jenson, *Graded Holiness: A Key to the Priestly Conception of the World*

107 C. van Houten, *The Alien in Israelite Law*

108 P.M. McNutt, *The Forging of Israel: Iron Technology, Symbolism and Tradition in Ancient Society*

109 D. Jamieson-Drake, *Scribes and Schools in Monarchic Judah: A Socio-Archaeological Approach*

110 N.P. Lemche, *The Canaanites and Their Land: The Tradition of the Canaanites*

111 J.G. Taylor, *Yahweh and the Sun: The Biblical and Archaeological Evidence for Sun Worship in Ancient Israel*

112 L.G. Perdue, *Wisdom in Revolt: Metaphorical Theology in the Book of Job*

113 R. Westbrook, *Property and the Family in Biblical Law*

114 D. Cohn-Sherbok (ed.), *A Traditional Quest: Essays in Honour of Louis Jacobs*

115 V. Hurowitz, *I Have Built You an Exalted House: Temple Building in the Bible in Light of Mesopotamian and Northwest Semitic Writings*

116 D.M. Gunn (ed.), *Narrative and Novella in Samuel: Studies by Hugo Gressmann and Other Scholars, 1906–1923* (trans. D.E. Orton)

117 P.R. Davies (ed.), *Second Temple Studies: 1. Persian Period*

118 R.J. Tournay, *Seeing and Hearing God with the Psalms: The Prophetic Liturgy of the Second Temple in Jerusalem* (trans. J.E. Crowley)
119 D.J.A. Clines & T.C. Eskenazi (eds.), *Telling Queen Michal's Story: An Experiment in Comparative Interpretation*
120 R.H. Lowery, *The Reforming Kings: Cult and Society in First Temple Judah*
121 D.V. Edelman, *King Saul in the Historiography of Judah*
122 L. Alexander (ed.), *Images of Empire*
123 E. Bloch-Smith, *Judahite Burial Practices and Beliefs about the Dead*
124 B. Halpern & D.W. Hobson (eds.), *Law and Ideology in Monarchic Israel*
125 G.A. Anderson & S.M. Olyan (eds.), *Priesthood and Cult in Ancient Israel*
126 J.W. Rogerson, *W.M.L. de Wette, Founder of Modern Biblical Criticism: An Intellectual Biography*
127 D.V. Edelman (ed.), *The Fabric of History: Text, Artifact and Israel's Past*
128 T.P. McCreesh, *Biblical Sound and Sense: Poetic Sound Patterns in Proverbs 10–29*
129 Z. Stefanovic, *The Aramaic of Daniel in the Light of Old Aramaic*
130 M. Butterworth, *Structure and the Book of Zechariah*
131 L. Holden, *Forms of Deformity*
132 M.D. Carroll R., *Contexts for Amos: Prophetic Poetics in Latin American Perspective*
133 R. Syrén, *The Forsaken Firstborn: A Study of a Recurrent Motif in the Patriarchal Narratives*
134 G. Mitchell, *Together in the Land: A Reading of the Book of Joshua*
135 G.F. Davies, *Israel in Egypt: Reading Exodus 1–2*
136 P. Morris & D. Sawyer (eds.), *A Walk in the Garden: Biblical, Iconographical and Literary Images of Eden*
137 H.G. Reventlow & Y. Hoffman (eds.), *Justice and Righteousness: Biblical Themes and their Influence*
138 R.P. Carroll (ed.), *Text as Pretext: Essays in Honour of Robert Davidson*
139 J.W. Watts, *Psalm and Story: Inset Hymns in Hebrew Narrative*
140 W. Houston, *Purity and Monotheism: Clean and Unclean Animals in Biblical Law*
141 G.C. Chirichigno, *Debt-Slavery in Israel and the Ancient Near East*
142 F.H. Cryer, *Divination in Ancient Israel and its Near Eastern Environment: A Socio-Historical Investigation*
143 D.J.A. Clines & J.C. Exum (eds.), *The New Literary Criticism and the Hebrew Bible*
144 P.R. Davies & D.J.A. Clines (eds.), *Language, Imagery and Structure in the Prophetic Writings*
145 C.S. Shaw, *The Speeches of Micah: A Rhetorical-Historical Analysis*
146 G.W. Ahlström, *The History of Ancient Palestine from the Palaeolithic Period to Alexander's Conquest* (ed. D. Edelman, with a contribution by G.O. Rollefson)
147 T.W. Cartledge, *Vows in the Hebrew Bible and the Ancient Near East*
148 P.R. Davies, *In Search of 'Ancient Israel'*

149 E. Ulrich, J.W. Wright, R.P. Carroll & P.R. Davies (eds.), *Priests, Prophets and Scribes: Essays on the Formation and Heritage of Second Temple Judaism in Honour of Joseph Blenkinsopp*
150 J.E. Tollington, *Tradition and Innovation in Haggai and Zechariah 1–8*
151 J.P. Weinberg, *The Citizen-Temple Community*
152 A.G. Auld (ed.), *Understanding Poets and Prophets: Essays in Honour of George Wishart Anderson*
153 D.K. Berry, *The Psalms and their Readers: Interpretive Strategies for Psalm 18*
154 M. Brettler & M. Fishbane (eds.), *Min'ah le-Na'um: Biblical and Other Studies Presented to Nahum M. Sarna in Honour of his 70th Birthday*
155 J.A. Fager, *Land Tenure and the Biblical Jubilee: Uncovering Hebrew Ethics through the Sociology of Knowledge*
156 J.W. Kleinig, *The Lord's Song: The Basis, Function and Significance of Choral Music in Chronicles*
157 G.R. Clark, *The Word Óesed in the Hebrew Bible*
158 M. Douglas, *In the Wilderness: The Doctrine of Defilement in the Book of Numbers*
159 J.C. McCann, *The Shape and Shaping of the Psalter*
160 W. Riley, *King and Cultus in Chronicles: Worship and the Reinterpretation of History*
161 G.W. Coats, *The Moses Tradition*
162 H.A. McKay & D.J.A. Clines (eds.), *Of Prophet's Visions and the Wisdom of Sages: Essays in Honour of R. Norman Whybray on his Seventieth Birthday*
163 J.C. Exum, *Fragmented Women: Feminist (Sub)versions of Biblical Narratives*
164 L. Eslinger, *House of God or House of David: The Rhetoric of 2 Samuel 7*
165 E. Nodet, *A Search for the Origins of Israel: From Joshua to the Mishnah*
166 D.R.G. Beattie & M.J. McNamara (eds.), *The Aramaic Bible: Targums in their Historical Context*
167 R.F. Person, *Second Zechariah and the Deuteronomic School*
168 R.N. Whybray, *The Composition of the Book of Proverbs*
169 B. Dicou, *Edom, Israel's Brother and Antagonist: The Role of Edom in Biblical Prophecy and Story*
170 W.G.E. Watson, *Traditional Techniques in Classical Hebrew Verse*
171 H.G. Reventlow, Y. Hoffman & B. Uffenheimer (eds.), *Politics and Theopolitics in the Bible and Postbiblical Literature*
172 V. Fritz, *An Introduction to Biblical Archaeology*
173 M.P. Graham, W.P. Brown & J.K. Kuan (eds.), *History and Interpretation: Essays in Honour of John H. Hayes*
174 J.M. Sprinkle, *'The Book of the Covenant': A Literary Approach*
175 T.C. Eskenazi & K.H. Richards (eds.), *Second Temple Studies: 2. Temple and Community in the Persian Period*

176 G. Brin, *Studies in Biblical Law: From the Hebrew Bible to the Dead Sea Scrolls*

177 D.A. Dawson, *Text-Linguistics and Biblical Hebrew*

178 M.R. Hauge, *Between Sheol and Temple: Motif Structure and Function in the I-Psalms*

179 J.G. McConville & J.G. Millar, *Time and Place in Deuteronomy*

180 R. Schultz, *The Search for Quotation: Verbal Parallels in the Prophets*

181 B.M. Levinson (ed.), *Theory and Method in Biblical and Cuneiform Law: Revision, Interpolation and Development*

182 S.L. McKenzie & M.P. Graham (eds.), *The History of Israel's Traditions: The Heritage of Martin Noth*

183 J. Day (ed.), *Lectures on the Religion of The Semites (Second and Third Series) by William Robertson Smith*

184 J.C. Reeves & J. Kampen (eds.), *Pursuing the Text: Studies in Honour of Ben Zion Wacholder on the Occasion of his Seventieth Birthday*

185 S.D. Kunin, *The Logic of Incest: A Structuralist Analysis of Hebrew Mythology*

186 L. Day, *Three Faces of a Queen: Characterization in the Books of Esther*

187 C.V. Dorothy, *The Books of Esther: Structure, Genre and Textual Integrity*

188 R.H. O'Connell, *Concentricity and Continuity: The Literary Structure of Isaiah*

189 W. Johnstone (ed.), *William Robertson Smith: Essays in Reassessment*

190 S.W. Holloway & L.K. Handy (eds.), *The Pitcher is Broken: Memorial Essays for Gösta W. Ahlström*

191 M. Sæbø, *On the Way to Canon: Creative Tradition History in the Old Testament*

192 H.G. Reventlow & W. Farmer (eds.), *Biblical Studies and the Shifting of Paradigms, 1850–1914*

193 B. Schramm, *The Opponents of Third Isaiah: Reconstructing the Cultic History of the Restoration*

194 E.K. Holt, *Prophesying the Past: The Use of Israel's History in the Book of Hosea*

195 J. Davies, G. Harvey & W.G.E. Watson (eds.), *Words Remembered, Texts Renewed: Essays in Honour of John F.A. Sawyer*

196 J.S. Kaminsky, *Corporate Responsibility in the Hebrew Bible*

197 W.M. Schniedewind, *The Word of God in Transition: From Prophet to Exegete in the Second Temple Period*

198 T.J. Meadowcroft, *Aramaic Daniel and Greek Daniel: A Literary Comparison*

199 J.H. Eaton, *Psalms of the Way and the Kingdom: A Conference with the Commentators*

200 M.D. Carroll R., D.J.A. Clines & P.R. Davies (eds.), *The Bible in Human Society: Essays in Honour of John Rogerson*

201 J.W. Rogerson, *The Bible and Criticism in Victorian Britain: Profiles of F.D. Maurice and William Robertson Smith*

202 N. Stahl, *Law and Liminality in the Bible*
203 J.M. Munro, *Spikenard and Saffron: The Imagery of the Song of Songs*
204 P.R. Davies, *Whose Bible Is It Anyway?*
205 D.J.A. Clines, *Interested Parties: The Ideology of Writers and Readers of the Hebrew Bible*
206 M. Müller, *The First Bible of the Church: A Plea for the Septuagint*
207 J.W. Rogerson, M. Davies & M.D. Carroll R. (eds.), *The Bible in Ethics: The Second Sheffield Colloquium*
208 B.J. Stratton, *Out of Eden: Reading, Rhetoric, and Ideology in Genesis 2-3*
209 P. Dutcher-Walls, *Narrative Art, Political Rhetoric: The Case of Athaliah and Joash*
210 J. Berlinerblau, *The Vow and the 'Popular Religious Groups' of Ancient Israel: A Philological and Sociological Inquiry*
211 B.E. Kelly, *Retribution and Eschatology in Chronicles*
212 Y. Sherwood, *The Prostitute and the Prophet: Hosea's Marriage in Literary-Theoretical Perspective*
213 Y.A. Hoffman, *A Blemished Perfection: The Book of Job in Context*
214 R.F. Melugin & M.A. Sweeney (eds.), *New Visions of Isaiah*
215 J.C. Exum, *Plotted, Shot and Painted: Cultural Representations of Biblical Women*
216 J.E. McKinlay, *Gendering Wisdom the Host: Biblical Invitations to Eat and Drink*
217 J.F.D. Creach, *The Choice of Yahweh as Refuge and the Editing of the Hebrew Psalter*
218 G. Glazov, *The Bridling of the Tongue and the Opening of the Mouth in Biblical Prophecy*
219 G. Morris, *Prophecy, Poetry and Hosea*
220 R.F. Person, Jr, *In Conversation with Jonah: Conversation Analysis, Literary Criticism, and the Book of Jonah*
221 G. Keys, *The Wages of Sin: A Reappraisal of the 'Succession Narrative'*
222 R.N. Whybray, *Reading the Psalms as a Book*
223 S.B. Noegel, *Janus Parallelism in the Book of Job*
224 P.J. Kissling, *Reliable Characters in the Primary History: Profiles of Moses, Joshua, Elijah and Elisha*
225 R.D. Weiss & D.M. Carr (eds.), *A Gift of God in Due Season: Essays on Scripture and Community in Honor of James A. Sanders*
226 L.L. Rowlett, *Joshua and the Rhetoric of Violence: A New Historicist Analysis*